Advance Praise for

Path of Light

"A much-needed, penetrating, and practical journey to the core of *A Course in Miracles*. Robert Perry offers unique insight that can help us make the Course real and meaningful in our lives. Living these masterful principles will change your life in wondrous ways."
—ALAN COHEN, AUTHOR OF *I HAD IT ALL THE TIME*

"Robert Perry is a first rate *A Course in Miracles* scholar. I like the simple, 'easy' way in which he clarifies seemingly difficult Course concepts. Reading *Path of Light* brings renewed excitement and interest to this modern spiritual classic."
—JON MUNDY, PH.D., AUTHOR OF *MISSOURI MYSTIC* AND *AWAKEN TO YOUR OWN CALL*

"I felt a sense of peace and trust as I read Robert Perry's superb introduction to *A Course in Miracles*. 'Here,' I thought, 'is a book worthy to rest beside the Course on anyone's night stand.' In many ways it resonates with the same friendliness and blessing, the same lovely quietness, that one feels when opening the Course itself. It is a softly illuminated portal that ushers us into the boundless room of light that is *A Course in Miracles*."
—HUGH PRATHER, AUTHOR OF *HOW TO LIVE IN THE WORLD AND STILL BE HAPPY*

"A superb introduction to the beautiful and enigmatic work that is *A Course in Miracles*. Highly recommended both for beginners and for old hands at the Course."
—RICHARD SMOLEY, AUTHOR OF *INNER CHRISTIANITY: A GUIDE TO THE ESOTERIC TRADITION*

"*Path of Light* is a skillful and elegantly understated presentation from the warm heart and brilliant mind of one of the most respected teachers of *A Course in Miracles*. Like a master storyteller, he uses simple words to relay the deep truth of a lengthy and complex spiritual teaching, organizing it in a logical and accessible way that makes the Course available to everyone. In *Path of Light*, Robert Perry serves as our guide for *A Course in Miracles*. With his help, we find the path much clearer, the teaching more relevant, the lessons and practices more accessible. *Path of Light* will deservingly rise to the top of the reading list of all sincere students of *A Course in Miracles*."
—ROBERT FERRE, ONE HEART, ST. LOUIS, MISSOURI

"A thoughtful approach to the Course that presents the key teachings very clearly. An important guide for anyone wanting to understand the Course."
—PETER RUSSELL, AUTHOR OF *FROM SCIENCE TO GOD*

"Robert Perry is simply the best Course scholar writing today. He thoroughly and accurately represents what the whole Course says and doesn't just focus on certain 'pet' passages which he believes represent the 'central' teaching while disregarding the rest. However, even his scholarship takes a back seat to his own teaching insights. When he relates our tendency to project blame and guilt to how we would 'instinctively' spit a scorpion out of our mouth, I get the teaching viscerally. Bravo!"
—REV. TONY PONTICELLO, CO-FOUNDER, COMMUNITY MIRACLES CENTER, SAN FRANCISCO

"Robert Perry's new book, *Path of Light*, presents a fresh appreciation of *A Course in Miracles,* as not only a map of consciousness, but also a vehicle of personal transformation. His fine book, useful to anyone interested in learning about *A Course in Miracles*, offers practical demonstrations of how the Course is directed not only at self help, but also at the much more lofty goal of self realization."
—RUSSELL TARG, AUTHOR OF *MIRACLES OF MIND: EXPLORING NONLOCAL CONSCIOUSNESS AND SPIRITUAL HEALING*

"*Path of Light* is just that; a step by step guide, brilliantly and systematically assembled by Robert Perry. What else would you expect from this teacher? You who would take the Course journey all the way will welcome the chart Robert Perry has drafted. Bon voyage!"
—HOWARD WESTIN, AUTHOR OF *LOVE LETTER TO HUMANITY*

"*Path of Light*, an exceptional book on spirituality, is sure not only to intellectually engage its readers, but also to inspire and transform them. Even for long-time students of *A Course in Miracles*, Perry sheds new light on this extraordinary teaching, and reawakens and reminds us of the exquisite possibility available to each of us in every moment."
—ROBIN CASARJIAN, AUTHOR OF *FORGIVENESS: A BOLD CHOICE FOR A PEACEFUL HEART*

"Robert Perry's *Path of Light* is a masterpiece that will illumine the way to a life of true peace and love for any sincere seeker of truth. With the depth that can only come from a lifetime's dedication to truly understanding and applying the mighty teachings of the Course, Robert breaks down powerful spiritual insights into pragmatic steps using straightforward language. Readers will gain all they need to live the transformative message of *A Course in Miracles*."
—ROBERT HOLDEN, AUTHOR OF *SHIFT HAPPENS*,
AND MIRANDA HOLDEN, AUTHOR OF *BOUNDLESS LOVE*

"Hang on to your seat belts—Robert brings a wonderful overdue sense of adventure to *A Course in Miracles*. Extremely helpful."
—DUANE O'KANE, FOUNDER, CLEARMIND INTERNATIONAL INSTITUTE, LANGLEY, BRITISH COLUMBIA

"I am so excited about this book. It is stunning, brilliant, an awesome read. I really believe that it is going to make a very significant contribution to the world."
—SARAH HUEMMERT, FOUNDER, EDMONTON MIRACLES CENTER, CANADA

"Robert Perry's dedication to thorough and scholarly examination of the message of *A Course in Miracles*, and his commitment to practicing its principles, are commendable and sincere. These qualities are embodied in this in-depth but eminently readable and practical overview. A book of this nature has been long overdue."
—IAN PATRICK, DIRECTOR, MIRACLE NETWORK, UK

"I am so grateful for this book. I find in it the essence and the spirit of the Course in a way that reaches deeply into my mind. *Path of Light* is a true blessing, not only for Course students, but also for those of the general public who are wanting a clearer view of what the Course is really all about."
—MIRKALICE GORE, FOUNDER, A PLACE FOR MIRACLES, LAS VEGAS, NEVADA

"*Path of Light* is a truly inspired work. It will have a major impact on making the wisdom of the Course more widely accessible. We are all grateful for Robert Perry's scholarship, commitment, and integrity. My expectation is that *Path of Light* will become the definitive guide to *A Course in Miracles*."
—JACK WEBER, DARDEN GRADUATE SCHOOL OF BUSINESS, UNIVERSITY OF VIRGINIA

Path of Light

Other Books by Robert Perry:

An Introduction to *A Course in Miracles*
Relationships as a Spiritual Journey: From Specialness to Holiness
Guidance: Living the Inspired Life
A Course Glossary: 158 Definitions from *A Course in Miracles*
Reality and Illusion: An Overview of Course Metaphysics

By Robert Perry and Allen Watson:

The Answer Is a Miracle
Let Me Remember You: God in *A Course in Miracles*
Bringing the Course to Life: How to Unlock the Meaning of *A Course in Miracles* for Yourself
Everything You Always Wanted to Know About Judgment but Were Too Busy Doing It to Notice

Path of Light

Stepping into Peace with *A Course in Miracles*

Robert Perry

Published by Circle Publishing
A division of The Circle of Atonement Teaching and Healing Center
P.O. Box 4238 • West Sedona, AZ 86340
(928) 282-0790 • Fax: (928) 282-0523
E-mail: info@circleofa.com • Website: www.circleofa.com

Cover design by George Foster; www.fostercovers.com
Design and layout by Phillips Associates UK Ltd
Author photo by Peggy Iileen
Printed in the USA

ISBN 1-886602-23-9

Library of Congress Cataloging-in-Publication Data

Perry, Robert, 1960-
Path of light : stepping into peace with A course in miracles / Robert Perry.-- 1st ed.
p. cm.
Includes bibliographical references and index.
ISBN 1-886602-23-9 (pbk.)
1. Course in miracles. 2. Spiritual life. I. Title.
BP605.C68P47 2004
299'.93--dc22

2004000047

This course was sent to open up

the path of light to us, and teach us,

step by step, how to return to the

eternal Self we thought we lost.

Workbook, Introduction to Review V

Contents

PART II: THE TEACHING

PART III: THE PROGRAM

PART IV: LIVING THE COURSE

List of Illustrations

Foreword

Because I am a student of *A Course in Miracles*, any book that illumines its teaching more deeply is a gift to me. Today, however, with a plethora of commentary on the Course, it is important not just for me but for all who care about its wisdom to discern whose work presents the most powerful insight.

I have always felt that Robert Perry is a writer and thinker whose understanding of *A Course in Miracles* is a teaching in its own right. As someone who wrote one of the earliest popular treatises on the Course, *A Return to Love*, I have always felt it is Perry who guides the Course student to the next step. He is one of our most brilliant teachers of the principles of the Course, and for those of us who consider ourselves serious students, his understanding impacts our own.

For those who feel that for them, *A Course in Miracles* is not to be missed, then I would venture to say that neither should *Path of Light*. Some gifts, though exciting, come with instruction manuals that are important to read. *A Course in Miracles* is such a gift, and *Path of Light* is such a manual.

Path of Light is a brilliant instruction, which takes the promise of the Course and delivers it home. It is more than a book, it is a blessing.

—Marianne Williamson,
author of *A Return to Love*

PREFACE

Assessing *A Course in Miracles*

A Course in Miracles—what a curious name! But if ever there was an occasion not to judge a book by its cover, this may be it. For despite its curious title and origins, hundreds of thousands, if not millions of people from all around the world are studying the Course, and finding it more than a match, not only for their intellect, but also for their deepest spiritual longings. Many notable thinkers—including Glen Olds, the former president of Kent State University; Willis Harman, former professor of Engineering at Stanford University; and Ken Wilber, one of the world's foremost philosophers and scholars of religion—have described the Course in extremely positive terms, and compared it favorably with the world's great contemplative traditions.

So what, then, is *A Course in Miracles*? From one perspective it is simply a set of curiously titled books. From another, it is a spiritual discipline comprising a systematic thought system and set of practices that claims to offer an effective and sufficient path to awakening.

This is obviously quite a claim! In fact it may be one of the most remarkable claims one can make—to claim to provide a discipline capable of guiding practitioners to the ultimate goal of life and of the world's great religions: the goal of enlightenment, liberation, *moksha, wu, fana*, *ruah-qodesh*, atonement, *satori* or salvation.

Assessing the Course

This raises an obvious question: how can we assess this claim? The easiest approach would be to simply ask practitioners. However, this is hardly a valid or reliable method. After all, a glance at any newspaper or history book makes painfully clear that there is hardly any philosophical foolishness or spiritual stupidity which does not appeal to some people, and sometimes to large numbers of people.

So how can we accurately assess the Course's value and validity, authenticity and effectiveness, legitimacy and liabilities? These are questions that will probably consume practitioners, scholars and researchers for decades. But what about those of us who would like some answers, even if only preliminary and provisional, right now?

One approach is to compare the Course's practices and thought system to those of the time-honored great spiritual traditions, and especially to their common core of practices and wisdom. For example, looking at the Course's practices, we might ask, "to what extent do they contain the central and essential practices common to the world's great spiritual traditions?"

There seem to be seven practices that each of the world's great religious traditions assume to be central and essential for anyone who would awaken to their true nature and highest potential.[1] These practices are:

1. Redirecting motivation away from egocentric material cravings towards altruistic, transpersonal and transcendent goals.
2. Transforming emotions. This includes two components: reducing painful, destructive emotions such as fear, hatred and jealousy; while cultivating positive, beneficial emotions such as love, compassion and joy.
3. Fostering an ethical lifestyle.
4. Calming and concentrating the mind.
5. Refining awareness and developing sacred vision.
6. Cultivating wisdom.
7. Practicing service and generosity.

One simple measure of a tradition may therefore be suggested by the number of these practices that it contains. For example, in its initial form

Confucianism offered a wonderful teaching emphasizing ethics, wisdom and service. However, it lacked other practices, such as for concentrating and calming the mind, and therefore constituted an extremely valuable way of life, but not yet a fully effective spiritual discipline. Centuries later, when it merged with Taoism and Buddhism to create neoConfucianism, a full and authentic spiritual tradition of enormous value and influence was created.

How then does *A Course in Miracles* measure up on these seven practices? In short, it seems to embody them all:

1. It places great emphasis on motivation. In fact, it states that a teacher's first and foremost challenge is to inspire a redirection of motivation. It certainly emphasizes the importance of reducing both egocentric craving and aversion, and of redirecting desires away from the "toys and trinkets of the world"[2] to healthier spiritual goals. And it suggests we do this for both our own benefit and in order to benefit others.

2. Emotional transformation lies at the heart of the Course. It offers devastating critiques of the dangers lurking in emotions such as fear, guilt and anger; offers multiple exercises for releasing them; and also contains a wealth of exercises for the cultivation of love, joy and compassion.

3. It also scores well on the ethical dimension. It emphasizes that all behavior, and even all thought, is to be directed away from egocentricity and attack, and towards loving and serving one's neighbor as one's Self. Certainly the Course would agree with the claim that "The foundation...of all authentic spirituality is a universal ethics."[3]

4. The Course recognizes the importance of cultivating concentration and calm. It paints a painful portrayal of our usual agitated state of mind and suggests that "a tranquil mind is not a little gift."[4] One of its central goals is the realization of "the peace of God," which according to both St. Paul and the Course, "surpasses understanding."[5] One of its central, and for some people most evocative, lessons states, "I want the peace of God."[6]

5. The Course certainly emphasizes the importance of refining perception. In fact, it suggests that this refinement can be carried to

remarkable degrees, in which we and others are seen as Christ and the children of God, and the world is recognized as a schoolhouse for our awakening. The Course describes this transcendental vision as "seeing with the eyes of Christ"[7] or as "vision," and this vision has obvious analogies to Plato's "eye of the soul," Taoism's "eye of the Tao," Sufism's "eye of the heart," and Tibetan Buddhism's "pure perception."[8,1]

6. "Get wisdom; get insight: do not forget" urges the Jewish Torah.[9] We can define wisdom as deep understanding of, and practical skill in responding to, the central existential challenges of life. Certainly the Course aims very explicitly at fostering wisdom, and it explores all the major existential challenges, such as meaning and purpose, sickness and suffering, aloneness and death.

   It recommends first looking unflinchingly at them and the amount of suffering they engender, a recommendation that any good therapist might offer. But it then goes on to make a second specifically spiritual recommendation. It suggests that the optimal strategy is to awaken from the ego-based identity which suffers to the transcendent Self which witnesses, but is not identified with or affected by, this suffering. Here, as in many places, the Course offers good psychology, but it also goes well beyond psychology.

7. The final, and in some ways culminating component of the seven practices, is fostering service and generosity. "The best people among you," taught Mohammad, "are the ones who are benefactors to others."[10] This is clearly one of the Course's strong points. It emphasizes repeatedly that spiritual practices are not done for ourselves alone, because actually we are not alone, or even separate. In fact, to try to do the Course exclusively for our own benefit is to buy into and strengthen the illusion of separateness. Rather, the Course emphasizes that service is both a means to, and an expression of, awakening and recognizing our true identity.

   In fact it goes even further to recommend that we explicitly aim to practice and awaken for the benefit of all. Students of comparative religion will recognize this as a contemporary restatement of the Buddhist Bodhisattva ideal. This may well be the highest ideal the human mind has ever conceived. For what goal, what aspiration could be more altruistic, more encompassing and more sublime than to aim to actualize and awaken ourselves in order to optimally serve the awakening and well-being of all?

While the Course shares this Bodhisattva ideal with Buddhism it also offers unique perspectives and practices for realizing it. Specifically, its primary focus is on healing and optimizing our relationships, with the goal of truly loving others as our Self. This emphasis on transforming our peer relationships, and the many practices it offers for doing this, are unmatched by any other spiritual tradition, and are probably a large factor in its wide appeal.

So *A Course in Miracles* seems to aim for the highest spiritual goals and to include all seven of the central and essential practices for reaching them. However, this raises further questions: how effective is it in helping people realize these goals? How many people does it speak to, and how quickly and completely does it transform them? And how does it compare to other spiritual traditions on these measures? As yet we have no firm data and nothing beyond testimonies to answer these crucial questions. Here is a fertile field for future researchers.

How Sophisticated Is *A Course in Miracles*?

Looking through the religion and spirituality section of any bookstore can be a disquieting experience. So many popular books offer simplistic thought systems, disciplines that include no discipline, and precious little in the way of authentic practices. Superficiality sells.

Is this also true of *A Course in Miracles*? Could this be why it is so remarkably popular? Here the answer seems clear, and it is a firm "No." No, the practices it offers are far from minimal. In fact, as described earlier, they are systematic, rigorous, and include all seven of the central practices.

And no, the Course's thought system is anything but superficial. In content it is a restatement of the perennial philosophy, or what we might call the *sophia commonalis*—the common core of wisdom and philosophy at the heart of the world's great religions. In addition it also offers a version of what Ken Wilber calls the "*psychologia perennis*"—the common contemplative understanding of the nature and workings of mind.[11]

Not only does the Course offer a version of the perennial philosophy and perennial psychology, but it offers a highly sophisticated version at that. A full discussion of this topic would take a book, and fortunately that is what Robert Perry is offering us.

However, we can take the Course's discussion of forgiveness as a useful example, since forgiveness is probably the practice that the Course most emphasizes. Having now devoted some thirty years to researching the world's religious and spiritual traditions, I can say that I have found nothing that matches the sophistication of the Course's analysis of the value of, and mechanisms underlying, forgiveness. Each tradition has its own strengths, and one such strength for the Course is its sophisticated understanding of, and many practices for fostering, forgiveness.

Dangers, Traps and Cults

One potentially painful question that must be asked of any spiritual tradition is "to what extent is it liable to misuse?" After all, there is no ideal so high, no tradition so venerable, no text so transcendent, that it cannot be misused by somebody.[12] What is the likelihood of the Course being misused? For example, is the Course a cult, or could it become one?

To answer this question we must first look at exactly what a cult is. A cult is a membership organization with a hierarchical, authoritarian power structure, which places authority outside the individual in the leader or authorities. It usually sees its members as uniquely special and superior to other people. It enforces rigid adherence to its belief system and behavioral norms, limits any questioning of these beliefs and norms, and often limits access to dissenting opinions and beliefs. Finally, it is easy to get into and hard to get out of.

A Course in Miracles is almost the exact opposite. There is no organization to join, and no hierarchy of power. There is no outside authority to obey; in fact, it suggests that the highest authority lies within us. There are no limitations on questions or access to other views, no methods of enforcement, and it sees all people—Course practitioners and others—as equal children of God. Finally, it is supremely easy to get out of; all one has to do is close the book. Anyone who believes that *A Course in Miracles* is a cult probably knows little about either the Course or cults, or both.

This is not to say that the Course could never be misused by cultic groups, but it is to say that there is little in the Course itself which supports such misuse. Likewise, the Course appears to score well on more formal measures of health and pathology in spiritual traditions, such as the Anthony Typology or Ken Wilber's spectrum model.[13] As such, the Course seems to be a refreshingly safe and low risk path.

Summary

Surveying all these issues, what conclusions can we reach? In *A Course in Miracles* we have a new spiritual discipline that uses Christian language to express the perennial philosophy, the perennial psychology, and the perennial practices in a surprisingly systematic, sophisticated and compelling way. It speaks to large numbers of people, yet certainly not by watering down either its message or its practices. In fact, it offers both a highly sophisticated thought system and an eminently practical set of exercises. You may not agree with *A Course in Miracles* and you may not decide that it is your path. However, the weight of evidence suggests that it is a most impressive document and an effective path that warrants serious attention by practitioners and scholars, and that the many people around the world who practice it are probably benefiting both themselves and others.

I am delighted that Robert Perry—a wonderfully sincere and dedicated practitioner and teacher of *A Course in Miracles*—is offering such an accessible introduction to it. Robert honors the sophistication of the Course's thought system, yet never loses sight of the fact that the Course is above all an eminently practical path to awakening. I trust that *Path of Light* will serve the awakening of many and the well-being of all.

—Roger Walsh, M.D., Ph.D.

Roger Walsh is Professor of Psychiatry, Philosophy, Anthropology, and Religious Studies at the University of California at Irvine. He has written and edited numerous books in the field of transpersonal psychology and spirituality, including Paths Beyond Ego: The Transpersonal Vision *(ed.) and* Essential Spirituality: The Seven Central Practices to Awaken Heart and Mind.

Acknowledgements

I wish to extend my heartfelt gratitude to the following people:

Ken Bauer, for his beautiful artwork, and all the time, care, and attention to detail that went into it.

Vin LoPresti, for his superb, insightful, and generous work as editor of this book.

André Gendron, for the selfless commitment and energy he has given to get this book into the hands of readers.

D. Patrick Miller, for his invaluable role as publishing consultant.

My colleagues at the Circle of Atonement—Nicola Harvey, Greg Mackie, Mary Anne Buchowski, and Allen Watson—who have set aside much of their own work, and given themselves tirelessly to making this book a reality.

Rick Baker, without whom the whole project simply would not have happened.

My grateful thanks also go to the following people: Bart Bacon, Gail Kump, Mick Phillips, Armando Brons, Maryglenn McCombs, George Foster, Val Scott, Dan Cavicchio, James Gregory, Mitzi Condit, and Margery Mackie.

Introduction

What is *A Course in Miracles*?[1] You may have friends who study it. You yourself may be a student of it. You may have heard Marianne Williamson or Wayne Dyer or Deepak Chopra quote from it. You may have seen it in the New Age section of your bookstore, or heard that it teaches forgiveness. You may also have heard some very strange things about it—that it was channeled from Jesus, or that it says the world is only a dream.

On the surface, *A Course in Miracles* is a book consisting of twelve hundred pages and three volumes: Text, Workbook for Students, and Manual for Teachers. It was not authored in the conventional sense, but rather channeled or "scribed" by Helen Schucman, a research psychologist at Columbia University. Since its publication in 1976, it has become a modern spiritual classic, selling over a million and a half copies and attracting a devoted following of tens of thousands of students.

These bare facts, however, do not really tell us what *A Course in Miracles* is. It is difficult, in fact, to ascertain exactly what it is. The Course does not fit conventional molds, and its author did not explain how it relates to our traditional academic or literary categories. In a manner of speaking, it just dropped out of the sky, leaving us with the task of figuring out what it is. For this reason, it has been given many public faces, depending on who is portraying it. And, as Richard Smoley notes in *Inner Christianity: A Guide to the Esoteric Tradition*, there is often a wide gap between how the Course is represented and what it really is:

> The fact remains that the Course, as thousands of people have found, is a powerful means of spiritual transformation. Although it is sometimes misrepresented as a compendium of feel-good nostrums, actually it teaches a rigorous form of mental discipline that, if scrupulously observed, would lead one to exclude all thoughts of hate and negativity. Anyone who carried out its teachings in full would be a saint.[2]

The purpose of this book is to present, as accurately as possible, the Course as it really is, underneath its various public faces. It is my firm belief that neither Course students nor the world as a whole has begun to tap the real power of the Course, largely because we are still trying to get a handle on what it is. As the above quote suggests, beneath its public faces lies a potent, transformative spiritual path, one which employs practical means to lead us, step by step, toward the goal of complete awakening. This book attempts to demystify the Course, clearly explaining its origin, its nature, its teachings, and its program. In particular, it aims to clarify what it means to walk this path. This, in fact, is the focus of the second half of the book, which explains what must be done to move forward on this path, answers the questions that come up at different points along the way, and describes the benefits gained from traveling this road.

For this reason, the book is primarily aimed at people who are open to exploring the Course as a spiritual path. This includes those who know little about the Course but are interested in incorporating more spirituality into their lives. This also includes people who are already students of the Course or have been in the past. For new students, this book attempts to supply them with everything they will need to begin working with the Course. For more experienced students, the value of this book is that it lays out a new vision of the Course, in both theory and practice, one that makes the most of the Course's practical nature.

There exists a single overall framework underpinning both the portrayal of the Course to the general public and the way it is perceived within its community of students—a single lens through which people tend to see it. This framework is that the Course is a spiritual *teaching*. In my experience, it is primarily seen as a collection of insightful, inspirational ideas, to be read, quoted, and discussed. We can see this reflected in the wise quotations from it that pepper various popular spiritual books. We can also see it in books written for Course students, books that often focus on the Course's metaphysical ideas while scarcely mentioning the practical discipline contained in the Workbook. I admit that this is not the only way the Course is perceived; most students do hold some of the other view which I will describe shortly. Yet, having said that, I still think that the vast majority primarily relate to it as a teaching.

Relating to the Course mainly as a teaching has been a fateful move, in my opinion, for it has automatically dictated an overall relationship with it. As a teaching, our main response to the Course is to *try to understand its ideas*. We especially seek to understand its basic orienting concepts—about God and the Holy Spirit, about the illusory nature of the world, about the details of the original separation from God. As a result, discussion of these concepts tends to fill Course books, study groups, and online chat rooms. Discussions of how to live the Course also fill these forums, but such discussions tend to be rather speculative. If the Course is mainly there to teach us its concepts, then we will probably have to figure out on our own how to apply it. The Course itself is often seen as so aloof from practical concerns that it is common to hear that once we have ingested its ideas, we need to set the book down so that we can go out and live it.

The problem with this notion is that the Course has set a very lofty goal for us. As the quote from Richard Smoley said, to embody its teaching is to be a saint. Yet if the Course is only a teaching, then it provides no way for us to achieve that goal. It merely points to a distant summit, tells us to arrive there, but then provides us with no path—no roadmap—for reaching that summit. At that point, we start hoping that we will be magically whisked there, perhaps in some earth-shattering mystical experience, or perhaps just by reading and discussing the book. But what a hollow hope that is! According to integral philosopher Ken Wilber, this dilemma is rampant in contemporary spirituality.

> You really have to have an understanding of the development of consciousness. Otherwise, just exhorting people to adopt new paradigms is pretty worthless. It's a goal without a path….What we're short on are actual paths for interior development that would deliver that goal.[3]

That is exactly how *A Course in Miracles* portrays itself. It does not present itself as a spiritual teaching, but rather as a spiritual *path.* It always depicts itself as trying to move us along a journey of inner development toward a goal of total realization. It is filled with imagery of traveling along a pathway; it urges us to walk swiftly along "the road this course sets forth."[4] It calls itself "an easy path, so clearly marked it is impossible to lose the way."[5] It calls itself "an organized, well-structured and carefully planned program."[6] What it most often calls itself is merely a "course"—a word which means a program of instruction, and which also means a path along which something moves. In the following passage, from which the title of this book is drawn, we see all of these things; we see the Course leading us one step at a time along a path to the goal of waking up to Who we really are:

> This course was sent to open up the path of light to us, and teach us, step by step, how to return to the eternal Self we thought we lost.[7]

This distinction between viewing the Course as a path versus as a teaching may seem to be a subtle one, but it makes a world of difference. It determines, in fact, our basic relationship with the Course. When we view it as a path, a different relationship with it arises than when we view it as a teaching. If the Course is a path, then our main response to it is to seek to *progress along the path toward the goal.* With this main response comes its own set of questions and priorities: What does the Course tell me to do in order to make progress? Am I doing those things? What results am I experiencing? In this mode, we still try to understand the teaching, but as a *means* to making progress on the path, not as an end in itself.

The whole concept of a path, of course, is that it offers a way to reach the goal, and that is exactly what the Course provides. It is filled with practical exercises. It tells us what to do and what results will obtain. It claims, in fact, to provide us with everything we need along the way, so that all that is left to us is to pay attention: "You need offer only undivided attention. Everything else will be given you."[8] We can see this in all three volumes, but it is perhaps easiest to see in the Workbook, which gives minute instruction in exactly how and when to practice the Course—including how to hold our mind while practicing and how to deal with those inevitable extraneous thoughts. Thus, we do not have to set the book down in order to live it; the book is what tells us how to live it. That is its whole purpose. It is a manual in how to progressively realize its teaching.

Viewing the Course as a path opens up a world of benefits, benefits that seem frustratingly out of reach when we view it as a teaching. Now, under the Course's guidance, when we get upset, we know how to dispel our negative feelings. When we face a difficult decision, we know how to listen to the Holy Spirit. When we are mired in interpersonal conflict, we know how to resolve it. When we are afraid, we know how to calm our fears. When we yearn to feel closer to God, we know how to experience that closeness. We know exactly what to do to put one foot in front of the other on this path. As a result, we get somewhere. In the midst of the same trials as before, we experience more peace, and this peace spreads to everyone we encounter.

The model of the Course that I will present in this book is grounded in careful scholarship. It is a purist model, in that it aims for complete fidelity to the words of the Course. Because such fidelity is only an ideal, details of this model will at times shift around; yet I have a great deal of confidence in the model's basic outlines. Normally, we assume that such devotion to "the letter of the law" kills the spirit, leading to a stale and rigid spiritual life. This is not true with the Course. Its words are soaked through and through with practicality. Thus, the deeper we go into those words, the more we contact the Course's urge to set us free and its very sensible counsel in how that freedom can be realized. As a result, this model has much greater practical relevance than we might expect from a scholarly-based model. It has transformed my own spiritual life, and I have seen it bring wonderful results into the lives of students, who now relate to the Course as a set of transformative tools, rather than a mere collection of ideas.

I write this book both as a student of the Course and as a teacher. I have been a student since 1981. It took me a few years, but I eventually fell in love with the Course, and that love has only deepened with time. For my first ten years with it, I too related to the Course primarily as a teaching. Only slowly, through close study of the book, did I come to realize that it is a "clearly marked" path. Once I came to this realization, I gradually began to treat it as such, attempting to incorporate all the aspects of the path into my life. As I did, the benefits the Course was able to give me mushroomed. I cannot even imagine my life now without the daily activity of walking this path.

I have taught the Course publicly since 1986. Initially, I quite naturally taught it within the Course-as-teaching framework I described above. I was thus mainly concerned that students understand its ideas. I also wanted them to apply it, but I acted as if each individual had to devise his or her own ways of doing that. Over time, though, my conception of my role has changed. I now see my job as helping students walk "the road this course sets forth." It has been extremely gratifying to watch students use the Course's practical measures and receive the benefits from doing so.

Those benefits, combined with my own personal experience with the Course and my scholarly investigations into it, have only caused my estimate of its stature to grow. A passion has arisen in me to spread the word about this remarkable path. For years the urge has grown in me to compress my overall vision of the Course—a vision I share with my colleagues at the Circle of Atonement—into a single book that could reach a large number of potential and actual students.

The purpose of this book is to present the Course as a spiritual path. It is a new spiritual path, one that, in my view, breaks significant new ground. It is bursting with fresh insights into the human condition and the way to God. Yet in many ways it is quite traditional. Many of its methods are ones that have been working for spiritual aspirants for thousands of years. Further, it is not shy about spiritual authority nor about good old-fashioned discipline. Though it shines with originality, there is nothing trendy about it. Its only concern is to propel us toward that ancient and most noble of all goals, the transcending of egocentricity. And for that, it is an extremely effective means.

A Course in Miracles is unconventional; it is on the fringe. But so was every spiritual tradition when it first began. The Course, in my view, has the potential to become an enduring spiritual tradition. Its ideas reach to the sky, but it manages to bring them down to earth and guide us in concretely applying them. In the end, the Course provides a complete framework in which we can conduct our whole journey to God. Many of us are hungry for such a framework. We have left conventional frameworks behind, and this has deposited us in a kind of no-man's land, saddled with an independence that is bewildering rather than liberating. We do not want to go back to the old structures that we discovered to be so deeply flawed, yet we want *some* kind of structure.

We just want one that sets us free, rather than imprisons us. We want a structure in which we can truly feel at home. The more deeply I have gone into the Course, the more convinced I am that here is a path in which seekers from a wide variety of backgrounds can find a home. Here is a path on which countless people can experience accelerated progress on the only journey that counts.

Path of Light

PART I

HOW IT CAME AND WHAT IT IS

Tolerance for pain may be high, but it is not without limit. Eventually everyone begins to recognize, however dimly, that there *must* be a better way.

Text, Chapter 2, Section III, Paragraph 3

Introduction to Part I

Normally, we want to know a few basic things about a book before we start reading. We want to know who the author is, what genre best describes the book, and how its content can be briefly summarized. These facts can usually be supplied rather quickly—that's the function of the book's jacket. We get a paragraph about the author. We are told what category the book fits in; for instance, science fiction or psychology or spirituality. Most of the jacket is devoted to telling us about the book's contents. We do not need to know how the book was written because we more or less already do know that: the author sat down at a desk, consulted his or her notes, and wrote.

With *A Course in Miracles*, however, these simple issues are not so simple at all. Before we even get to the question of its content, we face some rather formidable issues. Its authorship is an issue that will be debated for as long as the Course exists. What genre the Course fits into is almost impossible to define. Is it New Age? Is it Christian? What exactly *is* it? And how it was written is a whole story in itself.

So before we dive into what the Course teaches and what its program is, we need a couple of chapters to discuss what normally fits comfortably on part of a book jacket, or is not even mentioned on that jacket because it's common knowledge. In discussing these seemingly mundane issues, we enter a different world, where our ordinary assumptions do not apply and our familiar categories are much too limiting.

ONE

The Genesis of *A Course in Miracles*

The story of how *A Course in Miracles* came into the world is as unusual and unconventional as what the Course teaches. Indeed, the two can be seen as mirror images of each other. Somehow, the way the Course came to be is a reflection of what it teaches. Remarkably, the story of its birth is a *parable* of its teaching. In light of this, I would like to relate the history of the Course's genesis in a way that draws this metaphor out. At various points, I'll pause and discuss the theme in the Course's teaching that is demonstrated by that particular part of its story.

The story of *A Course in Miracles* begins in the late 1950's at Columbia University in New York City. In 1958, Bill Thetford (1923–1988) was hired as the director of the Psychology Department at Columbia-Presbyterian Medical Center. Shortly afterward, he hired Helen Schucman (1909–1981) as a research psychologist in his department. From the beginning, their relationship was fraught with conflict and friction. They respected each other and worked closely together, but their personalities were completely opposite. What's more, they felt surrounded by competition, suspicion, and backbiting in their department. This atmosphere of conflict was all-pervasive, extending to their relationship with other departments and even other medical centers.

After seven years of this, Bill had had enough. One day in June of

1965, before a weekly meeting that usually proved particularly unpleasant, he did something that was quite out of character for him. Normally quiet and unassuming, he gave an impassioned preplanned speech to Helen, insisting that "there must be another way"—a way in which people could get along. He in fact intended to try out this new way at that day's meeting. He would focus on the positive rather than focusing on people's mistakes. He would refrain from attack. He would cooperate rather than compete. The two of them, he said, had been going the wrong way, and it was time for them to head in a new direction. Helen wrote:

> When it was over he waited for my response in obvious discomfort. Whatever reaction he may have expected it was certainly not the one he got. I jumped up, told Bill with genuine conviction that he was perfectly right, and said I would join in the new approach with him.[1]

Though there appeared to be nothing at all spiritual about this event, later developments revealed it to have immense spiritual significance. Indeed, it was a classic example of what the Course would call a "holy instant," a moment when we let old patterns of thought fall away and leave an empty space for something new to enter in. Afterwards, we do not quite return to normal. Whatever entered in that moment will take on a life of its own and may whisk us off on a journey that we never anticipated.

This is exactly what happened to Helen and Bill. They knew this was a pivotal event in their lives, and they tried hard to implement their new approach. This actually resulted in significant improvement in the interpersonal dynamics within their department (though, unfortunately, not in their relationship). Yet the most significant results of their decision were totally unexpected. It was as if an inner switch clicked on inside Helen, as if she had been waiting for this event her entire life. She spontaneously began to have a series of dramatic inner visions, dreams, and psychic experiences. Helen had always seen inner pictures, but now these transformed into colorful moving pictures with their own storylines.

In the first series of inner images—which came to her both in the waking and dream state—she saw an ancient priestess, heavily wrapped in chains and kneeling. Over a period of weeks, she saw the chains fall away and the figure slowly rise, lift her head, and look at Helen, her eyes full of innocence and compassion. Helen was deeply moved, and understood this priestess to represent some holy person deep inside her, who had been imprisoned but was now being freed to resume her ancient function.

In the second series, Helen saw a number of scenes depicting her and Bill in what looked like past-life situations, although she recognized the situations as at least partly symbolic. The earliest picture chronologically was of an ancient time in which Helen again appeared as a priestess. This priestess lived in a temple and healed others via prayer, while Bill served as her devoted assistant. After this came several scenes in different time periods in which she and Bill were out of accord—either Helen needing the help of an unresponsive Bill or Helen assuming a superior role and regarding Bill with contempt. The series, however, came full circle in its final installment. She and Bill were in a church, where they knelt with Jesus before a simple wooden altar, on which was written the word "Elohim," the Hebrew word for God. She said simply, "We had finally reached our goal."[2]

The third series portrayed the spiritual journey upon which Helen was embarking. It began with Helen finding an old boat stuck in the mud, which she tried vainly to free. Then a man showed up whom she eventually recognized as Jesus. He helped her free the boat and then steered it through a violent storm before returning the steering wheel to her. The boat ended up traveling down a peaceful canal lined with beautiful trees, grass, and flowers. Helen, excited by the possibility of treasure, fished down in the water and pulled up a treasure chest which, to her disappointment, only contained a large black book. On the spine was printed in gold the word "Aesculapius," the Greek/Roman god of healing. It was a curious and seemingly anticlimactic ending to this inner saga; yet in later visions, she continued seeing this same mysterious book, once with a string of pearls around it, and once being carried in a bundle by a stork. While she was viewing this last scene, an inner voice said to her, "This is your book."[3]

In the midst of receiving these series of inner pictures, Helen began having episodes of knowing things she should not be able to know—primarily events happening at a distance, events that were later confirmed. She called this her "magic phase," and it aroused great anxiety in the hard-nosed scientist in her, as well as stirring pride and self-inflation in her ego. She didn't realize it, but she was in a crucial phase of deciding how to use an unusual ability that would be the source of her function: the ability to receive information through non-ordinary means. Would she use it for the glorification of her ego or in service of a higher plan? This question was finally decided in a pivotal inner vision.

In this vision, she found herself coming upon a very old scroll in a desert cave—a cave that she recognized years later when she visited the caves in which the Dead Sea Scrolls were found. She opened the scroll to see the words "God is" on the center panel. As she opened it further, tiny black letters began appearing on the side panels. An inner voice explained that on the left side she could read all of the past, and on the right side all of the future. After struggling with the temptation to look at the side panels, she made a firm decision:

> I rolled up the scroll to conceal everything except the center panel.
>
> "I'm not interested in the past or the future," I said, with finality. "I'll just stop with this."
>
> The Voice sounded both reassured and reassuring. I was astonished at the depth of gratitude that it somehow conveyed. "Thank you," it said, "You made it that time. Thank you."
>
> And that, it seemed, was that.[4]

A thread we see running through Helen's inner visions and psychic experiences is also a major theme in the Course: Each of us has been assigned a specific function in the overall plan for salvation. This function makes optimal use of our talents and abilities, but it may take a form we never would have guessed, and it may utilize abilities we never knew we had. It has been designed *for* us, not *by* us. It does not wait for us to fashion it but merely to accept it. We do so by making a single, genuine decision to see another person's interests as the same as our own (as Helen did by joining Bill in his search for a better way). By making this decision, we enter into a pact with God, even if we don't believe in God. We unleash forces beyond our control that will conspire to carry us into our function. Yet we cannot fulfill our function alone. We need companions (like Bill) who will stand by our side, and we need guidance from a heavenly presence (like Jesus) to steer us through stormy waters that we could not navigate alone. And, most importantly, we need to surrender our abilities to God, rather than using them to puff up our own ego. We need to stop with the center panel, just as Helen did.

Helen's decision to use her "scribal" abilities only for God marked the end of what was apparently a preparatory phase. Her cryptic line at the end of her above account—"And that, it seemed, was that"—implies that something had come to completion and that something new was about to commence. At this point, Helen remarked to Bill that she felt she was "about to do something very unexpected." Then, on the night of October 21, 1965, Helen heard the now familiar inner voice speak these startling words:

> This is a course in miracles. Please take notes.

Helen phoned Bill in a panic, asking what she should do. Bill wisely suggested that she do what it instructed and take down the notes. Then they could look them over at the office in the morning and see if they made any sense.

Thus began the seven-year process of scribing *A Course in Miracles.* Helen would take down the dictation in a shorthand notebook. Then, the next day in the office, she would read it to Bill, who would type it up. From the very beginning, they realized that this was the answer to their request for a better way. This highlights an important feature of the Course. Helen and Bill were not looking for anything spiritual—Bill had no religious beliefs, and Helen had adopted the pose of a "militant atheist"—they just wanted a way to get along with each other and with their colleagues. Yet, strangely, their decision to pursue plain old interpersonal harmony triggered a series of paranormal experiences, and these culminated in an inner voice dictating a spiritual tome. Further, this spiritual tome was all about how to find the better way they sought—a way to cooperate and not compete. This implies that interpersonal harmony has a genuinely spiritual significance. It implies that somebody up there cares about us humans getting along.

The Course teaches that we will only reach total spiritual awakening by transforming our "special relationships"—in which we essentially use others to make ourselves feel special—into "holy relationships," in which we join with another in pursuit of a truly common goal. According to the Course material, this is the only true road out of the illusion of separate selfhood:

> Each one must share one goal with someone else, and in so doing, lose all sense of separate interests. Only by doing

> this is it possible to transcend the narrow boundaries the ego would impose upon the self.[5]

It is no accident, then, that the cradle in which the Course was born was the joining of two people who had been at each other's throats for years. It seems only appropriate that a book which teaches that "salvation is a collaborative venture"[6] was itself the fruit of a collaborative venture.

The writing was not automatic. It required Helen's conscious cooperation, yet she did not decide when she would take dictation. Rather, she would "feel it coming on."[7] Thankfully, its timing seemed carefully designed to not conflict with her daily activities. It was also highly interruptible. She could put her notebook down in mid-sentence to speak to someone or take a nap, and when she resumed, the writing would pick up exactly where it left off. She could put it down for hours, days, or even weeks, without at all disturbing its flow of words and ideas. Further, she could take dictation anywhere, at home or at work, even on buses and subway trains. She did not need to find a special place or withdraw into a trance. In every way, the writing seemed designed to fit into the structure of her life, rather than requiring her life to fit into its structure.

This does not mean, however, that Helen did not put up a fight. Throughout the process, she often refused to cooperate, at times for weeks at a stretch. However, during these uncooperative periods, she found herself feeling acutely uncomfortable and even depressed until she returned to her scribal role. Moreover, as adamantly as she resisted *writing* what she heard, she found *reading* it aloud to Bill even more difficult. She would stutter, experience coughing attacks and prolonged yawning jags, and sometimes even lose her voice completely, making each page that Bill typed a difficult and exhausting journey. Without his constant support, in fact, the process would have been impossible. Bill later joked that he would type the notes "with one hand on Helen and the other on the typewriter."

Helen's resistance to the Course is legendary among Course students. She had long ago put away the matter of religion and now considered herself a strictly rational scientist. Her new role as the scribe of an inner voice that (as we'll see) claimed to be Jesus was a distinctly unwelcome one, which threatened to destroy her professional reputation. It was a role she never publicly identified with. Rather than using her position as scribe to collect throngs of adoring followers, she refused to become a public spokesperson for the Course once it was published, deciding instead to remain in the background. To the end of her life, very few of her family, friends, and colleagues were even aware of her role as the scribe of *A Course in Miracles*.

It was not only the role of scribe that Helen resisted; she also had tremendous difficulty with the Course's teachings. They represented a fundamental challenge to her entire way of being. Along with her razor-sharp intellect came a judgmental temperament. She also felt constantly victimized, was preoccupied with physical illness, and was insistent that she was the one in control of her life.[8] The Course's teachings called her to leave all of these things behind, to give up her judgments, control, and sense of victimization. Yet by all accounts, she did not have much success in doing so. She once told a friend, "I *know* the Course is true...but I don't believe it."[9]

Yet to emphasize only Helen's resistance would be unfair. There was a whole other side to her. As a child, she had been deeply concerned with matters of religion. Born Jewish, during her childhood she also explored Catholicism and the Baptist church. Her search for God, however, was ultimately unsuccessful, and in young adulthood, she resentfully tried to put the matter behind her. One gets the impression, though, that her claimed "militant atheism" later in life was more anger at God than actual belief that there was no God.

Helen had a decidedly mystical side to her. She clearly had paranormal abilities as well as an innate propensity for mystical experiences. The author of the Course once commented on this, saying, "You are *not* the average American woman....Your experience in your life has been atypical."[10] Perhaps her most dramatic spiritual experience came decades before the Course. Forced by circumstance to ride the subway, she found herself revolted by the sad display of humanity she saw around her. She shut her eyes and experienced a vision of herself as a child walking into, prostrating herself before, and then disappearing into a radiant light she knew to be God. When she opened her eyes she was overwhelmed with love for all the people she had been disgusted with just a moment before.

These two sides to Helen resulted in a deeply divided attitude toward her role as scribe of *A Course in Miracles*. She argued with the author, and at times even resorted to calling him names, yet she also had a deeply personal sense of connection with him[11] and never seriously considered not completing her assignment as his scribe. Here is how she put it:

> As for me, I could neither account for nor reconcile my obviously inconsistent attitudes. On the one hand I still regarded myself officially an agnostic, resented the material I was taking down, and was strongly impelled to attack it and prove it wrong. On the other hand I spent considerable time in taking it down and later dictating it to Bill, so that it was apparent that I also took it quite seriously. I actually came to refer to it as my life's work, even though I remained unconvinced about its authenticity and very jittery about it. As Bill pointed out, I must believe in it if only because I argued with it so much. While this was true, it did not help me. I was in the impossible position of not believing in my own life's work. The situation was clearly ridiculous as well as painful.[12]

Helen's split may strike us too as "ridiculous," but in fact she is a perfect symbol for how the Course views all of us. We may experience ourselves as reasonably unified in our personalities and our goals, but according to the Course we are all profoundly split inside. Our true nature, it says, is not just spiritual; it is *spirit.* In this part of us, experiencing oneness with God is as automatic as breathing, and our natural and spontaneous impulses are exactly the same as God's Will. Yet now our minds are identified with a *false* nature, which the Course calls the ego. It is the ego that is the driving force behind life as we know it, behind the rat race in which everyone relentlessly pursues the needs of a separate self. The ego does not just lead us in a different direction than God; it wages constant war on the spirit within us. It tries in every way possible to conquer our true nature, to keep it permanently submerged so that we will never look it in the face and side with it. As a result, our mind becomes a battlefield, constantly torn between the two sides, haunted by an unquenchable yearning for the heavens and yet driven by the urge to wallow in the mud; sensing that the spirit is our joy and yet finding ourselves morbidly attracted to misery. If any one of us examined our mind honestly and sensitively, we would find the same split in us that Helen described in herself.

The story of *A Course in Miracles* naturally raises an insistent question: Where did the material come from? Who (or what) actually authored it? I think it is impossible to maintain that it came from Helen's conscious mind, that she simply composed it and then tricked everyone into believing that it came from an inner voice. No one takes that possibility seriously. Could it, however, have come from her unconscious mind? Perhaps the material represents an amalgam of influences that she soaked up during the course of her life. This theory has been put forward, but it too has difficulties. Helen simply did not absorb many spiritual influences. Her chief influences were her childhood experimentation with being a Catholic and a Baptist and an adult interest in the Bible and the rituals of Catholicism. Yet these conventional Christian influences can hardly account for the depth of mystical and metaphysical thought that pervades the Course. She herself remarked, "I have subsequently found out that many of the concepts and even some of the actual terms in the writing are found in both Eastern and Western mystical thought, but I knew nothing of them at the time."[13] Patrick Miller, author of *The Complete Story of the Course*, concludes, "There is little evidence of 'new thought' or metaphysical schools exerting significant influence on Schucman before the transcription of the Course."[14]

It seems, then, that if the Course did come from Helen's unconscious, that unconscious must have been able to tap into broader influences than what she had personally encountered, or perhaps even to tap into the actual realities of which the Course speaks. Generous as this idea is, however, it is not the Course's account of its authorship, which can be gleaned from the following passages:

> If the Apostles had not felt guilty, they never could have quoted me as saying, "I come not to bring peace but a sword." This is clearly the opposite of everything I taught.[15]
>
> The "punishment" I was said to have called forth upon Judas was a similar mistake. Judas was my brother and a Son of God, as much a part of the Sonship as myself.[16]
>
> As the world judges these things, but not as God knows them, I was betrayed, abandoned, beaten, torn, and finally killed.[17]
>
> My resurrection comes again each time I lead a brother safely to the place at which the journey ends and is forgot.[18]

In light of these passages, it is unmistakable who the author is claiming to be. Also unmistakable is the fact that this voice claiming to be Jesus of Nazareth is trying to change our perception of the biblical Jesus. Each passage contains some element of this: He never taught that he came to bring the sword of God's wrath; he regarded Judas not as his betrayer, only as his brother and his equal; historically speaking, his crucifixion did *occur*, but in God's eyes it was not *real*; he experiences his resurrection all over again each time he leads one of us to complete awakening. The author not only believes he is Jesus, he also believes that history's image of him has instilled fear in people, and he wants to change that image.

Given that it is impossible to prove who or what authored the Course, each person must arrive at his or her own beliefs about this. Yet the Course's claim that Jesus authored it reflects important currents in its teaching. The Course teaches that our little minds are hopelessly inadequate when it comes to charting our course through life. Not only do we have limited intelligence and information, but our attachment to our egos also makes us literally insane. Left to our own devices, says the Course, we will inevitably decide against our own best interests. We therefore need the guidance of an inner voice which transcends our limited ego, which sees the big picture and knows the path to true happiness. This Voice can guide us to make sound decisions and, more importantly, can lead us down that path to happiness and sanity. The Course calls this Voice the Holy Spirit, yet also gives It a more personal face: Jesus. It says that Jesus is one of us who, through his awakening, became a pure extension of the Holy Spirit. It says that in his resurrection, he transcended being localized, confined to one place at a time, and gained the ability to be personally present to each and every individual on earth. To students who believe that Jesus wrote it, the Course itself is concrete testimony that Jesus is indeed present to us in a very personal way.

When the Course began coming through, Helen and Bill had no idea what it was. They didn't know if it was anything beyond the opening miracle principles. As time went on, though, they saw it slowly grow into a genuine course. The Text came first and took three years, reaching completion in 1968. Then came the Workbook, which was completed in 1971. Helen found the Workbook easier to scribe, due in part to the fact that its scope—a year of daily lessons—was set out from the beginning.

Finally came the Manual for Teachers, which was scribed during 1972.

If it had been up to Bill and Helen, *A Course in Miracles* would probably have remained a quiet thing, shared cautiously with a few people. Bill remarked on their fear of having their professional identities compromised: "The Course was our guilty secret! Professors at Columbia didn't *do* this kind of thing, particularly in the Department of Psychiatry. Can you imagine?—hearing voices, taking down material of this kind..."[19] The Course, however, seemed to draw to itself what it needed in order to get out of Helen and Bill's closet. The Course teaches that along the way, we will be joined by "mighty companions,"[20] and that is precisely what happened in this case. After the Course's completion, two key people with whom it was shared decided to join with Helen and Bill and devote their lives to the Course.

Ken Wapnick, a young psychologist, was about to embark on a life as a monk in a monastery in Israel. Though raised a Jew, he had become an agnostic in his youth, but had recently converted to Catholicism, having felt a calling to become a Catholic monk. Just before leaving for Israel to plunge into the monastic life, Ken met Helen and Bill. "Helen's book" was only mentioned in passing and Ken did not read a word of it, but while in Israel, he had two significant dreams about this book, and it began to loom larger and larger in his mind. When he returned to America to tie up his affairs, he was extremely eager to read the manuscript. Once he did, all of his plans changed:

> As I began reading the text from the beginning I quickly recognized the Course as being the most perfect blend of psychology and spirituality that I had ever seen. And I am sure that it did not take me very long to realize that *A Course in Miracles* was my life's work, Helen and Bill were my spiritual family, and that I was not to become a monk but to remain in New York with them instead.[21]

Ken became a key part of the early Course family. He helped Helen with the final editing of the manuscript, became her closest spiritual confidant, and, after her death, went on to become the Course's most influential interpreter.

The fourth member of this little family was Judith Skutch (now Skutch Whitson). At the time, Judy was living a busy life immersed in the world of parapsychology. She and her husband Bob were running the Foundation for Parasensory Investigation, which funded a number of seminal projects. Their Manhattan apartment often hosted several events at once, and Judy was in touch with the top names in the field. Yet as exciting as this life was on the outside, Judy felt a deep void inside, and one night she reached a breaking point. "Alone in my bedroom I began to weep, and without knowing how or where the words came from, I let out a desperate, wrenching cry: 'Won't someone up there please help me!'"

Things happened in rapid succession after this. Within days, a numerologist told her that soon she would meet an older woman who would become her teacher, and that within a year, she would publish one of the most important spiritual documents known to humanity. Nine days later she was introduced to Helen Schucman and Bill Thetford, ostensibly to discuss holistic healing. However, during the conversation, Judy turned to Helen and heard herself say something completely unexpected: "You hear an inner voice, don't you?" This startling comment prompted Helen and Bill to take Judy into their office and spill their whole story to her. Judy was shown the Course, and she read its introduction. "When I finished reading that first passage a great sigh of relief welled up inside me as I heard the inner voice proclaim, 'Here is your map home.' And I knew absolutely this was the answer to my call for help."[22] The circle of those whose lives were devoted to the Course had now grown to four, and these four began meeting almost daily to discuss and practice the Course together.

With Judy's arrival, the cat was finally out of the bag. She soon began sharing the Course with friends in San Francisco (a comfortable three thousand miles away from Columbia University), and it took off. Judy's copy of the Course was photocopied, and those copies were copied, and so on until the copies were getting too light to read. The four clearly perceived that the Course needed to be put in a form that was more user-friendly than twenty pounds of photocopied paper. So the group had several hundred photo-reduced copies printed, but these were snatched up almost as soon as they were printed. With interest in the Course growing exponentially, the original group reached the inevitable decision that the Course had to be published. In fact, several publishers approached them during this time, but all wanted to abridge the material, something which felt distinctly wrong to the small Course family.

The group met and sought inner guidance about the situation. Each one received a different bit of instruction: The Course was to be published in its original form (not abridged); by those whose lives were devoted to this alone; by a nonprofit organization; somehow they all should be involved. Surveying this guidance, they realized that they were the only ones who could meet all these criteria. It dawned on them that *they themselves* were meant to publish the Course. They had little money, but based on an inner directive to "make the commitment first," Judy pledged all of her assets to the Course's publication.

That proved unnecessary, however. The next morning, she received a call from a man in Mexico. Remarkably, he was studying the Course with a group there. He was calling to urge Judy to publish the Course in hardcover as soon as possible, and to altruistically offer the proceeds of a recent real estate sale to make this possible. With all obstacles out of the way, the Course was published in June of 1976 by the Skutchs' non-profit Foundation for Parasensory Investigation, whose name had now been changed (based on guidance received by Helen) to the Foundation for Inner Peace.

A Course in Miracles went on to become a unique spiritual phenomenon. Though it has primarily (and somewhat inaccurately) been associated with New Age spirituality, its appeal has cut across all boundaries. It has sold over a million copies. A number of translations have been published and more are in the works. Thousands of weekly study groups have been formed to discuss it. It has privately informed the life and work of a great many authors, psychologists, ministers, and Catholic priests and nuns. Centers devoted to it have sprung up all over this country and around the world. It has inspired literally scores of books, many of them bestsellers, such as Marianne Williamson's *A Return to Love* and Jerry Jampolsky's *Love is Letting Go of Fear*. In short, it has become a modern spiritual classic, whose influence is increasingly global.

In reflecting on the story of the Course's genesis, we can see that it corresponds amazingly well to what the Course teaches about the birthing-and-development process that spawns a holy relationship. The Course says that our special relationships, which are based on the ego, should not be cast aside, but should instead be given to the Holy Spirit. "However unholy the reason you made them may be, He can translate them into holiness."[23] This translation to holiness occurs, as I mentioned earlier, when two people experience an instant of joining in a truly common goal. Once they do, they no longer have to go it alone. A presence of holiness enters the relationship and shepherds it towards its goal. This presence, though, can only remain confined within the fence of this relationship for so long. As the Course says, "The holy light that brought you together must extend, as you accepted it."[24] The presence wants to reach through these two people to uplift the world. Thus, it designs for them a joint function, something they can do together for the sake of others. And as they do it, the holy presence adds its own power to their efforts, so that their impact is far greater than what they could have accomplished by their own strength. In the end, the Course promises, "Through your holy relationship, reborn and blessed in every holy instant you do not arrange, thousands will rise to Heaven with you."[25] This entire process I have just described is lifted straight from the Course's teaching, yet it is not difficult to perceive this exact same process in the Course's story.

Perhaps the main theme that strikes one about this story is that throughout, the impetus at least appears to have come from somewhere beyond the human realm. It would be one thing if Helen had bought tapes on how to channel—so that she and Bill could gather the material she would channel into a best-selling book. What actually happened, though, was something altogether different. Helen and Bill did not plan to produce a book, especially one so spiritually oriented, nor did Helen plan to be a channel of any sort. A voice came to her unsought, announced the title of its book, and then proceeded to dictate it. It did not just dictate a flow of words, it designed the overall structure of the book as well, which included three separate volumes, each with its own purpose and title. Once the book was complete, Helen and Bill did not have a clue what to do with it, yet events unfolded serendipitously and swept the Course into publication, almost as if the author wanted to make sure his opus reached a wider audience. From start to finish, the individuals involved seemed to be reluctant participants in someone else's script. It's easy to get the impression that whatever voice dictated the Course's words was also the driving force behind the entire story.

Even though the Course is often associated with the New Age and is laced with themes reminiscent of Eastern spirituality, its story looks more like something straight out of the Bible. We all know the classic biblical pattern. Into an unlikely, even inhospitable situation, God comes. He speaks to a reluctant nobody who cannot for the life of him fathom why God would choose him. This person balks and resists, but in the end accepts the difficult assignment of being God's mouthpiece. Initially, God may speak to this person in private, but the words are always meant for a wider audience. Eventually, what God says through this one person causes waves that reach far beyond that person's little sphere, and may in the end reach even beyond his culture and time period. For, from the beginning, God's eye is on the entire world.

The story of the Course, then, is reminiscent of the stories of the Hebrew prophets. Just as Moses asked God, "Who am I that I should go to Pharaoh?…I am not eloquent…but I am slow of speech,"[26] so Helen had a strikingly similar reaction when the voice first began dictating to her:

> "Why me?" I asked. "I'm not even religious. I don't understand the things that have been happening to me and I don't even like them….I'm just about as poor a choice as you could make."
>
> "On the contrary," I was assured. "You are an excellent choice, and for a very simple reason. You will do it."[27]

And so we see that the history of the Course's genesis echoes the familiar biblical pattern, but in a fresh way, and in a distinctly nonreligious setting. If we accept the Course at face value, instead of God coming to believing Jews, in this case He came to agnostic university professors.

What I find particularly striking about the story is that it does not just reflect the ancient spiritual theme of God working through chosen human vessels; it also reflects the particular teachings of *A Course in Miracles*, including the holy instant, the split mind, the special function, and the importance of human relationships. The Course's emphasis on interpersonal joining, for instance, is reflected in the fact that the Course had two scribes, as opposed to one solitary prophet. Somehow, woven into the events surrounding the Course's genesis were specific themes central to the Course itself. This gives the distinct impression that while the author was dictating the Course's ideas onto paper, he was also painting these same ideas on the canvas of Helen and Bill's lives. In fact, we can see him working on three levels, for Helen's inner visions, as we saw, also reflected Course themes. Thus, it is as if the author's message was being imprinted on the situation in multiple ways—in the form of the words that Helen took down, the inner pictures she saw, and the events of the Course's scribing and publication. All three carried the same themes; all three bore the unique stamp of the same author.

If, in fact, the Course's story is a parable of its teaching, what does this parable say? What meaning does it communicate to us? Before we consider the Course's teaching in more depth later in the book, I'll attempt here to take the various Course themes we've already seen highlighted in the Course's story and weave them together into a cohesive message for our lives.

Life in this world, as it is normally conducted, does not work. Our blind pursuit of our own self-interest inevitably entangles us in conflict with those around us. And since everyone else is caught in the same struggle, we find ourselves standing in the middle of ever-widening circles of interpersonal discord.

Yet all this can be changed in a single miraculous instant. For just a moment, we can choose to step outside our habitual patterns of thinking and relating. We can reach outside the bubble of our self-interest and join hands with another. In this moment, the two of us can forget our differences and unite in a common purpose. This instant is what the Course calls a holy instant. By momentarily stepping outside our egocentric ways, we allow something new to come in, something holy, and our lives will never be the same again.

In this instant, we invite God in. It doesn't matter if we believe in Him or not. It doesn't matter if we are surrounded by people and institutions that would ridicule the notion of God showing up in our lives. There is no one to whom God will not come, given just a tiny opening. There is nowhere that is too unclean for Him to enter. Once God enters, an entire prearranged plan will be set in motion, one that has been waiting simply for our readiness. From this point on, we will be led along a journey not of our making.

On this journey, we may discover new dimensions to our being that we had no idea were there. We may discover there is a part of us that experiences contact with God as completely normal. We may uncover a natural ability to hear the quiet voice of higher wisdom within ourselves. We may stumble upon powers that are usually considered supernatural.

We will also discover that we have been given a special function, a specific role in God's plan to save the world, one designed especially to fit our particular talents. The holy instant we experienced was, unbeknown to us, our act of accepting this function. From that moment on we will be led ever deeper into this function, first into preparing for it and then into fulfilling it. This process requires our cooperation, but once we have provided a sufficient amount of that, it will unfold of its own accord.

We will also be led through a transformation in how we relate to others. The reason we are encircled by conflict is that we are trying to bend others to our will so they can meet our needs. We must slowly emerge from this condition and acquire an ability to genuinely join with others in goals that transcend separate interests. Our lessons in this regard will, at least at first, be found mainly with the person with whom we shared that holy instant. This relationship is the classroom in which we must learn to step outside our ego's walls and join. Here is where we will initially be faced with the lofty challenge of transforming all our relationships from special to holy.

We do not, however, learn to join with others simply to enjoy a more pleasant earthly existence. Rather, joining with them is how we best learn to join with *God*. It is therefore part of a spiritual journey, a journey of inner awakening. In fact, everything we are going through now is part of this journey. Even our function in the plan for salvation is not just for the world, but for ourselves as well. By selflessly serving others we discover that true goodness, indeed holiness, lives within us. And thus we realize that we naturally belong with the Holy One.

This inner journey is in essence a process of letting go of our ego, and we will find this anything but easy. Just as we may uncover a part of us that is genuinely holy, we will also discover, to our shock, a part of us that is insanely resistant to all that is loving and happy, a part of our mind that is actually waging war on God. We will find ourselves in the uncomfortable position of being split down the middle, with our minds a battleground between sanity and insanity.

We may find, for instance, that our ego jumps in to claim our newfound powers as its own—as tools to elevate itself rather than as instruments for God to use to help others. We may observe that we are deeply ambivalent about our newfound function, perhaps fearing that it threatens the worldly identity we spent so long constructing. And we may find that joining with another person is not as easy as it sounds, for it ultimately requires saying goodbye to our precious ego.

Because we are so divided inside, we need a Guide along this journey. Without this One, we might easily wander off and spend all of our time hanging out in a roadside bar. Our Guide's single-minded intent makes up for our profound ambivalence. He is in charge of the delicate process of leading us through the relinquishment of our ego. He is in charge of keeping us on course in the maelstrom of our ego's storms. He, in fact, is in charge of the entire journey, on the inside and on the outside. We can travel downstream swiftly or lazily, we can even try for a time to paddle against the current, but as long as we stay on the river, it will have its way with us and carry us where it wants us to go.

In the end, our Guide has bigger plans than just our own awakening. We may follow Him in obscurity for years, but all the while, He is secretly readying the fruit of our efforts to leave the manger and go out into the world. We may want to keep our child at home, but the child is not ours to keep. It came here to accomplish something. It came here to fulfill a ministry. And in the end its ministry may touch countless lives and continue to do so long after we are gone, for it was not given only to us. Being from God, from the very beginning it was a gift to the world.

TWO

What Is *A Course in Miracles?*

A Course in Miracles is a spiritual path that shares basic themes with Christianity, Eastern mysticism, and modern psychology. Its central teaching is forgiveness.

Beyond this brief statement, answering the seemingly simple question "What is *A Course in Miracles*?" is surprisingly difficult. When you ask what something is, you are essentially asking, "What *sort* of thing is it?" "What *category* does it fit in?" And therein lies the problem: The Course fits no familiar category. There is nothing in the world quite like it. This may sound like an extravagant claim, but by the end of this chapter I hope you will see the truth of it.

We depend on familiar categories. Let's say you ask someone what Jainism is. When you are told "it's a religion," that essentially tells you what you wanted to know. You already have a category called "religion" built up in your mind, a category complete with a list of characteristics. Now, you simply apply those characteristics to this particular case: "Oh, I see. Jainism is a tradition that probably has a belief in God or some ultimate spiritual principle, most likely has scriptures and forms of worship, perhaps has temples or sanctuaries, maybe some sort of priesthood," etc. By applying to Jainism the label "religion" and all the characteristics that go along with that label, you instantly have some idea of what it is.

The Course, however, is notoriously difficult to categorize, something which has frustrated students and commentators alike. In *Hidden Wisdom*, authors Richard Smoley and Jay Kinney claim that the Course has been miscategorized, that it has been made by its popularizers to sound like "another update of the gospel of positive thinking," when instead, "In its hard-headed rigor it resembles the teachings of the Desert Fathers."[1] They end up categorizing it as Esoteric Christianity rather than New Age: "In its inner 'turning' toward God through the mediation of Jesus Christ, the Course is indeed Christian."[2] Patrick Miller, in his book *The Complete Story of the Course*, speaks of three "forces" associated with the Course: academic psychology, mystical spirituality, and the New Age. He then says that these three forces

> are sufficiently dissimilar in essence to have spawned a great deal of confusion about the true nature of *A Course in Miracles*. Their confluence in one phenomenon has made the Course appear to be a variety of things to students, critics, and the public at large.[3]

I believe that, rather than straining to find the appropriate category for the Course, we should recognize that there *is* no appropriate category, and that this is part of the nature of the Course. Instead, the Course fits many seemingly disparate categories. Each one captures some facet or aspect of the Course, each one by itself paints only a partial picture; but when we look at the Course from all of their angles at once, we finally get a sense of it "in the round." We finally see a more or less adequate answer to the question "What is *A Course in Miracles*?"

In this chapter I will sketch the main categories I think we need in order to arrive at a roughly accurate sense of what the Course is. Once I have done that, I will explore the implications of this curious phenomenon in which the Course straddles so many categories yet is encompassed by none of them.

1. An educational course

One need only look at the Course's cover to see that it places itself in the category of "educational curriculum." It explicitly calls itself a "course" and has a text, a workbook, and a manual for teachers. The Text, like so many texts, supplies this course's "theoretical foundation,"[4] or "abstract level."[5] It sets forth a system of ideas that is often highly intellectual. As with any text, we are urged to study this one carefully.[6] The Workbook, as we might expect, contains a series of exercises, which are intended to help the student apply the Text's ideas on a more practical level. The Manual for Teachers—again, not unexpectedly—provides support for those students who will go on to teach this course to their own "pupils."[7] All in all, like any course, *A Course in Miracles* is designed to take students on a journey of the mind, in which they gradually learn a body of ideas and how to apply those ideas in practice.

A Course in Miracles, however, is *not* like any educational course. Its goals are profoundly different. A conventional course has the underlying goal of helping us stand on our own two feet as capable persons in society. If your childhood education is successful, then in the words of the Course, "By the time you reach 'maturity' you [can]...meet the world on equal terms, at one with its demands."[8] In this light, formal education is a part of the larger process of socialization, in which the world trains us to fit into our social environment. The Course, on the other hand, claims that its training "is directed toward achieving a goal in direct opposition"[9] to the training that turned us into responsible adults. It claims that true learning means the *unlearning* of everything the world has taught us, so that we at last emerge from the collective fog of society and enter the limitless freedom enjoyed by the world's spiritual greats.

The very title signifies the difference in this course. Rather than a course in math or anthropology, this is a course in *miracles*. What an odd thing for an educational course to teach us! A miracle is usually considered to be a gift from above. How many educational courses aim at teaching us to receive gifts of grace from the Divine? Miracles come to set us free from the bondage of the world; one thinks of Jesus setting people free from paralysis or blindness. In the Course's view, such outer imprisonment ultimately stems from our inner bondage to the human ego. Its miracles, therefore, have the purpose of liberating us from this inner bondage, and thus from the entire human condition. Conventional courses end up teaching us how to better punch the world's time clock. How many of them aim at setting us free from the world?

2. A channeled spiritual teaching, as found in the New Age

Someone unexpectedly begins hearing an inner voice. It seems there is a being from the other side who wants to speak through her. This being, who claims to have lived on earth long ago, speaks his wisdom into her mind, wisdom which she is instructed to pass on to others. As he continues to speak, an overall spiritual philosophy emerges, one that bypasses earthly traditions, coming as it does, straight from "upstairs." He says that divinity resides in each person, and that everyone has access to God without having to go through institutions. He says that all is one, and that our task on earth is simply to awaken to that oneness through the series of lessons presented to us by earthly life.

This pattern that we associate with the New Age fits the Course to a tee, yet it was not very familiar when Helen Schucman began scribing the Course in 1965. That changed, however, in the 70's and 80's, as the New Age movement mushroomed, and the public heard of various channeled entities such as Ramtha, Lazaris, and Emanuel. Now, this pattern constitutes a recognizable category in which we can place the Course.

This raises a thorny issue: Is *A Course in Miracles* "New Age"? Along with many Course students and teachers, I believe the Course has been far too closely identified with the New Age. A balanced view, in my opinion, is that the Course does contain themes that are considered New Age, yet it also contains themes and characteristics that fall well outside the New Age worldview. Rather than referring to the Course as New Age, I prefer to say that it "overlaps" the New Age. Dutch scholar Wouter Hanegraaff, in his voluminous study *New Age Religion and Western Culture*, locates the Course within the New Age but acknowledges that it is "decidedly atypical":[10]

> True other-worldliness [where one seeks the ultimate goal of existence in a radically different mode of being than that found in this world] is very rare in the New Age movement. The only unambiguous example in our corpus is *A Course in Miracles*. According to this text—which has correctly been characterized as a Christianized version of non-dualistic Vedanta—our world is just an illusory chimaera, which has nothing to offer but violence, sorrow and pain.[11]

Notice the difficulty Hanegraaff has in categorizing the Course. He includes it in his study of the New Age, but admits that it is not a good fit and then goes on to label it a Christianized version of Vedanta. This lends support to my point that the Course fits no single category and is best described in terms of multiple categories.

3. A purported communication from Jesus Christ

No one has shaped our world more than Jesus of Nazareth. Two billion people claim to be his followers. Imagine if a contemporary message could somehow be authenticated as coming from him. That message would have monumental significance for a third of the world's population. Yet how could such a message ever be authenticated?

Here we face one of the more controversial aspects of *A Course in Miracles*, for the Course claims to be just such a message. It does not emphasize this claim, but there is no question that it does make it. The author speaks of his birth, his miracles, his Apostles, his experience in Gethsemane, his crucifixion, his resurrection, the way he is portrayed in the New Testament, and the way he has been characterized by Christianity.

But how can we know if this really is Jesus? This issue is just like the dilemma that early Christians grappled with in identifying Jesus as the Messiah. Such an identification could never be proven. Hence, their conviction had to come from within. When Peter proclaimed Jesus to be the Messiah, Jesus responded, "Flesh and blood has not revealed this to you, but my Father who is in heaven."[12] Students of the Course are in much the same position. The only way they can come to believe that Jesus authored the Course is through an inward recognition, through perhaps the same still, small voice that spoke to Peter.[13]

There is, however, an immediate obstacle to believing this book was authored by Jesus: The Course's Jesus simply does not square with the traditional Jesus. He does not claim to have a uniquely divine nature, to be the only begotten Son of God, and he does not call for us to believe in him and his sacrifice on the cross. However, this may be more of an advantage than an obstacle. Historians have long recognized that the historical Jesus did not claim or ask these things *either*. In fact, as New Testament scholars peel away the layers of tradition that obscure the original Jesus, many of them find a figure who is strikingly reminiscent of the Course's Jesus. They find a challenging figure who is more than anything else a teacher, a teacher of a way or path which aims for a deep-level transformation in us. This teacher turns upside-down our normal perception of the world, overturning our conventional assumptions as if they were the tables of the moneychangers. He asks us to envision God as an amazingly gracious Father who pours out His love on sinner and saint alike. And he calls us to respond to the world's slings and arrows with an egoless love that mirrors the way God responds to us. Strikingly, all of these elements are central to *A Course in Miracles*.[14]

If the Course really is a message from Jesus, what exactly does he have to say to our modern world? Does he address conditions in the Church? Does he sound the alarm about the environment or warn of impending judgment? No. His message is both more timeless and more personal. He says simply, "Forgive your brother." No matter what he did to you, how unfair it seemed, or how strongly you feel impelled to defend your interests, forgive him; not out of duty, but out of a profound realization that there is ultimately nothing to forgive. If you do, you will make peace with yourself, you will awaken to an untouched innocence within you, you will realize you are God's beloved Son, and you will help save the world.

4. A new system of psychology, with ties to Freud

Modern psychology has changed how we all think about ourselves. It has taught us that there is more to our minds than we realize, that beneath the conscious mind lies an immense unconscious filled with mysterious dynamics. And it has taught us that many if not most of our problems have their source in the mind. Hence, we cannot solve things simply by putting our outer affairs in order; we must attend to the healing of our minds.

A Course in Miracles is deeply psychological. It contains a remarkably extensive and intricate theory of the mind, of its fundamental nature, how it works, what makes it sick, and how it can be healed. On one level, this theory has much in common with modern psychology, especially Freudian psychology—more than most Course students would like to admit. Like Freud, the Course sees the conscious mind suspended over a dark unconscious, filled with buried thoughts and desires the conscious mind finds too frightening to face. This includes impulses that seem more animal than human. Like Freud, the Course views the mind as a veritable battleground, filled with conflict between the conscious and unconscious, between the base and the noble, between the desire for life and the urge for death. And like Freud, it depicts us habitually relying on defense mechanisms, such as denial and projection, to keep from our awareness that which we fear to confront.

The Course, however, ranges far beyond Freud, extending its psychological insights into realms that would be called spiritual or even theological. In fact, one of the most striking things about the Course's psychological system is that it routinely takes insights that we can read in psychology texts or observe in our daily lives and stretches them to mind-boggling extremes. For example:

- Just as Freud taught us to see the conscious mind as only the tip of the iceberg, the Course sees the Freudian unconscious as being the tip of an even larger iceberg. Beneath it lie vast realms of mind which eventually open up to the infinite.
- We know that individuals can go insane and have a break with reality. The Course, however, makes the bold claim that this has happened to all of us. We are all mad. We have had a primordial break with true reality, which is limitless spirit. As a consequence of that rupture we have acquired the false delusion that we are separate beings, and this delusion has caused us to hallucinate a world of time and space, which is not actually there.
- We know from experience that when we feel guilty we also fear that our just deserts will catch up with us. The Course takes this notion to its logical extreme and claims that all fear, without exception, stems from (mostly unconscious) guilt. All fear is, in the final analysis, fear of punishment.
- As we all have experienced, giving to others feels good because it makes us believe that we are good. The Course sees this as an example of a basic law of mind that operates not only in this world but also in the Mind of God. Selfless giving will ultimately save us, but not because it will earn us a ticket through the pearly gates. Rather, it has the psychological power to show us that holiness is basic to our nature.

5. An inspired scripture, in the lineage of the Bible

Scriptures have exerted a powerful influence over human culture for thousands of years, and it is no wonder why: If a book really did contain Heaven's will for the earth, then it would have every right to tower over our landscape and shape our lives and our civilizations. We all know the classic pattern, especially as it has manifested in the West: A book appears, which was written by specially chosen human messengers working under divine inspiration. This book is seen as literally putting the divine will on paper, and so its words carry an exalted power and authority for its followers, becoming their guide in personal, social, and religious matters.

A Course in Miracles fits this pattern perfectly, in two obvious ways. First, its story gives the appearance that it was written by a specially chosen messenger, in this case not merely under divine *inspiration*, but via direct *dictation*. In this sense, the Course is like the Islamic Koran, which, according to tradition, is comprised of direct revelations sent down from God to a single passive receiver, Muhammad. Second, the Course has taken on the kind of authority among its followers which is the defining characteristic of scripture. Once again, Dutch scholar Wouter Hanegraaff echoes this view:

> If we were to select a single text as "sacred scripture" in the New Age movement, the sheer awe and reverence with which the Course...is discussed by its devotees would make this huge volume the most obvious choice. Indeed, it is among those channeled texts which refute the often-heard opinion that channeling only results in trivialities.[15]

The Course clearly appears to see itself in the line or lineage of the West's primary scripture. It frequently refers to the Bible (containing over eight hundred allusions to biblical passages), uses terms and symbols from the biblical tradition (about three dozen by my count), and has the same major figure (Jesus).

The Course, however, sees itself as possessing an authority greater than that of the Bible. It demonstrates this in hundreds of biblical allusions in which its author feels no compunction about selectively affirming certain biblical themes while freely correcting others. For instance, consider this familiar Bible verse: "God is not mocked: for whatsoever a man soweth, that shall he also reap."[16] Here is the Course's reinterpretation: "'God is not mocked' is not a warning but a reassurance. God *would* be mocked if any of His creations lacked holiness."[17] To show what a dramatic reinterpretation this represents, let us draw out the meaning of both passages:

> *Original meaning:* Be warned—when you break God's Laws, His power still has the last word. He will make sure you pay for your sins.
>
> *Course reinterpretation:* Be reassured—when you appear to turn yourself into a sinner, God's power still has the final say on who you are. You are still His holy Son.

Here, the same affirmation that "God is not mocked" yields precisely opposite views of God's relationship with sin: "He will not allow sin to go unpunished" versus "He will not allow sin to *be real*." And this reveals the Course's main problem with the God of the Bible. In its view, a God Who allows sin to be real and is then compelled to respond to it with wrath is not a God of Love. The Course agrees with, and often quotes, the biblical declaration that God is Love, but it goes further than the Bible in emphasizing that God is *only* Love.[18]

In addition to frequently overriding the Bible's authority, the Course also never binds its students to the authority of the Bible. Nowhere, for instance, are students urged to observe the Jewish Sabbath or practice Christian baptism. Instead, the Course charts a new way, a new spiritual path, whose authority is contained completely inside its own covers, as well as in the presence of the Holy Spirit within each student's heart.

6. A path of enlightenment, as found in Eastern spirituality

For over a century now, masses of people in the West have been turning to the East for spiritual light. There, they seek what they perhaps failed to find in the religion of their birth: direct access to spiritual reality; inner liberation that is available now, in this life; teachers who have tasted that liberation; and techniques that can open up that same experience to anyone.

Whereas in the West the classic pattern for the birth of a religious tradition involves the Divine speaking through a chosen messenger, in the East the pattern focuses on the crucial significance of a man who awakens to his oneness with the Divine.[19] This man has freed himself from the tight strictures of his personal ego, with its attendant bitterness, anger, and worry. He has shaken off the illusion that he is a separate self and has awakened to who he really is, which, he discovers, is limitless. He now lives in the awareness that he is one with the All. He has been liberated. He is enlightened.

Now, this enlightened individual teaches others the way out, leading them along the same road that he followed. The path he teaches is somewhat unique to him, following, as it does, the particular contours of his own journey. However, it leads to the same ultimate goal as other paths. His way consists of both teachings and practice. The *teachings* re-educate the student's worldview, instructing him that his suffering is due to the illusion of being a separate ego, and that release from suffering lies in awakening to his true unbounded nature. These teachings may also reveal that the entire phenomenal world is an illusion, and that true reality abides in a transcendental realm beyond time and space, a realm in which there is no separate selfhood, for all is one. The *practice* consists of disciplined mind training, especially in the art of meditation, which allows each individual to detach from his false identity and directly experience who he really is. By following the teachings and doing the practice, the student is eventually freed from his ego and ushered into the same state his teacher found—the state of enlightenment.

This pattern, which one so readily associates with Eastern mysticism, fits the Course as well. Every one of the sentences in the above description accurately portrays the Course. *A Course in Miracles*, then, despite its American origin (through a person who said she knew nothing of Eastern mystical thought) and its biblical language, can be seen as joined with the great river of Eastern spirituality that is flowing into Western culture. How curious that its author, who claims to be Jesus Christ, the divine savior of the West, also resembles an enlightened master of the East!

7. A literary work of art

The Course presents a rigorously consistent intellectual system. We might expect such a system to be expressed in dry, technical language that aims at plain explanation and leaves little room for misinterpretation. Yet the Course is trying to do more than just *inform*; it is trying to *transform*. It wants to move us, to change us. To accomplish this it adopts the forms of art, which are designed for just such a purpose.

This aspect of the Course meant a great deal to Helen Schucman, who once said, "It is quite a literary thing and it does require a certain background….I happen to like this stuff from a literary viewpoint." My colleague Greg Mackie has studied the artistic elements in the Course and sums up his findings in the following paragraph:

> Rather than linear, the Course, as Ken Wapnick has pointed out, is written *symphonically*: it introduces themes, develops them, lays them aside, and then brings them together, exploring their connections much like a symphony. Rather than simple sentence structure, the

> Course is written *poetically*: large portions are written in iambic pentameter, and even those parts not written in this poetic meter have a poetic quality, even occasionally using alliteration and rhyme. Rather than straightforward language, the Course often resorts to the *literary* language of simile, metaphor, symbol, personification, imagery, and allusion. And rather than carefully defining its terms, the Course, like much literature and poetry, uses terms that are more *suggestive* than definitive. Terms are rarely strictly defined, but instead have flexible meanings that depend upon the context of the words around them. All of these techniques enhance depth; they reveal deeper layers of meaning and beauty, free words from the limitations of strict definition, and open them up to deeper connotations and connections.[20]

Even the Course as an intellectual system has an artistic quality. Its system is composed not only of concepts, but also of *characters* (God, the ego, the Holy Spirit, you, your brothers) who interact with each other and move through *places* (Heaven, the world, the borderland, the gate of Heaven, roads and pathways) and *events* (the separation, the Last Judgment, the Second Coming, the final step) in three acts: from a tranquil beginning, through an extended crisis, to a final resolution. This intellectual system, then, also has the flavor of an epic story.

Perhaps the most significant poetic device in the Course is iambic pentameter, also called Shakespearean blank verse. In this kind of verse, each line has five "feet" of two syllables each, and in each "foot" the second syllable is stressed. This results in lines of ten syllables with every other syllable stressed. I'll illustrate this with a line from the Course, in which I divide the feet and emphasize the stressed syllables:

> The *hush*• of *Hea*•ven *holds*• my *heart*• to*day*.[21]

Here is a passage from the Text laid out in verse:

> The blood of hatred fades to let the grass
> grow green again, and let the flowers be
> all white and sparkling in the summer sun.
> What was a place of death has now become
> a living temple in a world of light.
> Because of Them. It is Their Presence which

has lifted holiness again to take
its ancient place upon an ancient throne.[22]

If you read these lines sensitively, you will notice that the iambic pentameter lends a song-like rhythm to the material. Since every other syllable is stressed, it almost feels as if there is a heart beating within each line. The use of iambic pentameter goes on unbroken for hundreds of pages in the Course. About one fourth of the Text is written in this form of verse (beginning in Chapter 24), about two thirds of the Workbook (beginning in Lesson 98), and key portions of the Manual for Teachers. Remarkably, the Course started coming through in this way some time before Helen and Bill even noticed it.

For millennia, art has been a tool for reaching us in a deeper, more personal way than purely logical or analytical ideas generally can. The Course uses the *techniques* of art because it shares the *aims* of art. The aim of art is to move us emotionally and to usher us into a new way of seeing. That is the aim of the Course as well. Its whole goal is to *move* us into a *new perception,* for that, in its eyes, is how we wake up.

8. A manual for interpersonal healing and harmony

There is a plethora of books on the market about relationships, telling us how to get the love we want, how to live romantically every day, how to talk to our children, etc. *A Course in Miracles* is also a book that promises to reveal the path to truly happy relationships. It sees this topic, however, in its broadest dimensions, lumping together a number of subjects that may seem distinct and separate to us:

- healing our painful romantic relationships and friendships
- joining in a common goal with another and undertaking a joint developmental journey
- reaching out to help those who feel alone and in need
- healing the sick in mind and body
- saving the world

This interpersonal focus should not surprise us. After all, *A Course in Miracles* came as an answer to a request for "another way" for people to relate, a way for people to get along. Understandably, students often lose sight of this dimension of the Course. The Course lays out a path of inward realization, in which we withdraw the needs we have laid on others, realize the world is illusory, and turn within ourselves to discover a glorious reality waiting there. The Course, in other words, is beckoning us to embark on the ancient quest to find our inmost center. However, it sees this quest as occurring primarily in our everyday relationships, in how we see and relate to other people, and even in *conjunction* with them. The Course tells us bluntly, "It is impossible to remember God in secret and alone."[23]

What is the Course's prescription for a happy relationship? Rather than arming us with various strategies for getting our needs met, or for skillfully consolidating both partners' needs into a creative "win-win," the Course teaches a radical approach. It says that our happiness lies not in how well we are treated, but in how lovingly *we* see and treat others. It says that real happiness comes not from coaxing (or manipulating) our partners into doing it right, but from *forgiving* them for doing it *wrong*. We would be much happier, in its view, if the real message behind our every communication was not, "Why can't you get it right?" but rather, "Awake and be glad, for all your sins have been forgiven you."[24]

If we can impart this message with real conviction, says the Course, we can work miracles in our relationships and in the lives of anyone we encounter. This, in fact, is the meaning of the Course's title. Students of this material often see a miracle as something strictly internal, yet the Course itself usually speaks of a miracle as an interpersonal event in which something healing passes from one person to another and joins them together. *A Course in Miracles* is therefore, quite literally, a course in how to heal others and heal relationships.

Contemplating the categories

Now we can go back and answer our original question. What is *A Course in Miracles*? What category does it belong in? The answer: Rather than fitting inside a single category, the Course sits astride at least eight categories. Only when we see it as a montage of these eight can we get an adequate sense of what it is. You might want to read down the following list and silently add "that is also" to the end of each item.

A Course in Miracles is…

1. An educational course
2. A channeled spiritual teaching, as found in the New Age
3. A purported communication from Jesus Christ

4. A new system of psychology, with ties to Freud
5. An inspired scripture, in the lineage of the Bible
6. A path of enlightenment, as found in Eastern spirituality
7. A literary work of art
8. A manual for interpersonal healing and harmony

This list answers one question, but in doing so it immediately raises another: How can one thing fit all eight of these categories? How on earth could one book be all these things? Our minds are always captivated when something breaks out of old molds and breaks new ground. That is, after all, the mark of true creativity. Yet how could one thing break *this* many molds?

Our minds are category-bound. According to the Course, we perceive our world through the lens of familiar categories. We thereby impose a grid onto reality that chops a continuous fabric into little separate boxes. We thus perceive things not according to what they are, but to the label of the category we slap onto them.[25] We even confine *ourselves* to categories, unconsciously behaving within the patterns they dictate. If we are writing a textbook, for instance, we unthinkingly write according to our "textbook" category, which dictates how a textbook should sound. In the end, without even realizing it, we become the slave of our categories.

The author of *A Course in Miracles* is refreshingly free of this enslavement. He does not make an occasional creative leap that breaks out of our categories; rather, walking through their walls is his normal way of being. To see how regularly he does this, try asking yourself the following questions:

- How many educational courses are also inspired scriptures in the lineage of the Bible?
- How many purported communications from Jesus Christ are also psychological systems with ties to Freud?
- How many inspired scriptures in the lineage of the Bible are also Eastern-style paths of enlightenment?
- How many new psychological systems are presented as literary works of art?
- How many educational courses are also channeled spiritual teachings?

- How many new psychological systems are also inspired scriptures in the lineage of the Bible?

To my knowledge, the answer to each one of these questions (and many others we could ask) is: *one*. Just *A Course in Miracles*. That is why the Course exists in a category by itself. There is nothing like it. Humans are by nature imitative. What we produce automatically falls into the shape of familiar categories. Yet whoever (or whatever) the author of the Course may be, his mind does not work that way. He thinks outside all the boxes.

Yet although he thinks outside them, he willingly steps *inside* them. He uses them, rather than turning up his nose in repugnance. For instance, even though he voices deep criticisms of conventional education (calling it a fruitless effort to "teach the mind a thousand alien names, and thousands more"[26]), he still freely adopts its forms. Why? The following passage from the Course provides an answer. It says that once you have a holy instant, an experience of true reality, you should

> then step back to darkness [the sensory world], not because you think it real, but only to proclaim its unreality in terms which still have meaning in the world that darkness rules.
>
> Use all the little names and symbols which delineate the world of darkness. Yet accept them not as your reality. The Holy Spirit uses all of them, but He does not forget creation has one Name, one Meaning, and a single Source Which unifies all things within Itself. Use all the names the world bestows on them but for convenience, yet do not forget they share the Name of God along with you.[27]

We can boil this passage's counsel down to one sentence: *Speak of reality in a language the world understands, even if you do not accept that language as defining reality*. This, says the author of the Course, is what the Holy Spirit does, and this, apparently, is what *he* does as well. He uses our familiar categories in order to reach us, even though he does not believe in the limits they impose.

As I contemplate all this, my mind naturally thinks of God. This is how I imagine God would be if He were to express Himself in our world (and the Course teaches that He does all the time, through the Holy Spirit and Jesus). His Mind would naturally transcend the little mental boxes we have built up through human culture. He could never fit into our tiny categories. At the same time, He would not turn up His nose at His children's boxes. He would gladly use them if, by doing so, He could speak to us in a way that we could comprehend. What he would do with them, though, would far surpass our narrow abilities. He would find some masterful way to join those little boxes together into a much larger space, an airy mental room that would expand our horizons and liberate our minds from their tiny compartments. And He would do all this simply because He wanted to reach us, to "kiss us through the dark," as a poet once said. What is *A Course in Miracles*? Perhaps it is an instance of God doing just that.

PART II

THE TEACHING

I am teaching you to associate misery with the ego
and joy with the spirit.

Text, Chapter 4, Section VI, Paragraph 5

Introduction to Part II

Now that we have looked at how *A Course in Miracles* was written and what it is, we can turn to the crucial question of what it teaches. The Course, as I stated in the introduction, is more than a teaching, but even so, its teaching is its foundation. All of its practical methods are just applications of the ideas it teaches. In a way, the teaching is also the goal, for the program of the Course is simply a way of leading students step by step into the full embodiment of the teaching.

The purpose of this teaching is to usher us into a different perception of reality. It is designed to turn the world we see upside down, and it has an uncanny ability to do just that. This can be disorienting, but this is also the medicine; this is how the Course expects to cure us. As it says, "Only perception can be sick."[1] By healing our perception, it plans to heal us through and through.

Therefore, as you read the following three chapters, try not to be disconcerted if you find yourself feeling disoriented. That just means the medicine is working. The Course speaks of this disorientation and says, "Fear it not, for it means only that you have been willing to let go your hold on the distorted frame of reference that seemed to hold your world together."[2]

The first of the three chapters that follow, Chapter 3, is especially challenging. It is designed to peel away layer after layer from our picture of ourselves. By doing so, it attempts to give us a different understanding of the source of our suffering, one that locates the problem within us, where it can be changed, rather than outside us in the world, where it cannot. If you can make it through that chapter, things get much brighter. Chapter 4 then describes the Course's vision of reality. This vision is so different from the conventional view only because the Course teaches that true reality is perfect, and the "reality" we live in now is anything but. Finally, Chapter 5 describes the Course's answer to our problem, telling us how we can walk off the battleground and into everlasting peace.

THREE

The Problem

What would you say is the problem with your life? Forget, for the moment, what your religious or philosophical beliefs may counsel you to answer. Just take a moment and reflect on these questions:

- When you feel angry or afraid, what sorts of things do you see as the cause of those feelings?
- What things do you complain about at the end of the day?
- In your eyes, what (or who) has deprived you of something that could have made your life complete?
- Can you think of one or two problems whose solution would dramatically change how happy you are?

Those questions probably brought to mind many specific things, but I would guess that the majority of them could be classed under a single heading: external circumstances. Surely, that's the problem with our lives. Circumstances are not the way we want. Our car breaks down, our spouse is hard to please, our boss is in a bad mood, our body comes down with the flu, our workload is too heavy, our status too low, our finances too thin. We are surrounded by difficult circumstances and always have been. We have been paddling hard our whole lives, yet we still just barely manage to stay afloat.

"Difficult circumstances" is really a polite way to put it.

Circumstances are more than just difficult; they appear to be actively assailing us. Everyone is looking out for themselves, and while they're at it, they're likely to step on us. At times they almost seem to be in league against us, in a conspiracy that involves not only our family and coworkers, but even impersonal forces like traffic and the weather. In short, the world seems—either zealously or lazily—out to get us. External circumstances appear to be attacking us. A hundred times a day, they peck at us; occasionally, they try to crush us. Perhaps we resist seeing life through this gloomy lens, but I suspect that somewhere inside we still do, and that in moments of frustration, this lens fills our vision.

In the midst of the world's insane obstacle course, we are quite simply doing our best. Our intentions are good. We may occasionally lash out or inadvertently hurt someone, but whenever we do, there are pressures on us that, if recognized, make our actions perfectly understandable. We do get blamed, but only by those who do not see the whole picture. In truth, we are just trying to make the best of a difficult situation. And if we can work hard and long enough, maybe we can climb above all the strife, and on some peaceful hilltop, build a little paradise for ourselves.

The face of innocence

In a way, nothing could seem more obvious than the above account of our fundamental problem. Who of us has not felt beset by difficult circumstances? Who of us does not believe that if only things on the outside were different, we could be happy? However, according to *A Course in Miracles*, the entire scenario I just presented is utterly false. It could not be further from the truth. The problem is *not* external circumstances. Our intentions are *not* so good. In espousing the above scenario, we are simply wearing what the Course calls "the face of innocence":

> It is this face that smiles and charms and even seems to love. It searches for companions and it looks, at times with pity, on the suffering, and sometimes offers solace. It believes that it is good within an evil world.
>
> This aspect can grow angry, for the world is wicked and unable to provide the love and shelter innocence deserves. And so this face is often wet with tears at the injustices the world accords to those who would be generous and good.

> This aspect never makes the first attack. But every day a hundred little things make small assaults upon its innocence, provoking it to irritation, and at last to open insult and abuse.[1]

Who cannot identify with those statements? Indeed, the Course sees the face of innocence as the conscious self-image of virtually everyone alive. Yet calling this the *face* of innocence carries a chilling implication: It is nothing but a face we put on, a mask we wear over something else—a something not so innocent. This something, says the Course, is the real cause of our suffering. What, then, lies beneath the face of innocence? Since this face is essentially the posture of the conscious mind, to delve beneath it is to plunge into the realm of the unconscious, which the Course sees as having several layers. We will now explore these layers one by one, winding ever closer to the real heart of the matter.

The enraged victim

According to the Course, just below the mild-mannered face of innocence lies what might best be called *rage*. It is difficult for us to imagine that something as dark and frenzied as rage is lurking beneath all these smiling faces. Most of us seem so nice and so sincere. Yet consider this: Perhaps the difficult circumstances we discussed above have left you feeling more wounded and more angry than you would ever guess. Perhaps if you opened your conscious mind to your true feelings—allowed it to savor the bitter taste of how brutalized you really feel at the hands of the world—you would be too overwhelmed to function. And so you keep a lid on it and let only small amounts into your awareness. At one point, the Course says, "You will become increasingly aware that a slight twinge of annoyance is nothing but a veil drawn over intense fury."[2] That slight twinge is like a jet of steam escaping from the ground at your feet, coming from a vast field of seething underground magma.

The Course graphically describes this level. It says that in this place we point at the world with our "accusing finger...unwavering and deadly in its aim,"[3] and hatefully declare, "I am the thing you made of me, and as you look on me, you stand condemned because of what I am."[4] Please read that line again and imagine actually saying it to someone. Is there perhaps someone in your life to whom you *want* to say it? Consider the possibility that on this level of your mind, you are constantly saying it to everyone—in fact, to the entire world. That is the kind of rage the Course is talking about.

People often uncover this place in psychotherapy, and when they do, it seems as if they have at last hit on the real truth. "No wonder my life has been such a mess! Look at what they did to me!" Yet this level is a façade, just like the one above it. The benign face of innocence, as we saw, is a mask we wear to cover the face of the enraged victim. And this face, in turn, is also a mask, a lie. It too serves to cover something else.

The victim in us claims to be furious because of what others have done to us. Our rage is seen as a justified response to real injustice. And if, in our righteous anger, we strike back, we believe we are within our rights. After all, our hand was forced; we were attacked first. Is that not what we all maintain? I doubt I've ever heard anyone say, "Yes, it's true. I attacked first, totally unprovoked. I just thought that assault would be a good way to get what I want." We all claim to attack only because someone else attacked us first. Yet we cannot *all* be telling the truth, or there would be no first attacks to provoke anyone, and thus no attacks at all. Some of us must be lying.

The ego

What if we are *all* lying? What if every one of us attacks first? What if there has *never* been any real provocation, any real justification for our attacks? What if we attack just because we like it, but then concoct an excuse to make our attack seem innocent? That is the value of being a victim, right? As a victim, you can attack yet be innocent, even heroic. What if our whole victim stance is just a ploy to grant carte blanche to an insatiable aggression in us that we have covered up?

This, indeed, is what the Course claims to be true. It says that we only perceive other people as attacking us in order to justify our own attack. Perception is a very subjective thing. What we perceive has far more to do with our own interior dynamics than with the world outside. According to the Course, we see a world of enemies not because they are really out there, but simply because we want to attack. The Course puts it succinctly: "I make all things my enemies, so that my anger is justified and my attacks are warranted."[5] I see enemies only because I want a justification to attack. It may be hard to understand how this could be true, yet if it is, it means that we have never truly been attacked.

It means that we have no real cause for all our anger and resentment. This is actually the source of our deliverance, for as we will see in Chapter 5, this is the basis of forgiveness.

For now, though, we are still working our way down through the levels of the mind. In the following powerful passage, the Course first describes the victim level and then describes the ruthless victimizer that lies beneath it:

> A brother separated from yourself, an ancient enemy, a murderer who stalks you in the night and plots your death, yet plans that it be lingering and slow; of this you dream. Yet underneath this dream is yet another, in which you become the murderer, the secret enemy, the scavenger and the destroyer of your brother and the world alike.[6]

This is strong language, but appropriately so, for it mirrors the intensity of these buried levels of the mind. On the victim level, we do see a world that stalks us and plots our death. Yet that is the disguise; that is the lie. The level below tells a shockingly different story. There, the roles are reversed: *We* are the murderer. *We* are the destroyer. This level of the mind is consumed with rage, aggression, hostility, even murder—not because the world has mistreated us, but just because attack is the lifeblood of this level. This is what the Course calls the *ego*. The ego dominates all three levels we've discussed so far, but here, on this level, is where it shows its true colors. The other two levels are masks the ego wears. Here is where we see its true face.

What is the ego? It is often described as the belief that we are a distinct self, separate from everything else, the belief that "I am me and you are not." That is an accurate definition (and I'll elaborate on it in the next chapter), but we need to expand it to make the picture complete. The ego is the belief that since I am me and you are not, I am *end* and you are *means*. My gain is what counts; you're here to serve that. Under the sway of this belief, I inevitably seek to gain at your expense. I habitually seek to benefit from your loss. I repeatedly attack you to get what I want. I don't have to think about it; in fact, I usually don't think about it—it's just second nature. This notion that by attacking others I can gain at their expense is at the core of the ego. It instinctively grabs from everyone else's plate in order to feed itself.

It is frightening to consider that such a parasitic entity exists in us; so frightening that it is extremely difficult to *really* consider it. Even as I write this, I find my mind trying to push the idea away, thinking, "Sure, this may exist in others, but in *me*?" The urge to push this idea away is almost uncontrollable. Indeed, this urge is what produced the two masking levels above the ego's "core." They are nothing but disguises aimed at showing the world *and ourselves* a nicer picture, a picture of an innocent victim, who only attacks once pushed into a corner. And these disguises have worked. They have convinced us all that we're the good guy, doing our best, underappreciated and unfairly treated by a harsh world.

According to the Course, however, the evidence of this inner hostility lies all about us. For the ego in us is the main actor on the stage of our lives. It is primarily what struts about the stage, speaking its lines and doing its deeds. It just does so while wearing the face of innocence, like a killer who, even while he murders, wears the benevolent mask of a saint. The ego's hostility is still expressed, only in friendly packaging. Attack *in disguised form* is therefore the main dynamic in human life.

This is why human relationships are so conflict-ridden. This is why society is plagued by violence. This is why the world is so full of war. This, quite simply, is why humans cannot get along. Beneath all the neighborliness is a whole other agenda. This other agenda is fairly visible in our relationships with our enemies. It is much harder to see in our relationships with our friends and loved ones. Yet even there, it is in full force, and can be seen if we know what we're looking for.

Special relationships

The Course calls our relationships with friends and loved ones "special relationships." In our minds, having a *special* relationship is a good thing. We see these islands of love and warmth as our greatest consolation in this cold, hard world. Yet the Course sees the exact same dark dynamics operating in these relationships as in the rest of the world. In its view, the islands are just mirages, shimmering atop an uninterrupted sea of hate. This is a deeply unsettling perspective. It threatens to shatter our whole view of our lives. The Course, however, has a very compelling way of unmasking our "loving" relationships, a way which simply amplifies observations we ourselves make all the time.

Let's begin the unmasking process by defining what, in the Course's parlance, a special relationship is. Special relationships include all of the "positive" relationships from which we draw comfort, fulfillment, and security, but the dynamics behind them find their core expression in the romantic relationship. This is where the prizes are biggest, and where the illusion of love is the most convincing. We can define a special relationship as one in which:

- I have a special arrangement (an exclusive relationship) with
- and receive special treatment from
- a very special person
- so that I can feel more special.

Just reading that list can be exciting. After all, the special relationship promises a most treasured thing. It promises to make us feel really special. And that, according to the Course, is the prize we seek above all else, not only in romance, but in *every* area of life. In our minds, being special is the basis for self-esteem. It is synonymous with being a worthy person. How much worth can we have if we're nobody special?

Does anyone really question the unparalleled value of being special? We've spent our lives pursuing it, through landing the perfect husband or bagging the babe, through excelling in school or knowing the right people, through talent, achievement, recognition, career, wealth, sports—all of the ways in which we try to feel "more than." Yet there is a dark side to specialness, one we're aware of but prefer to look away from. To be special is to be better than, to be superior, to be set above others. By definition, you can only be special if someone else is *not*. You can only be set above if someone else is set below. Specialness is thus inherently competitive and inherently attacking. "He who is 'worse' than you must be attacked," says the Course, "so that your specialness can live on his defeat."[7] I think we all recognize this, which is why we try not to celebrate our specialness too loudly within earshot of the one we just defeated. And why we'd never murmur to our loved one, "Honey, it means so much to me that I am better than you." Specialness is an attack—and we know it.

You can see the quest to put everyone below us in our search for the ideal romantic partner. First, to win this person's heart we have to beat out the competition; put all of *them* below us. Once we do that, we hope that the two of us will be the golden couple, the envy of all; that everyone will gaze up at us in our castle and exclaim, "How I wish I were one of them!" Clearly, wanting all of them below us cannot be a loving impulse. We also hope that particular people from our past will witness the incredible catch we just landed and rethink their opinion of us.[8] We want them to think that perhaps we really *did* deserve the love and respect we sought from them in vain. With our new trophy in hand, we hope to show them just how wrong they were.

It is like being in a war. Before, when we were alone, the odds against us were too great, our enemies too numerous. But now, side by side, the two of us can face the world's battlefield together. Together, we might even end up on the top of the heap, as king and queen in our own lofty castle. In our private haven, we have the comfort of knowing that even if we're at war with the world, we're on each other's side. Or so it appears. The sad truth is that even though it seems like you and me against the world, the exact same war is raging between the two of us. In truth, it is you and me against *each other*. From start to finish, as we'll now see, the special relationship is an attack on our "beloved."

The special relationship as attack on our partner

It all starts when we find ourselves attracted to someone, perhaps even in love with that person (whom I will call "he" or "she" at different times). In our eyes, he should be flattered, honored, even elated by our love, because our feelings are living proof that he is a special person. As we all know, though, he is quite likely to feel unflattered, burdened, even stalked. Why? Because our love wants something from him. It wants to own him, to possess him. It wants to consume him in order to satisfy our own appetite.

The Course puts it this way: "Whoever seems to possess a special self is 'loved' for what can be taken from him."[9] We want someone who is really special, who comes to us with his own "bank account" of specialness. Once we own him, he is no longer his own person, and all of his specialness becomes our possession. In effect, he loses his identity, his "special self," and we gain it. Quite simply, we want him for the specialness we can take from him. We want to walk into a room with that other and almost hear people think: "Wow, is she fortunate to have landed him!" That is why our love may not make him feel like the king of the world, but instead like the Christmas turkey. Being an object of desire is not always a welcome thing.

That is what our "love" tends to do—turn people into objects. Since the body is an object, being attracted to someone's body amounts to regarding her as an object. We even have a word for this: We call it "objectifying" her. This is why, when seen as a sex object, a person so often feels not exalted, but degraded. To be seen as an object is simply demeaning. The following Course passage refers to this process and takes it one step further:

> Even the body of the other, already a severely limited perception of him, is not the central focus as it is, or in entirety....[Certain parts are] centered on and separated off as being the only parts of value.[10]

Seeing someone as a body is "already a severely limited perception" of who that person really is. Yet we then limit our perception of her even further, focusing on the particular body parts we value. We mentally carve her up and view her as a small pile of our favorite parts. No wonder she feels like the Christmas turkey!

I am making it sound as if all we're doing is taking from our partner. What about all the giving that is going on? Isn't that what separates the special relationship from everything else in the world? It is so filled with love and giving. Not so fast, says the Course, for it calls our acts of love "giving to get."[11] We call this same phenomenon a gift with strings attached.

When we give, whether it be of our time, energy, or money, we believe we lose what we give. We believe we're sacrificing something. Since we are not in the habit of simply throwing away things we value, we usually give only because we expect to get back something even better. The Course has strong words about this: "Such 'gifts' are but a bid for a more valuable return; a loan with interest to be paid in full."[12]

Sadly, even these pseudo-gifts are not made without reluctance. There is an unsocialized child in us, usually hidden below our conscious mind. This brat would prefer to just take what it wants, without having to give at all, or at least without having to give as much. If only we could just *take* the gold, this part of us thinks, we could come out ahead in the deal, and would not have to lose so much in the process. Though this desire is usually unconscious, it does come to the surface. Have you ever had thoughts about stealing something you wanted but could not afford? Or forcibly taking something that another refused to give you? On a milder level, the evidence for this child in us is the simple, everyday fact that we give cautiously, reluctantly, begrudgingly, measuring every ounce. We secretly resent the loss entailed in giving, and because of this, our gift carries a hidden angry message: "I lost for the sake of your gain. You gained from my loss." Surely we've all felt that at one time or another.

If you will, pick a specific person in your life and imagine this person speaking those very lines to you: "I lost for the sake of your gain. You gained from my loss." How would you feel? If you're anything like me, you'd have a sinking feeling in your gut that we commonly call *guilt*. Isn't this the feeling you've had so many times when someone made sacrifices for you? If so, then you must have internalized this same message from their sacrifices. You must have heard in your mind those same lines spoken to you, even though nothing of the kind was overtly said. The Course would say that you were not mistaken. That message was really there. And now that you have got the message, how would you try to *alleviate* this feeling in your gut? By giving something back, right? This shows you *really* got the message. This was the point of the "gift" from the beginning: to make you feel obligated to give back.

This is the Course's dark view of most giving in this world (though not all—the Course does say that true giving occurs). Our gift carries a hidden anger—anger at the fact that we are making a sacrifice, incurring a loss—which is designed to make the other person feel indebted, *guilty*. To relieve this guilt, the other person must then pay off his debt by giving us something of comparable value. The whole process can be summed up in this message, which is attached like an invisible card to most gifts: "You hereby gain from my loss (and are therefore guilty). You owe me." The Course puts it this way: "And for this sacrifice [the 'gift' he gave], which he demands of himself, he demands that the other accept the guilt and sacrifice himself as well."[13]

This view can sound so depressing, yet the truth of it is revealed when the other person consistently does *not* give back. Then, all the messages that were hidden beneath our face of innocence come out into the open. We start openly heaping on the guilt, saying, "Look at all I gave you! And what have you given back?" We find all kinds of dramatic and devious ways of saying, "You gained from my loss (and are therefore guilty). You owe me!" Shockingly, both our "giving" and our blaming carry the same angry message, only in the second case we openly display what in the first case we concealed.

This progression from gifts that carry *covert* anger to finger-pointing that expresses *overt* anger is the history of most special relationships. In the beginning, we shower our new love with gifts. We give him our time, our attention, our affection, our body. All of this appears to be given happily, but our happiness really lies not in the giving, but in the promise of future returns. After all, he is racking up quite a debt. In view of all that we are giving him, the only way he can possibly pay us back is to give us all of himself, give us the deed to his soul. That is our goal, for just as owning a special car makes us feel special, owning a special person makes us feel even more so. And when we finally get that deed (as we slip the ring on his finger), we figure it is time to ease up on giving and start reaping the rewards of our generosity. Unfortunately, however, he is thinking the same thing (for he has been going through the same process), and so his giving also slacks off. Consequently, we begin to feel swindled. As we do, our strategy slowly switches from "giving" to outright blaming: "You are not keeping up your end of the bargain! I have done all the sacrificing, while you have reaped all the benefits! You owe me, *big time*!" Even though later we'll say we didn't mean it, chances are that this message will, by this point in the relationship, sum up our whole perspective on it.

The destiny of the special relationship is that we end up *disillusioned*. Think about that word. It means that the love we thought he felt for us, and we thought *we* felt for *him*, was really an *illusion*, an illusion which we no longer have. We have been dis-illusioned. The Course would heartily agree. The love *was* an illusion. And it is only here at the bitter end, in the awful moment of disillusionment, that you get what was going on all along. He did not really love you. He was just using you. He wanted to get something from your special body, from its special parts. He wanted to own your special identity, so that he could feel more special himself. And all of his giving was just a way to instill guilt in you so that you would feel obligated to give him what he wanted. He was not giving, he was taking. He was not loving you, he was attacking you. Yet your disillusionment, insightful as it is, does not go far enough. The crucial element is missing. For you do not admit to yourself that you were doing *the exact same thing*.

I have laid this out in some detail because here is precisely what I was talking about before. Here is the ego's hostility expressing itself through a loving disguise. Here is pure attack running the show within love's inner sanctum. If attack is in charge even in romance, the most "loving" area of human life, then surely it is in charge everywhere else. And that is exactly what the Course sees. No matter where it looks on the face of this earth, it sees the ego as the dominant influence. It sees the ego doing what the ego does, trying to gain at the expense of others, trying to climb to the top of the heap by stepping on the heads below, yet all the while putting on the smiling appearance of a caring friend.

The call for help

Our tour through the dark layers of the unconscious is almost over. We have just one more layer to go and then, thankfully, things will brighten considerably. Years ago, a friend read a booklet I had written on special relationships and said, "It scared the hell out of me—or maybe it was the hell *in* me." I suspect that is why we tend to find material like this disturbing. Something in us feels fingered, something we would prefer to keep comfortably concealed. The Course, however, sees great value in unearthing these dark regions, for then and only then can they be transformed.

Let's now explore the next level down. Underneath the ego lies its real experiential results, or perhaps I should say its real psychological consequences. The Course speaks about the ego level as a "dark cornerstone" filled with hatred and grandiosity, and then speaks about what lies below it:

> For beneath [your ego's illusions]...is the loving mind that thought it made them in anger. And the pain in this mind is so apparent, when it is uncovered, that its need of healing cannot be denied....Beneath all the grandiosity you hold so dear is your real call for help.[14]

Based on this passage, I refer to this level as "the call for help." This is the dumping ground in which the ego deposits its waste products. Here is all the pain inherent in believing that one is an ego. Indeed, this level is like an underground reservoir of pain, pain that constantly yearns for release, that ceaselessly cries out, "Won't somebody up there please help me?" This pain consists primarily of two emotions: guilt and fear.

If you truly thought that everything in the preceding pages was true about you, if you really believed you were primarily (though not entirely) driven by a diabolical ego that doesn't really love anyone but just wants to devour others to feed itself, what would you feel? You would probably feel *guilt,* guilt so profound that it would be hard to carry on. According to the Course, this is what we do believe, every single one of us. In a deeply buried place in our minds, we are convinced we are that diabolical ego. The Course describes how we see things in this buried place:

> You think you are the home of evil, darkness and sin. You think if anyone could see the truth about you he would be repelled, recoiling from you as if from a poisonous snake. You think if what is true about you were revealed to you, you would be struck with horror so intense that you would rush to death by your own hand, living on after seeing this being impossible.[15]

We had hoped that by burying the ego under successive masks (the face of innocence and enraged victim), we could escape the monumental guilt that goes along with it. But we did not escape any of it. We just covered it over. There is a place in our minds where we look, with eyes that have no lids, upon the ego unmasked, undisguised. As a result, in this place we are perpetually awash in a sea of guilt.

To understand guilt we must first understand the concept of *sin.* We may not use the word "sin" much, but the meaning behind the word pervades our minds. We see it everywhere we look. I like to define sin as:

- An attack that attempts to do harm for the sake of selfish gain.
- An attack that succeeds, which results in real harm.

Given this definition, the connection between sin and the ego is obvious. They are virtually the same thing. Both involve attacking others for the sake of our own gain. Thus, believing we are an ego automatically means believing we are a sinner, and this has devastating consequences for our self-image. Our "sin" may apparently wound another, but it seems to inflict an even deeper wound on us. It may bruise the other's pride or even injure his body, but it seems to corrupt our very soul. It appears to wield a frightening power over our identity, changing us from good into bad, turning us into a grotesque monster. Finally, it seems to make us deserving of punishment, as the just reward for our crime, as the fitting treatment for the hideous thing we have become.

What is guilt? Guilt is simply the emotional experience of the belief that I am a sinner. Imagine believing the following things:

- I harmed another for the sake of my own selfish gain.
- I thereby corrupted my identity, changing myself from good into bad.
- Now, all I deserve is punishment, for what I did and for what I am.

How could one really believe all that and *not* feel guilty? Guilt is simply what we call how it feels to believe those things. Guilt is an emotion that is based on a story we tell ourselves, a story of the bad we did in the past, the bad we are in the present, and the bad we deserve in the future.

In its account of human suffering, the Course assigns a startling role to guilt. It says, "Guilt is...the sole cause of pain in any form."[16] How can this be? The Course is fully aware that for most of us, guilt would not even make it onto our list of what is causing us pain in our lives.[17] How, then, can it be the *only* cause? The reasoning is simple. According to the Course, the mind is so powerful that *it* is the cause of everything it feels. Our feelings are produced by our internal beliefs, not by external circumstances. Now imagine that our primary belief about ourselves is guilt, which says, "I deserve to suffer; I deserve to be unhappy." If we really do believe that (however buried that belief may be), and if our beliefs really do produce our emotional states, then what else could that belief do but produce a condition of misery? In the Course's view, all suffering is self-imposed punishment for presumed sin.

Our guilt does show up in our experience, though usually in altered form. Although its full proportions may lie deep in the unconscious, it continually oozes to the surface through a thousand pores. It surfaces through a host of negative beliefs about ourselves: I'm not good enough. I'm not worthy. I'm not enough. I don't deserve to be happy. I'm going to get caught. I'm embarrassed. I'm ashamed of myself. All of these add up to one pervasive feeling: *Something is wrong with me.* This belief undermines our entire emotional landscape, leaving us with no sure footing, no place to stand where we feel perfectly secure. We ascribe this feeling to all sorts of causes: to not being smart or pretty enough, to what our teachers said about us, or to how our parents treated us. But these "causes" represent a denial of the true, underlying cause: *We believe we are a sinner*. We believe that our nature, like that of a predatory animal, condemns us to attack others in order to feed ourselves. Deep down, that is what we really think is wrong with us. Our low self-esteem is the distant echo of subterranean guilt.

Our guilt shows up in yet another form: *fear*. If guilt says we deserve punishment, what can it lead to but *fear* of punishment? Think of the ways in which we express guilt's message: one day you'll reap what you've sown; sooner or later you'll have to pay the piper; the chickens will come home to roost; you have it coming to you. How do you feel when told, "You have it coming to you"? Imagine that, deep inside, there is a voice whispering that to you all the time.

This voice leads us to see ourselves forever encircled by threat, both known and unknown. It prompts us to constantly look over our shoulder, wondering when the boom will be lowered, wondering when we'll get our comeuppance. And it leads us to unconsciously interpret difficult circumstances as our just deserts. Thus, even while we ask aloud, "What did I do to deserve this?" somewhere inside, a resigned voice says, "I had it coming." It leads us, like the murderer in Poe's *The Telltale Heart*, to see accusation in situations that need not carry that message at all. We chronically—and needlessly—see events making frightening statements about us. We see endless variations on a terrifying theme: if *this* happens it means *this* about me. If I say this inappropriate thing, it means I'm a stupid person. If I don't attend my daughter's awards ceremony, it means I'm a bad father. If I'm unable to pay my bills, it means I'm irresponsible. We live in fear of these messages, but the messages are not in the events themselves, only in our minds. The question is, why are our minds so ready to see these damning messages everywhere? Why are we so prone to see outer events pointing an accusing finger at us? Once again, it is the voice of guilt whispering in our ear.

The logical connection between guilt and fear can open our minds to a radical possibility. What if *all* of our fear comes from guilt? What if *all* of our fear is fear of punishment for past misdeeds? This is what *A Course in Miracles* teaches, and though the idea is very difficult to accept, it follows directly from the idea I mentioned earlier: Our feelings are not caused by outer circumstances, but by our own beliefs. In this case, our feelings of *fear* are caused by our belief in our *guilt*.

If guilt is what causes fear, then guilt is responsible for our entire condition. For according to the Course, fear is not an emotion we experience intermittently. It is the state we live in. It is the human condition. We think that we are often free of fear only because most of

LEVELS OF THE MIND

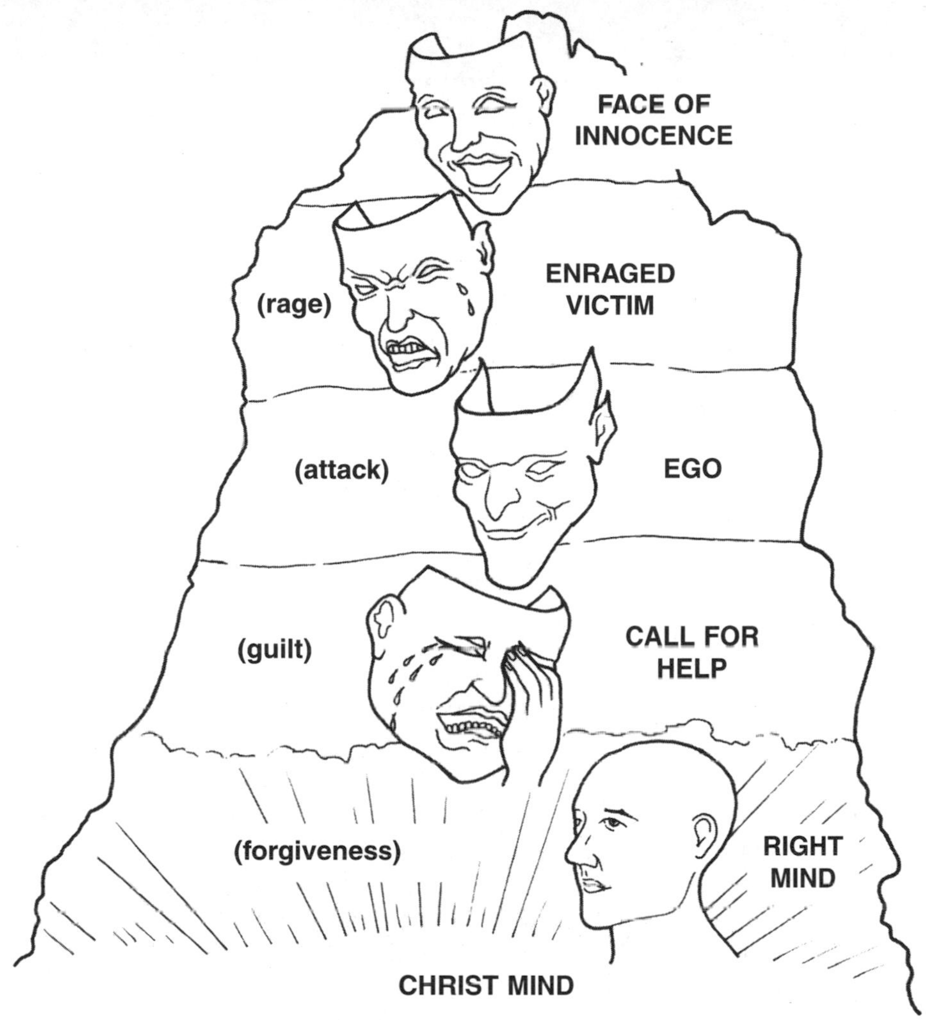

LEVELS OF THE MIND

The top level is the stance of the conscious mind. With each level down we get further away from our normal consciousness. The material on these lower levels breaks through into consciousness only rarely. From top to bottom the levels are:

The face of innocence: Here, on the conscious level, we see ourselves as the well-intentioned good guy, doing our best in an ill-intentioned world.

The enraged victim: Here, we hate the world that we believe has mangled us beyond repair.

The ego: Here, we attack without provocation, simply to gratify our needs at the expense of others. This is the hidden content of the above two levels.

The call for help: Here, we are awash in guilt over our ego's attacks and we yearn for redemption, even while we despair of ever finding it.

The right mind: Here, we are healed, redeemed. We abide in the reflected light of our true Self. We see with Christ's vision and love everyone with a pure, egoless love.

The Christ Mind: This is our true Self, beyond all levels, beyond time, space, and form. Here, rather than being loving, we are love itself.

us never experience *real* absence of fear. Only in rare spiritual experiences of oceanic peace does anyone touch a state that is truly free of fear. There is another reason we do not appreciate fear's real significance: We are strongly motivated to not admit how afraid we are. It is too humiliating. It makes us seem weak and pitiful. Who wants to stand up and announce, "Hi, my name is _____, and I'm afraid all the time"? Yet the Course suggests that if we are truly honest with ourselves, we will realize this is the case. The vast bulk of our fear is kept safely unconscious, yet even the tiny amount we let into our awareness is enough to keep us anxious, edgy, insecure, apprehensive, nervous, and worried all the time.

Summary of the problem

We began by asking, "What is the problem?" What is the cause of human suffering? We are finally in a position to appreciate the Course's radical answer. Our common belief is that the problem lies out there, in a barrage of outer circumstances that buffet us every day. The problem, we believe, is that the world is constantly attacking us. The Course turns this conventional view completely upside down. It says that the problem lies within us. The problem is that we are attacking the world. Underneath our friendly face of innocence and our posturing as the outraged victim lies the ego, a place in our mind that is pure attack, that is always on the offensive. The ego disguises its brutality by wearing the masks above it, and so its actions present an outer form of kindness and goodwill while carrying an inner content of hate and attack.

How does this explain human suffering? I would like to revisit a passage we saw earlier, and this time include a sentence I omitted:

> Yet underneath this dream [of being the victim] is yet another, in which you become the murderer, the secret enemy, the scavenger and the destroyer of your brother and the world alike. *Here is the cause of suffering.*[18]

"Here is the cause of suffering"—our own murderous ego. Our suffering is not caused by others trying to gain at our expense, but by *our* attempt to gain at *their* expense. It is not caused by the cruel world, but by the cruelty in our own hearts. This cruelty convinces us that we have sinned, that we have destroyed our original innocence and turned ourselves into a devil. The guilt that results is the root of all our suffering. It says we deserve to suffer as punishment, and so leads us to unconsciously see ourselves as creatures who *should* suffer. Thereafter, we live in a perpetual state of fear, as we nervously wait for our sins to catch up with us.

This is probably the last message we want to hear. We've spent our lives telling ourselves that we're sincere, that we're the good guy, that the other guy started it. We've spent our lives believing that the real story is what they did to us. The last thing we want to hear is that the real story is what *we* did to *them*. I completely understand that. I too find this message disturbing, yet I also find it refreshing, and you may be experiencing it that way too. For this message is the complete opposite of what our egotism would say. It undoes all our double standards and applies to ourselves the same perceptions we apply to others.

Moreover, there is really no need at all to find this message disturbing, for in actuality, it opens up a door to a remarkable perspective on ourselves. We want to keep the ego hidden away because we consider it to be the ugly truth about us. Deep down, we believe that it is who we really are. The Course, however, wants to bring it to light, to show us that it is *not* who we really are.

The ego is an imposter, "a stranger...who wandered carelessly into the home of truth and who will wander off."[19] It insists, over and over again, that it is who we are. Yet "underneath this constant shout and frantic proclamation, the ego is not certain it is so."[20] It senses that who we really are is something altogether different, and this makes it profoundly insecure. Accordingly, all that the ego urges us to do is designed not for our happiness, but rather to convince us that *we* are *it*. Indeed, this is why the ego urges us to attack—not for our benefit, but because it wants to frame us, to manufacture proof that we are a sinful ego. It is like a "friend" who urges us to commit a crime, ostensibly so that we can get rich, but secretly because he wants to see us go to jail. The ego wants to convict us, in the court of our own mind, of being a guilty sinner, deserving of eternal punishment. Yet the ego is trying to prove something that can never be proven. It is trying to convince us of a "truth" it senses to be false. For the ego, too, is just a mask, a mask of evil worn by a being of pure love.

FOUR

Reality and Illusion

In the previous chapter, we peeled off one mask after another. After removing our phony face of innocence, we eventually uncovered the real cause of our suffering, which turned out to be our own attacking ego. In the end, however, we saw that the ego is just another mask. What, then, lies beneath all the masks? What is the enduring reality that was there prior to the masks and will remain when they are gone?

A Course in Miracles has a radically different view of reality than what we are accustomed to. It takes most students some time to get used to this view, but it is the entire foundation for the Course's teaching and practice. In this chapter, therefore, we'll leave the comfort of our familiar mental surroundings and allow the Course to take us on a rollercoaster ride, turning us upside-down, challenging our every idea of what is real. This ride may leave our head spinning, but it's well worth it, for in this new view of reality lies the promise of release from all the pain and heartache of the "reality" we see before us now.

REALITY

God

The Course's view of reality starts with its view of God, the Creator of reality. The single most important thing to understand about this view of God is that it characterizes God as totally egoless; in fact, it depicts God as the complete and precise opposite of the ego.

Voltaire said that God created us in his image, and that we then returned the favor. It doesn't take a genius to observe that the God of many religions looks suspiciously like a rather large, overblown ego. Many of us left the fold of the church for this very reason. And yet to actually see God as nothing like an ego is easier said than done. After all, that is our only experience of living beings. They all have egos. They all police their personal space. They all protect their bodies. They all look out predominantly for their own interests. They all respond unhappily to being attacked. This is not just true of humans, but of any being with any sentience at all. The Course sees the ego as so deeply entrenched in this world that only the rarest of people get free of it entirely; most who claim to be without it are making that claim from their egos.

Thus, given our experience in this world, we regard the concept of *living being* as synonymous with the concept of *being that has an ego*. When we are told, therefore, that God is a living being, we unconsciously project an ego onto Him. What else would we do? As a result, it actually takes a long time for us to really think of God as not having an ego. In the next few pages, however, I hope to shorten that time by discussing as clearly as I can what it means to say that God is egoless.

Let's begin by returning to the two fundamental principles of the ego:

1. *Separation*: "I am me and you are not."
2. *Attack*: "I am end and you are means."

What does it mean to project these two principles onto God? It means, first of all, that we assume that God is a separate being. Being separate, His sphere of concern is primarily around Himself; it encompasses His goals, His rules, His agendas. God is first and foremost concerned with matters of God. Secondly, it means that He sees others as a means to His ends. That is their primary significance in His eyes. Thus, how He regards them is dictated by how well they serve His ends. If they serve His ends well, He gives them the royal treatment. If they do not, He sends them plagues and boils and casts them into the outer darkness; He goes "Old Testament" on them. His attitude toward different people, therefore, is extremely different, and His attitude even toward the same person differs from time to time, depending on that person's behavior.

Admittedly, this is a very crude conception of God, and we may have left such a picture behind long ago. My experience, however, is that we tend to *soften* the picture, rather than abandon it altogether. We may, for instance, assume that God is very tolerant of misbehavior, but still unconsciously imagine that His attitude toward us changes as our behavior changes. Or we may believe that He does not really punish, yet we may picture Him distancing Himself from us on those days when He is not high on our list of priorities. We may see Him as more loving than the portrait I painted above, but we probably still picture Him doling out His love selectively; for instance, loving Jesus Christ more than Adolf Hitler—or us.

A Course in Miracles invites us to step outside this picture completely. It invites us to envision a God Who falls completely outside our experience of what beings are like:

> You cannot understand how much your Father loves you, for there is no parallel in your experience of the world to help you understand it. There is nothing on earth with which it can compare, and nothing you have ever felt apart from Him that resembles it ever so faintly.[1]

"Nothing on earth" can prepare us for the overwhelming generosity of God, the pure egolessness, the undivided will to give without conditions and without any strings whatsoever. It is beyond our comprehension. Even so, we can still move our minds in its direction. A first step is to recognize that God contains the total reversal of the ego's two fundamental principles of separation and attack. Here are God's counterpoints to those principles:

1. *Oneness*. God knows us as one with Him, part of Him, not separate.
2. *Giving*. Giving is God's Nature. It is His joy.

If, as the first principle says, we are part of God, then by giving to us, He is giving to Himself. If, as the second principle says, giving is what brings God joy, then again, by giving to us, He is giving to Himself. Both principles yield the same conclusion. There is no possibility for God to be serving some agenda of His at our expense. Giving to us *is* His agenda. The Course at one point captures God's Nature in six brief words: "Giving Himself is all He knows."[2] Think about that line. If giving Himself is all He knows, then it is not the case that He is aware of the option of not giving but has rejected it. He does not even know about it.

In our experience, giving is always partial; we always hold something back. We do not give all of our love, all of ourselves. Our giving, then, is a *mixture* of giving and not-giving, and the proportions of the mixture differ based on whom we are giving to. Perhaps we give a 70/30 mixture (70% giving and 30% not-giving) to our spouse but only 10/90 to our next-door neighbor. Our spouse simply gets a lot more of our time, energy and attention than our neighbor. With God, however, there is no mixture, because He only knows about *one* of the ingredients in the mixture. This single fact carries enormous implications. It means the following three things:

1. There is no mixture in relation to you right now. He is giving *literally* all of His Love, all of Himself, to you right now. He is not holding anything back. (You, of course, are not aware of this, but the whole point of the Course is to bring you to the point where you are.)

2. There will be no mixture in relation to you in the future. No matter what you do, how well you play by His rules, how you treat people, how spiritual or worldly or even criminal your lifestyle becomes, there will never be a mixture.

3. There is no mixture in relation to anyone else, nor will there ever be. God does not have an inner circle of cronies who get to attend the banquet of His Love, while the rest of us have to subsist on crumbs. He does not give Mother Teresa a 95/5 mixture and Hitler a 5/95 mixture. *There is no mixture*. Not in relation to anyone, ever. The Course states it plainly: "God is not partial. All His children have His total Love, and all His gifts are freely given to everyone alike."[3]

How can we begin to grasp a Love such as this, a Love that goes outside all of our experience here? One way is to appeal to those elements *of* our experience that are most like this Love. That is what the author of the Course does in the following moving passage. In reading it, you may want to change the opening phrase of each sentence to "God loves *me*" (rather than "you") to make its message hit home:

> He loves you as a mother loves her child; her only one, the only love she has, her all-in-all, extension of herself, as much a part of her as breath itself.
>
> He loves you as a brother loves his own; born of one father, still as one in him, and bonded with a seal that cannot break.
>
> He loves you as a lover loves his own; his chosen one, his joy, his very life, the one he seeks when she has gone away, and brings him peace again on her return.
>
> He loves you as a father loves his son, without whom would his self be incomplete, whose immortality completes his own, for in him is the chain of love complete.[4]

Other passages speak of the liberating joy that comes when our expectations of how God will regard us encounter the reality of how He actually *does* regard us. In one passage, the Course portrays us as being afraid to go before "God's Own Higher Court,"[5] since we assume that His verdict will simply mirror the condemning verdict we have already laid upon ourselves. Yet, to our surprise, instead of His verdict sending us to hell, "His verdict will always be 'thine is the Kingdom.'"[6] Notice how this passage depicts God speaking to *us* a line that we are used to saying to *Him*.

In another passage, the Course describes us as hesitant to "come in honesty to God and say we did not understand," because we think admitting our shortcoming will just confirm His negative view of us and thus unleash His wrath. Instead of punishing us, however, He *rushes* to answer us, saying, "'This is My Son, and all I have is his.'"[7] Those familiar with the Bible will recognize this last line as drawn from the parable of the prodigal son, a parable that the Course retells because the story so poignantly captures its view of God. The parable, in fact, contains the exact same pattern as the above two images: Wayward person comes before authority figure expecting wrath, but instead finds himself met with the unbridled love of a father who wants only to give his son everything he has.

To appreciate the power in this idea, you might try to visualize the following scene: You stand before God (visualize God however you like) while He opens up the book of all your thoughts, words, and deeds, and scanning them, prepares to pass judgment on you. Who wouldn't feel afraid in this situation? To your surprise, though, you see God set the book aside, and you hear Him say to you (take time to imagine this), "My verdict will always be 'thine is the Kingdom,'" and then, "You are My Son, [insert your name], and all I have is yours." I have imagined this many times, yet I still find myself unexpectedly moved each time.

I realize that all this talk sounds very anthropomorphic. I'm talking about God as "He," as "Father." Is the Course teaching that God is male? Definitely not. In the Course's view, God's reality—as well as our own—is beyond the divisions of gender. You could say that male and female are nothing more than masks worn by eternal, genderless beings. In calling God "Father," the Course is simply employing a familiar cultural symbol to speak of that which lies beyond all symbols. In truth, God is no more literally a man than He is literally "a mighty fortress." We saw in that passage above that God is also likened to mother, brother, and lover. The earthly symbols are flexible. Their only purpose is to point our minds in the direction of That which transcends earthly categories.

Is God a person? Not as we understand personhood. When we think of a person, we imagine a being that is bounded by some kind of form, particularly a body. God, however, is pure spirit, without body, without form, without limit of any sort. However, I think that the word "impersonal" is even less appropriate when it comes to the God of the Course. That label implies that He is less than a person, while in truth He is more.

The following thought experiment can help us resolve this dilemma. Begin by imagining a loving father on earth, a father so loving that he is virtually egoless. If you cannot think of a father in your personal experience that fits this description, perhaps you can imagine a fictional father, maybe from television, film, or literature. Now imagine this father expanding, becoming larger than the earth, larger than the solar system, larger than the galaxy. As he expands, so does everything within him, including his personal qualities. Imagine him finally becoming so vast that he literally stretches to infinity. Being infinite, he would also be without boundary, meaning that he would be formless, without limitation, and without end. Rather than a finite being moving around within a larger space, he would now *be the space* within which other things moved. Now ask yourself: Would this formless father be void of personal qualities like love, caring, thought, and intention? Would he be empty of personhood? How *could* he be? He started out with those qualities, and throughout the process, all he did was expand. Would not those qualities simply expand with him, rather than suddenly disappearing? By the end of the process, wouldn't his love and thought and intention be literally infinite? Rather than being impersonal, would he not possess *infinite personhood*?

This helps us understand the God described by *A Course in Miracles*. He is formless and boundless, like the sky, yet He genuinely possesses the traits of personhood, only without the limitations we normally associate with it. He thinks, but His Thoughts are not little mice scurrying about, like human thoughts. Rather, each of His Thoughts is an eternal, unbounded reality. He wills, but an act of His Will is not a tiny effort pitted against larger obstacles. Instead, it is a limitless power with nothing standing in its way. He loves, but His Love has none of the fickle favoritism of our love. As we saw, He loves each one of us with all of His Being all the time.

It is important to remember, however, that all of this talk about God can only vaguely approximate something beyond our current comprehension. Ultimately, speech must fail to describe the Indescribable, and so there is a time when words must cease and we simply acknowledge God in silence: "We say 'God is,' and then we cease to speak, for in that knowledge words are meaningless."[8]

The Son

God's boundless impulse to give had an inevitable result. In the timelessness of eternity, He created a Son. In doing so, He held nothing back. He gave the Son everything that He is. The Son, therefore, also possesses infinite personhood. Like God, he too is pure, limitless spirit, without body, without form, without boundary. Perhaps the best visual metaphor for the Son is that of an endless field of radiant light, without gaps or shadows, and without end.

The Son is not a separate being. To create a separate Son would be entirely against God's Nature. Therefore, says the Course, "Nowhere does the Father end, the Son begin as something separate from Him."[9] Yet somehow, there is still a *relationship* between them, though not in the conventional sense of the word. This relationship is so perfectly united that the author of the Course refuses to call it a "one-to-one relationship," instead simply calling it "One Relationship."[10] The Father and the Son experience such endless joy in this One Relationship that all they do for eternity is sing of their love for each other. "Endless the harmony, and endless, too, the joyous concord of the Love They give forever to Each Other."[11] This relationship, quite literally, is Heaven.

This sounds very distant from our day-to-day concerns, but it's not. This, in fact, provides the answer to the riddle of who we are underneath all those masks. Again and again, the Course proclaims a breathtaking idea—that beneath all our self-images, beneath the face of innocence, the victim, the ego, and the call for help, we are none other than this perfect Son: "You are the spirit lovingly endowed with all your Father's Love and peace and joy."[12] The significance of this idea cannot be overstated. We spend all our lives uncertain of who we are, depressed because we seem so riddled with weaknesses, guilty because we seem so selfish. Yet, from the Course's point of view, all this is needless. Who we really are is cause for *limitless* self-esteem. If you will, repeat to yourself the following lines from the Course (which I have laid out in iambic pentameter), and try to imagine how you would feel if you knew from direct experience that they were true.

I am God's Son, complete and healed and whole,
shining in the reflection of His Love.
In me is His creation sanctified
and guaranteed eternal life. In me
is love perfected, fear impossible,
and joy established without opposite.
I am the holy home of God Himself.
I am the Heaven where His Love resides.
I am His holy Sinlessness Itself,
for in my purity abides His Own.[13]

If you really knew these lines were true, beyond a shadow of a doubt, would you have a problem with self-esteem ever again?

The Course speaks of a single Son, yet also of a plurality of *Sons*, sometimes in the same passage:

> It should especially be noted that God has only *one* Son. If all His creations are His Sons, every one must be an integral part of the whole Sonship. The Sonship in its oneness transcends the sum of its parts.[14]

We are these Sons: "We are creation; we the Sons of God."[15] Each one of us is a *part* of the one Son, yet we should not read that as "a small part," for these are not like parts in this world. In Heaven, just as in a hologram, each part literally contains the entire whole. "Every aspect *is* the whole."[16] So each of us is both a part of the Son, and at the same time, *all* of the Son. Another way of making this same point is to say that as Sons we do not each have our own unique self. Instead, at the core of each Son is the exact same Self, a universal Self which the Course calls the Christ. "Christ is the Self the Sonship shares."[17]

Because our nature is simply the extension of God's, we too have no ego whatsoever. "The Son of God is egoless."[18] In Heaven, therefore, we have not the slightest impulse to compete or attack. Like God, all we do is give, graciously shining our love out in all "directions." "In the state of being the mind gives everything always."[19] This is what the Course means when it says (as in the passage quoted above) that we share the very sinlessness and purity of God. Like Him, giving ourselves is all we know, and so, like Him, we are absolutely pure.

The Course calls this dynamic of giving *extension.* It is a central principle in the Course. It is what the mind naturally does, whether in Heaven or on earth. In fact, even when this dynamic is blocked, the mind will still do it in twisted forms.

Finally, our giving has the same result as God's: creation. As God created the Son, a limitless expanse of spirit, so we have our own creations, which, you could say, are "new" fields of limitless spirit. They are, in essence, the same as everything else in Heaven. And just as we love God for giving us life, so our creations love us. "Your creations love you as you love your Father for the gift of creation."[20]

Heaven

As water produces an oasis, so God's egoless Love produces a paradise beyond our imagination. The Course calls this paradise

Heaven. It is, of course, not a place in the sky with clouds, harps, and pearly gates. It is a transcendental realm of pure spirit, pure oneness:

> Heaven is not a place nor a condition. It is merely an awareness of perfect oneness, and the knowledge that there is nothing else; nothing outside this oneness, and nothing else within.[21]

Heaven is the complete absence of all the painful and limiting elements we experience here on earth. We spend our lives trying to avoid suffering here, yet our suffering is an automatic consequence of the basic nature of space and time. *Space* involves finite objects that are separate from each other, that often clash and collide, and that are vulnerable and eventually disintegrate. So what? you might ask. The problem is that in space *we* are one of these objects, which means that we experience ourselves as tiny, alone, in conflict, easily damaged, and doomed to die. *Time* means change. Time is a churning river in which objects constantly arise, change, and pass away. While we ride this river, we are at its mercy. *We* arise and change and pass away, and we see everything around us do the same. Nothing is stable; nothing can be counted on. We see friends turn into enemies, we see loved ones disappear, and we see our own body begin to crumble, before the river's current drags it down and it vanishes.

The very nature of space and time chews us up and spits us out. How can we be happy in such a realm? That is why people have always yearned for a realm that transcends the suffering inherent in this world, a realm that transcends time and space. The Buddhists call it nirvana; the Course calls it Heaven. There, in place of space, there is *infinity*: a single, unified expanse of pure spirit, without form and without end. Thus, rather than tiny and alone, we are infinite; we are everything. In place of time, there is *eternity*: a single boundless moment that never changes and never passes away. Rather than temporary and unstable, we are forever. In Heaven, therefore, we are like a limitless sun that is always rising and never setting. In this exalted state, we are free, free from all the brutal symptoms of time and space.

This, however, is only half the picture. Heaven is also the *presence* of the happy elements of life on earth, only expanded to an infinite degree. What are the things we search for so incessantly in this world? First on the list is love. We want to find someone whom we love with all our heart, and who will love and cherish us in return; we want to join with that person so completely that we lose sight of where we end and he or she begins. In addition, we want to make a contribution. We want to give something of ourselves that makes a difference in the lives of others. We want to produce a lasting legacy. Further, we want to belong to something bigger than ourselves, some family or community which we love, and which grants us an honored place within it. Ideally, we want this family to be one in which everyone is united in accomplishing some grand purpose, and we want to play an essential part in that glorious project. Finally, we want all of these elements to come together, at least for one brief and shining moment.

It is the dream of utopia. It is the hope for Shangri-la. It is the longing for a new age. It is what sends us back to nature to live in communes. It is the yearning to return to the Garden or be lifted into the new Jerusalem. It is the dream of social reform. It is what gave birth to democracy, and what sent the world into communism. It is the hope that rises in us whenever we try out a new church, or enter a new school, or join a business. And it is the hope that fades in us with each passing year.

If only we could find this paradise! Little do we realize that these deep longings in us are not about some place—or some situation—in this world; rather, they are distant memories of Heaven. They are the last remaining notes of an "ancient song you knew so long ago and held more dear than any melody you taught yourself to cherish since."[22] These longings are the testament to how much we miss home, and how deeply we desire to return.

Every element I sketched in the utopian picture above is really an arrow pointing to Heaven. There, we *do* know love, a love that is beyond our current comprehension. And we do not just unite with one person; we experience "relationships without limits."[23] There, we *do* belong to a glorious family, the unlimited family of God, and we *are* a cherished member: "Without you there would be an empty place in God's Mind."[24] This family *is* perfectly united in a glorious purpose: "the increase of the Kingdom,"[25] which occurs through God and His Sons joining in creation. And we *do* play an essential part in this purpose; through our creating, we leave a legacy that will literally last forever. Only in Heaven lies the paradise we have hoped to find around every corner on earth.

Yet how can a Heaven of pure, changeless oneness include *parts*, *relationships*, *extension*, and *increase*? Because Heaven is not something our brains can grasp. The mystics of all ages have said that

Heaven can only be described in the language of paradox, and the Course is no exception to this rule. It is filled with paradox: All is one, yet there is a Father *and* a Son. Nothing changes, yet creation happens. There is no use in trying to resolve such paradoxes with our brains. Perhaps the most useful thing we can do is simply take in the fact that Heaven is the absence of all earthly pain and limitation, and the presence of all earthly happiness infinitely magnified. To help us in this, the Course provides us with a brief exercise,[26] which I have broken down into four parts.

1. "Try to remember when there was a time,—perhaps a minute, maybe even less—when nothing came to interrupt your peace; when you were certain you were loved and safe."
2. "Then try to picture what it would be like to have that moment be extended to the end of time and to eternity."
3. "Then let the sense of quiet that you felt be multiplied a hundred times..."
4. "...and then be multiplied another hundred more."

"And now," says the Course, "you have a hint, not more than just the faintest intimation of the state your mind will rest in when the truth has come."[27] What is Heaven like? If you take the happiest, most peaceful moment of your life and imagine it multiplied in intensity ten thousand times and lasting forever, you'll have only the faintest hint of what Heaven will be like.

All of the peace the Course holds out to us, all of the freedom and deliverance it promises, are based on a single, potent idea: that Heaven is the only reality there is.

ILLUSION

The separation

Something, of course, went wrong. Before there was a physical universe, before time began, something appeared to shatter the limitless peace of Heaven:

> Into eternity, where all is one, there crept a tiny, mad idea, at which the Son of God remembered not [forgot] to laugh.[28]

What happened? The Course tells a strange story. It says that while we were in the boundlessness of Heaven, an outlandish, insidious idea came into our minds. We had the insane notion of separating from God.[29] The Course portrays this notion as motivated by two thoughts. First, we asked to be God's favorite Son, to receive more love than His other Sons—a request that made no sense to Him. Second, we decided that it was intolerable that we had been created by Someone Else, that we were the effect of some prior Cause. We wanted to be our own creator. We wanted to be First Cause.

We had conceived *the ego*, an idea that was the absolute opposite of everything Heaven stood for. In contrast to Heaven's oneness, the ego was the notion of separateness—"I am me and you are not." It was the idea of being a separate self, independent of God and split off from our brothers. In contrast to Heaven's pure givingness, the ego was inherently attacking—"I am end and you are means." It viewed everything as either food or potential food. In the last chapter, I elaborated on the second of these principles, that of attack. Let me now elaborate on the first. "I am me and you are not" means that I am a separate self, with my own mind, my own body, my own choices and feelings, my own life. As a separate self, who I am is not preset. As I make my choices, I actually determine who I am. If I do cruel things, I turn myself into a bad person. If I achieve great things, I turn myself into someone important. To a significant degree, I am self-made.

What could seem more obvious than all this? These ideas feel so self-evident that it seems virtually impossible to question them. Yet there was a time when they were inconceivable. And when they finally *were* conceived, they seemed to set off a kind of cosmic disaster, which the Course calls *the separation*. The idea of the ego was so antithetical to Heaven that it actually appeared to destroy Heaven, shattering its radiance into a billion shards; turning its countless stars, whose light had shone so generously, into selfish little lumps of clay:

> What is the world except a little gap perceived to tear eternity apart, and break it into days and months and years? And what are you who live within the world except a picture of the Son of God in broken pieces, each concealed within a separate and uncertain bit of clay?[30]

The making of the world

This is the Course's story of how the world was made. To complete the story: We simply took the bits of clay and organized them according to our liking. We took "a thread from here, a scrap from there, and wove a picture out of nothing."[31] This is hardly the respectful tone we expect to hear from a story of the origin of the universe. In fact, this is nothing like any story that we are accustomed to. To begin with, it says that we, not God, made the world. The Course means this quite literally. It means that the entire universe, including the dimensions of time and space, is the product not of God's Mind, but of *our* minds (this includes the minds of *all* of God's separated Sons). All of it tumbled directly out of our original thought of separation. To claim that we made the world can at first can sound rather arrogant and grandiose. The Course, however, masterfully answers that objection in the following passage:

> Is it not strange that you believe to think you made the world you see is arrogance? God made it not. Of this you can be sure. What can He know of the ephemeral, the sinful and the guilty, the afraid, the suffering and lonely, and the mind that lives within a body that must die? You but accuse Him of insanity, to think He made a world where such things seem to have reality. He is not mad. Yet only madness makes a world like this.[32]

If we believe that God made the world, this passage should give us pause. This world we claim God created is full of suffering. What kind of crazy world is it in which everyone suffers and everything dies? In which all our minds are locked up inside fragile bodies? In which we live in constant loneliness and fear? Haven't we all said in moments of exasperation that this world is insane? Hence, if we see God as its Creator, are we not accusing Him of insanity? And isn't *that* arrogant? This, in fact, is the exact point the Course makes in the line after the above passage. It says that it "is arrogance"[33] to claim that a God of Love made a world like this. This completely turns the tables on our original reaction. It's not arrogant to think *we* made the world; it's arrogant to think *God* did.

In conventional thinking, the beginning of the world was a glorious thing. Even scientifically minded atheists have quasi-religious feelings about the Big Bang that started it all off. The Course begs to differ. It sees the beginning of the universe as a profoundly negative event. Three times it calls it "the time of terror."[34] After all, this was when reality seemed to mutate from a perfect, limitless Heaven into a nightmarish universe pervaded by suffering and death. This was "the single instant when the time of terror took thc place of love."[35]

In our culture, we tend to see the universe as either a divine expression or a positive natural phenomenon. The Course departs from both views, seeing the universe as the expression of *insanity*. In its view, the process that generated the universe was akin to hooking up a movie projector to the mind of a madman. For, under the pressure of the ego, we *did* go mad, and out of this madness spilled the physical universe, a universe that is just the picture of everything contained in the ego:

- The ego was the belief in separation, and out of this belief streamed physical space, a matrix of separateness, containing a multitude of lonely separate objects. Space, in other words, is merely the outer picture of the crazy notion of separateness.
- The ego was the belief that there was a boundary around our minds, a membrane that cordoncd us off from the rest of reality. Out of this came the body, a physical boundary, which "seems to be a wall of flesh around the mind, keeping it prisoner in a tiny spot of space and time."[36]
- The ego was an apparent change introduced into a changeless domain, and out of it, flashed the realm of time, in which everything is constantly changing. Time, according to the Course, is just the outward projection of the insane idea of change.
- Finally, the ego was a thought of guilt. It introduced overwhelming guilt into our minds because it meant turning our back on God, leaving Him. And out of this guilt came a universe that is forever hounding us, always punishing us for some nameless crime we do not remember committing.

Everything we see around us is a picture of the idea of the ego. This is not just the result of blind cause and effect; it is a means to an end. It serves a psychological purpose. Let me explain. The ego, though just a belief, is a belief with which we identify. On a very deep level, we think we are the ego. And so our natural impulse of self-preservation gets channeled into preserving it. We think that keeping ourselves in existence means keeping our egos from dissolving. Losing our familiar boundaries and awakening to boundlessness feels to us as if we are falling into the void of annihilation. In the ego-state, therefore, we constantly struggle to hang onto the conviction that the ego is real, that the ego is us.

This brings us to the psychological purpose of the universe. According to the Course, the universe was projected from our minds to serve as visible proof that the ego is not madness, but truth. If this is so, the universe does its job well. Every single thing we see is convincing testimony on behalf of the ego. It is a "world in which the proof of separation seems to be everywhere."[37] Looking around us, separation seems to be more than a mere belief, it appears to be the only truth. Believing in it seems to be not just some choice, some whim, but the stern decree of reality itself. Very simply, "In a world of form the ego cannot be denied for it alone seems real."[38]

Think about it. Hasn't your experience of living within space convinced you that separateness is real and that you are separate? Hasn't your experience of being in a body convinced you that you are vulnerable, as well as finite? Hasn't your experience of living in time convinced you that nothing stays the same, that everything is unstable? After all you've seen, doesn't doubting the reality of separation, limitation, vulnerability, and change feel like an enormous effort, and doesn't believing in a perfect, limitless Heaven feel like some pie-in-the-sky fantasy? Onto these universal elements of the human experience, the Course would merely add the following question: *What if you made the world to achieve this very psychological result?* What if you made it to convince yourself that you really are an ego, and that therefore you need never worry about the terrifying prospect of losing your boundaries in the limitlessness of God? If you did, then your plan has worked very well indeed.

IT WAS ONLY A DREAM

Given what we've just discussed, the separation looks like a tragedy of unimaginable proportions. Thirteen billion years of time and space, a war-torn world in which millions of living things die every second—these seem like very serious matters indeed. And from this perspective, we'd naturally imagine God's response to be one of anger, or at least alarm. Yet the Course calls the separation "a tiny, mad idea," and can tiny, mad ideas actually come true? Can they really work? Imagine that someone told you, "I have a plan to blow up the world. You see, all my life I've stirred my coffee clockwise, but today I'm going to stir it *counterclockwise.* And this will blow up the world!" Would you be alarmed? Or would you laugh? That is exactly how Heaven reacted to our plan to blow up eternity—with "gentle laughter."[39] It knew our crazy idea could never work.

Regardless of how massive the effects of the separation appeared to be, the truth is contained in this one momentous statement: *"The separation never occurred."*[40] Nothing really happened. The separation was not a real event in which we literally left Heaven and actually made a physical world. Rather, it was merely a *psychological* event, in which minds that remained *within* Heaven merely fell asleep and had a dream. Meanwhile, in the daylight of reality, nothing at all changed. Everything continued as it always had. And as it still does. Even now, at this moment, only Heaven is real. Only Heaven has ever been real. In the Course's teaching, Heaven *is* reality; they are one and the same thing. Everything else is pure illusion.

Yet how can this be? How can everything we experience as real *not* be real? The Course presents plausible and thought-provoking answers to this question, which we'll explore in the following four sections.

1. There is no world.

The world appears to be our home. In the midst of all of life's uncertainty, it's good to know we can count on the fact that we're standing on solid ground. Yet according to the Course, we *cannot,* because we *are* not. This world is literally the stuff of dreams, no more real than our dreams at night—in which, of course, the ground *also* seems solid. True, this world is dreamt out of a much deeper part of our minds than our nighttime dreams, and so it is more stable and is also a collective dream rather than a private one. What really makes this dream harder to question, though, is the fact that we do not regularly wake up from it. With a nighttime dream we can look back from the waking state and see how insane and irrational it was, how it simply couldn't have been real. The Course is saying that one day, we'll awaken from *this* dream, and make the exact same observation.

Nighttime dreams, as the Course observes, make a powerful and disturbing statement about what the mind is capable of. They prove that we have the desire and ability to make a world that *seems* real, *seems* external to our mind, even though it is actually just a batch of images *inside* our mind. The Course then points out, very reasonably, that this desire/ability does not leave us when we get out of bed. How, then, can we be sure that we are not using it right now?

> You seem to waken, and the dream is gone. Yet what you fail to recognize is that what caused the dream has not gone with it. Your wish to make another world that is not real remains with you. And what you seem to waken to is but another form of this same world you see in dreams. All your time is spent in dreaming.[41]

If the world is only a dream, only a collection of mental images inside our mind, then there literally is no such place as this world. If you dreamt of some fantastic country that existed only in your dream, when you awoke would you try to travel there? This is how the Course sees our world, and this is what leads to its bold proclamation:

> There is no world! This is the central thought the course attempts to teach.[42]

2. There is no such thing as time.

Time appears to govern our existence. We live by the clock, and even when no clocks are in view, time is still graying our hair and grinding all things down to dust. Our thinking is so time-bound that after reading the above section, we probably assume that even if the world is a dream, that dream must still be playing out *over time*.

According to the Course, there is no such thing as time: "It is a joke to think that time can come to circumvent eternity, which *means* there is no time."[43] Eternity is not an endless string of incredibly happy moments. Rather, it is only one endless moment: "Eternity is one time, its only dimension being 'always.'"[44] To capture the sense of this passage, you could say that while in paradise it's always spring, in eternity it's always *always*.

Eternity came first and it rules out even the possibility of time. Hence, there is no room for time to exist. And so, even though we seem to be passing through different moments, everything must really be happening all at once. This means that the different moments of time are really all the exact same moment, just filled with different scenery. Time really contains only one moment. This single, all-encompassing instant is like the light of a projector, a light that is always the same yet *appears* different because it shines through different frames of film.

Consequently, this current moment, right now, is the same moment as when the dinosaurs roamed the earth, as when Jesus was born, and as when we will finally awaken from the dream. The light is the same; only the frames are different. We are somehow playing a giant mental trick on ourselves, fooling ourselves into believing that we are experiencing these different scenes sequentially, when actually, we are experiencing them all at once. If you find your mind tied in knots by this idea, be reassured; the Course tells us that it is impossible for our current minds to comprehend this. "And so you are not asked to understand the lack of sequence really found in time."[45]

As strange as this may sound, there is comfort in this idea that all of time is taking place inside one single instant. It means that the seemingly endless nightmare of the separation in reality lasts only a "tiny tick of time."[46] Even better, says the Course, that instant is *already over*. It came and went, and now we are simply reliving memories of it. "For we but see the journey from the point at which it ended, looking back on it, imagining we make it once again; reviewing mentally what has gone by."[47] Time is not some evil fun house in which we are trapped forever; it is a short film which is already shot, already in the can, and which we are watching from the safety of our home in eternity.

3. We are not who we think we are.

We scarcely question the basic "fact" that we are a human being, an imperfect mind living in a mortal body. Some of us have been taught that in addition to this "lower self," there is also a buried spark of divinity within us. Thus we have two selves, a higher and a lower.

As useful as this teaching is, however, this is not what the Course is teaching. Think, for instance, about someone in a mental institution with delusions of grandeur. Let's say his name is John Smith, and he's convinced he's Napoleon. Are there two selves here: John Smith *and* Napoleon? Or is there just one: John Smith *believing* he is Napoleon? Think about someone with severe amnesia. Let's say Sally Jones wakes up one day, far from home, having totally forgotten who she is. She eventually assumes a new life in a new town as Jane Doe. Again, are there two selves here? Or is there just Sally Jones who mistakenly *believes* she's Jane Doe?

To understand how the Course applies these insights to you, we first have to mentally divide you into two characters. The first is the character you experience yourself as. This would include your name, your personality traits, your body, your station in the world, your personal history and projected future—all the specifics that make up your sense of identity. The second is the "you" who experiences yourself as this collection of things. This is the "you" who is directing your eyes to scan across this page, who is feeling the sensation of whatever seat your body is sitting on, who thinks and comprehends, who feels pain and makes mistakes; you know—*you*. This "you" is not the eyes, the sensations, the thoughts, the pain, the mistakes; it is the one behind them, the one who experiences them and sets them in motion. It is an elusive creature, one you never actually see. Since you are the seer, seeing "you" would be like seeing your eyeballs without a mirror (just try it). There is some question, therefore, about what exactly this "you" is.

So, we have two characters: 1) the collection of things you experience as yourself, and 2) the "you" who is the experiencer. What is the relationship between them? In normal thinking, they are one and the same thing. In your eyes, "you" *are* that collection of things. We all know, however, that we can be wrong about ourselves, so there could conceivably be at least *some* distance between "you" (second character) and who you think you are (first character). The question is: how much distance?

From the Course's standpoint there is far more distance between these things than you would ever imagine. The distance, in fact, is virtually unlimited, for the first character is nothing, while the second is everything. The first character is just a pile of illusions. It is a person who never existed and never will. It is a papier-mâché mask, pasted together from this and that, and worn by a being whose true face could not be more different. For the second character—the "you"—is the holy Son of God, "a perfect being, all-encompassing and all-encompassed, nothing to add and nothing taken from; not born of size nor place nor time, nor held to limits or uncertainties of any kind."[48] The Son of God is not some buried aspect of yourself, some hidden part of you, some higher self. "The Son of God is you."[49] The very "you" who is trying to understand this paragraph is the Son of God. The very "you" who is so convinced that you are [fill in your name], from [fill in your place of origin] is the holy Son of God. That "you" you've never seen, that "you" right on the other side of your thoughts and feelings, that being is God's perfect Son.

You are that infinite being right now, this instant. You're just delusional, convinced you're some fictional character. You just have a severe case of amnesia, have forgotten who you are and have come to believe that you're someone else, living in some other place. But you are still the being you started out as, all those eons ago. You haven't changed one bit. You may "know" in your bones that you're just an ordinary human, not some divine spirit. Yet what does that mean? In the end all it means is that you're just as convinced you are a human being as the guy in the mental hospital is convinced he is Napoleon. And might it not be that you're just as wrong?

4. We are not where we think we are.

We probably go our whole lives without questioning where we are. We know without thinking: we are here in this world, in some particular place, in this body, in this head, behind these eyes and between these ears. What could be more obvious? Yet this unquestioning confidence is curious when you recall that we regularly experience being somewhere we are not.

Every night when we dream, we have the very convincing experience of being in a place we are not. And while in the dream, we do not question where we are—we just "know." We even experience ourselves as being inside a body which, upon awakening, we recognize as a mere mental image—a dream body. Though we appear to be inside the dream environment and inside the dream body, the truth is the exact reverse: *it* is inside *us*. It all takes place within our minds while we lie asleep in bed. This daily (or rather, nightly) experience has taught every one of us an undeniable fact: Our mind can give us a false sense of location, and a convincing one at that. Which leads to a question we may never have asked: *How do we know that isn't happening right now?*

A Course in Miracles claims that is exactly what is happening. According to it, we're not in this world and never have been. After all, there is no world. And we're not inside these bodies, either. They're just dream bodies that last a little longer than the ones at night. All of it, the entire dream, the entire universe, is just a tiny island of images floating inside our limitless minds while we lie asleep in our real home: Heaven. The Course sums it up with a touch of irony: "You are at home in God, dreaming of exile."[50] While we dream of being banished from home, we are asleep *at* home.

HEAVEN AND THE SEPARATION

HEAVEN AND THE SEPARATION

While God, being formless, cannot be literally depicted, we might envision Him as endless light, without form or boundary. Out of God extends His Son, the Christ, represented by the light shining in the center of the picture. The heads in the foreground are the sleeping Sons of God, parts of the one Son who have fallen into separation. In the separation, these sleeping Sons did not leave Heaven or change their nature. They merely fell asleep and dreamt of living outside of Heaven, in a world of space and time. This world, however, is just a dream image inside their sleeping minds. Eventually, as with the Son at the bottom of the picture, they will all awaken. For purposes of the illustration, the minds of the sleeping Sons are shown quite large in the overall scheme of Heaven. We should think of the separated mind, however, as infinitesimally small. The Course likens it to the tiniest ripple on the ocean—the ocean being the Christ.

This point, combined with the preceding three, turns our reality completely upside down. There is no world; there is no time; we are not who we think we are; we are not where we think we are. These four ideas take everything we experience, look it straight in the face, and give it a radically different explanation. All four explanations are based on a single, undeniable fact: Our mind can play tricks on us. We know from experience that our mind can dish up a false world for us. We know it can give us a false sense of identity. We know it can conjure up a false sense of location. We know it can even alter our experience of time, stretching it or compressing it. We know all this, but we unconsciously, naively, assume that this takes place within safe, reasonable bounds. Why do we assume that? What if there are no bounds? What if our entire universe is a trick being played on us by our own limitless mind?

Try, if you can, not to treat this as bad news. For it means that in spite of everything that seems to have occurred, Heaven remains the only reality.

CONCLUSION

What relevance, you may ask, does this have for our lives? Well, if this is true, then this changes everything. I mean *everything*. This is the Big Fact. This is the Good News. The Course puts its significance this way:

> In your own mind, though denied by the ego, is the declaration of your release. *God has given you everything.*[51]

If the Course's message is true, then there is a perfect, egoless God Who loves you with all His Being, right this instant. You are His Son, and all He has is yours. If this message is true, then you are an ancient, holy being, shining with God's Own purity. This being is not what you will someday become; this is not some spark within your overall makeup. This is what you are right now. You, this ancient divine being, have merely fallen into the delusion that you are this tiny, struggling human.

If this message is true, then God has given you an eternal home which exceeds an earthly paradise as the ocean exceeds a grain of sand.

You will not only spend eternity there, but you are there right now, this instant, merely dreaming that you are shipwrecked on this island of misery. For it is the only reality there is. If this is true, then you are not subject to any of the sources of pain that beset you now. They have no actual power over you whatsoever. They are just dreams. If this is true, it changes everything. No wonder the Course asks you,

> Why are you not rejoicing? You are free of pain and sickness, misery and loss, and all effects of hatred and attack.[52]

Please don't make the mistake of thinking that this is only relevant for some far-off future, maybe after you die. It is totally relevant now, and for a simple reason: Your emotions emanate from your picture of what is real. No matter what your eyes see, your feelings are determined by what your mind decides is real. If you were homeless and on the street, yet your mind knew for a fact that you were receiving a check for a million dollars tomorrow, would you feel depressed? If you were in a dream surrounded by monsters, yet you knew with crystal clarity that it was only a dream and that your real life was wonderful, would you have to wait until you awoke before you could be free of fear?

Likewise, if you decided that this message were true, and really embraced it in your heart, your emotional state would instantly reflect this picture. And what a state that would be! You'd lean back and bask in pure joy. You'd rest in the peace of knowing that you are loved forever. And you'd look upon every frightening appearance that came along as the lucid dreamer looks on those dream monsters. As the Course points out, "You would not react at all to figures in a dream you knew that you were dreaming."[53] Regardless of the conditions in your life—rain or shine—you would live in the serenity of knowing that all is very, very well.

If you truly, deeply accept this message, then, you are free. The struggle is over. The question is: *How* can you truly, deeply accept this?

FIVE

The Answer

We have now seen two pictures, which could not be more opposite. We have seen the ego brooding in the murky depths of our minds, the essence of divisiveness and attack, so terrifying to look upon that we have covered it over with successive masks. Little do we realize that from its hiding place it has authored our world, a world that is one massive battleground. On this battleground, there is no safety. The shells can come right through the walls of our house; indeed, they often come from the other side of the bed. All we know is that we live in fear.

And we have seen God, a God Who is totally egoless, Who is Love itself. "Giving Himself is all He knows."[1] We have seen that His overflowing Love created us as a Self Whose "shimmering and perfect purity is far more brilliant than is any light that [we] have ever looked upon."[2] His Love also created a realm that is the polar opposite to this world, a Heaven of perfect unity and bliss. Finally, we have seen that only Heaven is real, which means that getting from this world to Heaven is a simple process of waking up to what is. The essence of this process is captured in this beautiful prayer from Workbook Lesson 323, "I gladly make the 'sacrifice' of fear":

Here is the only "sacrifice" You ask of Your beloved Son;
You ask him to give up all suffering,

all sense of loss and sadness,
all anxiety and doubt,
and freely let Your Love come streaming in to
his awareness,
healing him of pain,
and giving him Your Own eternal joy.
Such is the "sacrifice" You ask of me,
and one I gladly make.[3]

The question still remains, however: How exactly do we accomplish this? How do we "give up all suffering" and let His Love come streaming in to our awareness? This is what we'll explore in this final chapter on the Course's teaching.

True perception or vision

According to the Course, we cannot leap directly from our current state of mind into the knowledge of Heaven. The gap between the two states is too great. Right now we live in the state of *perception*, in which we try to know a reality that is frustratingly outside ourselves. We can only see this reality through the plate-glass window of our physical senses and mental interpretations—a window that is anything but clear. In the end, in fact, this window functions more like a *mirror*. Rather than seeing reality, we end up seeing the reflection of our own state of mind. That is the problem with perception. It encloses us in our own subjective bubble and cuts us off from direct contact with what is real. That is why our ultimate goal is *knowledge*. In the state of knowledge, we are no longer separate from reality. The subject-object dichotomy has collapsed and we are one with the truth. No longer are we mired in shifting interpretations and subjective opinions. Now, we *know*—purely, immediately, with absolute certainty. There are no more questions; even the possibility of questions has disappeared.

As I said, we cannot get to knowledge directly. The shock would be too great. The total loss of boundaries would feel like utter annihilation. What we need, says the Course, is *true perception*, a kind of perception that so closely mirrors heavenly knowledge "that transfer to it is at last possible."[4] This "transfer" the Course calls *the final step*. It is taken by God Himself because only He can lift us across the gap that still remains between true perception and knowledge. Once the last step has been taken, we are permanently out of the world of time and space.

Our task, then, is to move from *false perception* (where we are now) to *true perception*. We do so through the power of choice. Most of the choices we make are inconsequential; we choose between different forms of the same content. But the choice of how we will perceive determines the world we live in. Because we have chosen false perception, we live now in a world of fear. Yet if we choose true perception, though the forms outside us stay the same, we will step into the *real world*, a world of safety and love.

What is false perception? In false perception, we rely upon our eyes and our other senses. We look out upon a world of bodies, meaningless forms. It is then up to us to interpret what those forms mean. We generally give them a somewhat unfavorable interpretation, simply because those bodies are so often doing things we don't like. If only they could get it right!

True perception, which the Course usually calls *vision*, is completely different. It is not a case of our brains giving a "nicer" interpretation to those bodies out there: "I think she meant well when she said that." It is a whole different mode of perception. Instead of our eyes looking on bodies, our *minds* look *past* all the forms. There, beyond each misbehaving body, we gaze upon the radiant light of holiness. The Course speaks of Great Rays streaming out from behind each body, "so unlimited that they reach to God."[5] When we see this, we are actually seeing a piece of reality, a little part of Heaven. "The golden aspects of reality that spring to light under His loving gaze are partial glimpses of the Heaven that lies beyond them."[6]

We don't see this light of holiness with our eyes. Rather than physical perception, it is more like the "seeing" we experience when we get a sudden insight and say, "Ah, I *see*." In that case, what we "see" is pure understanding, not visual forms, not shape, not color. It is the same with vision. Furthermore, this seeing is not merely one more interpretation cranked out by our brains. Mentally affirming that the light of holiness is behind that body can *lead* to vision, but is not itself vision. Rather, vision *dawns* upon us. It is infused into our minds from the Christ in us. It is not a thought we manufacture, but an experience we have. The Course suggests that, undiluted, it is an overwhelming one.

Two passages can give us a better sense of what vision is. The first comes from Workbook Lesson 158:

> Christ's vision has one law. It does not look upon a body, and mistake it for the Son whom God created. It beholds a light beyond the body; an idea beyond what can be touched, a purity undimmed by errors, pitiful mistakes, and fearful thoughts of guilt from dreams of sin. It sees no separation. And it looks on everyone, on every circumstance, all happenings and all events, without the slightest fading of the light it sees.[7]

This passage presents a series of contrasts between what vision does and does not see. In doing so, it captures how you would look upon someone in the state of vision. To begin with, you would look past her body. You would also look past her mistakes, all those misbehaviors that came from attacking thoughts, all those negative personality traits that seemed to taint her purity. In the end, you would look past everything that separates or distinguishes her from you or anyone else. As you look upon her, your eyes would still see what they have always seen, but your mind would be caught up in another vision entirely. You would be gazing on "a light" that is also "an idea" that is also "a purity" that is also "the Son whom God created." You would see what I am calling the light of holiness. As your focus moved from her to others, the shapes in your visual field would shift, but the light in your mind would remain constant. Behind every person, behind every situation, you would see this exact same luminous backdrop, the reflected light of Heaven.

The second passage is from the Text. It does not so much define what vision is as reveal the effect it will have on us:

> Can you imagine how beautiful those you forgive will look to you? In no fantasy have you ever seen anything so lovely. Nothing you see here, sleeping or waking, comes near to such loveliness. And nothing will you value like unto this, nor hold so dear. Nothing that you remember that made your heart sing with joy has ever brought you even a little part of the happiness this sight will bring you. For you will see the Son of God.[8]

To really appreciate the impact of this passage you must personalize it:

- Think about something lovely you have imagined in a fantasy. Then realize that someone you see through vision will look far lovelier.

- Then think about some incredibly beautiful sight you have seen, either in waking life or in a dream, and understand that this comes nowhere near the loveliness of vision.
- Think about something in your life that you hold dear, and consider that you will hold what vision shows you far more dear.
- Then think of some event that "made your heart sing with joy," and realize that it did not bring you "even a little part of the happiness this sight will bring you."

What is the source of this overwhelming joy? The Course says it simply: "You will see the Son of God." This, in other words, is a kind of religious vision, in which the veils momentarily part and you see eternity. One thinks of those children who have seen visions of Mary and how absolutely transfixed they are, heedless of their surroundings as they are caught up in the ecstasy of the vision. The Course claims that in the state of vision, this is how we will experience looking on *anyone*.

This vision, claims the Course, is already within us, in our right mind, a layer of our mind that lies beneath the ego and the call for help—which means that for most of us, it is deeply unconscious. But it is there. Our task is to bring it to the surface.

The Holy Spirit

We are not going to bring it to the surface by ourselves, however. We need help in order to see truly. The reason goes back to the mirror-like nature of perception. It is as if we are trapped inside a bubble with a reflective interior surface. Everywhere we turn all we see is the reflection of our own state of mind. We think we are looking on reality, yet instead we are merely seeing our own belief system in picture form.

Before this bubble can disappear, we need to hear a voice from outside of it, a voice that knows reality as it truly is, free of our subjective colorations and distortions. This voice can tell us what is real, even if we cannot yet see what is real. And as its messages lead us to greater sanity and peace, we gradually learn to trust it, and finally to see through the bubble; to see what it sees. This voice is the Holy Spirit.

The Holy Spirit "came into being with the separation."[9] He is God's loving response to our falling asleep in Heaven. According to the Course, God is aware that the constant outpouring of His Love has hit a blockage. He knows that "His communication channels [His Sons] are not open to Him, so that He cannot impart His joy and know that His children are wholly joyous."[10] He therefore responds, simply and immediately:

> So He thought, "My children sleep and must be awakened."
>
> How can you wake children in a more kindly way than by a gentle Voice That will not frighten them, but will merely remind them that the night is over and the light has come?[11]

The Holy Spirit is this gentle Voice. His role is to enter our dream and lead us to the glad awareness that "the night is over and the light has come."[12] Like God and Christ, you could say that He is a limitless, bodiless Person. Yet whereas the function of God and Christ is to increase the Kingdom through creation, the Holy Spirit's function is to restore the wholeness of the Kingdom by awakening all of God's children.

The key to this function is that He stands on both shores at once. "He knows because He is part of God; He perceives because He was sent to save humanity."[13] His Mind is awake in Heaven, yet He is perfectly aware of every last detail of the dream. This allows Him to perceive the dream *in light of reality*, and this is the perception He bestows on us.

An analogy might help us understand His function. Imagine a psychic hired to help a patient who is comatose because he is stuck in a demented dream and is deeply resistant to waking. This psychic has the very special gift of being able to enter the patient's dream, move around, and act in it with total appropriateness toward the dream, yet at the same time maintain open-eyed awareness of the hospital room in which the patient lies. Being aware of the room, the psychic sees the dream for exactly what it is: just a dream. While in the dream, the psychic befriends the patient, and then gradually instructs him in a special kind of sight. In this sight, the patient still sees the dream, but behind each dream image he also sees the light of the hospital room. At first this light is only the faintest glow, but with time, it grows increasingly bright and inviting. And the more it does, the more his fear of waking up to the room falls away, until at last he opens his eyes to his true surroundings, where his family waits to joyously greet him, with the psychic smiling beside them.

The mechanics of perception

Seeing with true perception means that we look on the same old people and situations as before, but see a whole new meaning in them. It means seeing a different reality, one that has been right in front of us all along, but which we failed to notice. And this requires acknowledging that we're not seeing things correctly *now*. It means admitting that our current perceptions are seriously off the mark. To admit this, it's helpful to understand *how* they are off the mark, what went wrong. And to acquire that understanding, we need to delve into the mechanics of perception.

In our view, of course, our perceptions are basically correct; we're seeing things more or less the way they are. It's as if light from the objects out there is traveling through two windows in our skulls and imprinting photographic images onto our minds. In this view, our perceptions are caused from the outside; they are the footprints of reality itself in the soft clay of our minds.

For instance, when someone yells at you, the sights and sounds of this event come streaming in through your senses, impressing themselves on your mind. Yet this is not all that seems to come streaming in. The *meaning* of the situation also appears to come in from the outside. You probably experience being yelled at as a bad thing, and this "badness" appears to exist in the situation itself. It seems to thrust itself onto your mind, coming in right alongside the sights and sounds, and *making* you feel bad.

This perceived meaning—which the Course calls *content*—is the crucial thing, for shape and color by themselves produce no feeling, no emotion. If you saw a batch of images that meant absolutely nothing to you, would it evoke any feeling in you? You have probably seen abstract art that struck you in just this way. "Whatever," you say, and walk on. Or think of when you've seen a married couple interacting, and suddenly one partner gets upset with the other for no apparent reason. Some trivial thing has been said that carries huge symbolic meaning within the relationship, yet to an outsider, it means absolutely nothing. Only when a meaning is assigned do feelings arise. Yet where does this meaning come from? The Course makes an obvious point:

> It is surely the mind that judges what the eyes behold. It is the mind that interprets the eyes' messages and gives them "meaning." And this meaning does not exist in the world outside at all.[14]

You cannot see meaning with your eyes, in the way you see the color red. Meaning is assigned by the mind; it comes from within the mind.

Let's explore how the mind assigns meaning.[15] This, as you might guess, is where things go wrong. This is where "errors in perception enter."[16] We begin the process with a laundry list of categories of things we want to see out there. Have you ever noticed that when you look at a scene, your eyes immediately search for and pick out things that interest you, while totally disregarding other things? Think of parents attending school plays; do they even *see* the other parents' children? We all know that people focus on certain things while ignoring others. Advertisers take advantage of this principle to put the very things in front of people that will catch their eye. Indeed, we all use this principle, for we're all advertising something. Even animals use it. I always think of that angler fish, which dangles a fake worm above its mouth to catch the eye of passing fish so it can eat them. It is counting on the fact that "worms" are high on the list of categories those little fish want to see.

We have all seen this principle at work, but we do not often understand how much it makes the world we see our own subjective invention. The Course says, "Perception selects, and makes the world you see."[17] If I look for acts of kindness, I'll live in a different world than the person who focuses on acts of callousness, and each of us will live in a different world than the guy who has a shoe fetish. What we focus on makes our world.

The subjectivity, however, doesn't stop there. Once our eyes alight on an item that seems to match one of our preferred categories, we instantly slap the label of that category onto it, and with that label, all of the meaning we have built up in that category. The category is like a file folder, in which we have been filing things away for years. When we see that item, we dump the whole fat folder onto it.

This is how we assign meaning to this new item; this is how we interpret it. We say, "This item is a member of this category, and therefore is like all the other items in this category." We generally do this with extreme carelessness and haste, for the very simple reason that we *want* to believe we've found a member of our desired category. That's what we were looking for in the first place. That hastiness can get us into trouble, as it certainly does those poor little fish.

To finish the whole process off, now that we've found an item that "obviously" fits our category, we take it as hard evidence that our category is indeed true.[18] After all, we ask ourselves, if the category was false, how could it fit things in the world so accurately? Having "confirmed" our category, we restart the cycle.

Stereotypes of people provide great—though rather sensitive—examples of this process. Let me, therefore, summarize the steps I have covered, using the stereotype of the "dumb blonde" (blondes, please forgive me; this was the least charged stereotype I could think of, and one I certainly do not believe in).

1. We have preferred categories, certain kinds of things that we want to see.

Let's hypothetically say that for some reason you want to see dumb blondes. Perhaps you find them attractive, or gullible, or easy to poke fun at. Perhaps you had a bad experience with a blonde, and as a result you just enjoy judging them. Whatever the reason, your eyes will unconsciously want to see them show up in your visual field.

2. This leads us to look for and focus on items that seem to fit our preferred category.

Without realizing it, you're looking for dumb blondes (along with a hundred other categories), and this causes you to notice and focus on anyone you think might even remotely fit the bill.

3. Once we find one, we interpret it by projecting our pre-established category onto it.

Almost as soon as you see a blonde, you automatically slap the label of "dumb blonde" onto her. This means that you interpret her according to all the meaning that has accumulated in your mental file folder marked "dumb blondes": poor reasoning skills, nonsensical speech, inappropriate giggling, etc. To make this label stick, you tend to ignore or explain away any evidence to the contrary.

4. Thus interpreted, we take this item as confirmation that our category is true.

You think, "Look at her. I was right: blondes really are dumb."

Of course, what is really dumb is this process. The Course says, "Can this confused and senseless 'reasoning' be depended on for anything?"[19]

The whole process is driven not by external evidence, as it should be, but by the internal desire to see something from our category. We see it, then, not because it *is* there, but because we *want* it to be there. And we never really discover we were wrong. If our desire is strong enough, the category can reinforce itself in the total absence of evidence; it "sees" the evidence out there even when it is not. We watch this happen all the time. We see it happen with the racist and the bigot. We see it happen with all manner of stereotypes and prejudices, which can persist uncorrected for centuries. People see what they want to see.

The Course boils it all down to three simple words: "Projection makes perception."[20] Perception is internally generated; caused not from the outside in, as we assume, but from the *inside out*. "What is seen as 'reality' is simply what the mind prefers. Its hierarchy of values is projected outward, and it sends the body's eyes to find it."[21] As this passage suggests, this process does not apply only to isolated instances. Rather, it produces the "reality" we see, a reality that is just the projection of our hierarchy of preferred categories.

Yet surely this cannot be true of us. We try to see accurately. And we do modify our categories in light of experience. One encounter with that fake worm was enough for us; we're not going near there again. This may be true (though probably not as true as we think), but remember—the important aspect of perception is not the *form* but the *content*, the meaning. That's what causes our emotions. We may modify our view of how the forms work out there, how things behave, but what about the meaning? If we had a certain meaning that we really desired to see in the world, what would stop us from seeing it as much as we wanted? What would stop us from painting our whole world in its color, and being totally convinced we were seeing not our own projection, but reality?

The perception of sin in the world

Unfortunately, that meaning exists. And we *have* painted our whole world in its color, and we *are* totally convinced that we're seeing not our projection, but reality. There is a category that is literally the mother of all categories, the stereotype of all stereotypes, the prejudice of all prejudices. It supplies the content of countless smaller categories, and contributes some content to all our categories. It is the category of *external sinner.* To one degree or another, we've projected this category onto everyone in our lives. The Course says, "There is no one against whom you do not cherish grievances of some sort."[22] Let's look at how this category gets projected onto the world, using the four-step process I described above.

1. We have an overpowering desire to see sin out there.

In Chapter 3, we discussed the ego, the self-concept that lies beneath the masks of the face of innocence and the enraged victim. The ego is filled with the pure intent to do harm for selfish gain. Therefore, as I pointed out in Chapter 3, it *wants* to see a world of enemies, a world of sinners, for such a world justifies its own attack. As long as the impulse to attack lives within us, we will have a powerful need to see sinners out there. Have you ever noticed that when you want to attack someone, your mind will automatically start building a case against this person, a case that conveniently justifies your attack?

There is another reason why we desire to see sin outside of us. Given that our ego is so rapaciously attacking, it generates an enormous amount of guilt. We instinctively respond to its presence with self-loathing and self-punishment. As the Course says, we believe we "have made a devil of God's Son."[23] Who wants to look inside and see *that*? If you actually felt all this in you, what would be your first instinct? Let me ask another question. If you felt a scorpion in your mouth, what would be your first instinct? That's what we do with the sin we see in us—try to spit it out, onto the world. The Course talks about a child who has murderous thoughts, say, toward his parents, but these thoughts are so frightening to him that he has to see them as outside himself. So he displaces them onto his toys. Now it's his toy soldier, not him, who wants to kill his parents. "This does the child believe, because he fears his thoughts and gives them to the toys instead."[24] The child, of course, is every one of us. We fear the sin in us, and so we have a simply overpowering desire to see it out there instead of "in here."

These two factors—the need to justify our own attack and the need to see sin outside us rather than within—come together to give birth to our favorite preferred category, that of the external sinner.

2. This leads us to look for and focus on sin in the world.

The Course claims that the main thing our eyes look for in the world is evidence of external sin. It is not an implausible idea. Think how much of our attention goes into fault-finding. Think how nimble our eyes are at picking out the tiniest flaws in other people. The Course likens our eyes to "dogs of fear,"[25] vicious hunting dogs sent out by our ego to find sin. "No little shred of guilt escapes their hungry eyes. And in their savage search for sin they pounce on any living thing they see, and carry it screaming to their master [the ego], to be devoured."[26] It is a harsh image, to be sure, but we can probably relate.

3. Once we find a suitable candidate, we project the meaning of "sinner" onto that person.

If our hunting dogs detect the faintest scent of someone behaving in an unwelcome manner, we slap onto him the label of "external sinner" and all the meaning contained in that category. We've done it a million times. We know we're not just making it up; we know we're peering into the truth about this person. We have no idea that we're just superimposing onto his face the devil that we secretly believe lurks inside of us. The desire we see in him to attack for the lowest of reasons is really our own hidden desire. The guilt we see in him is our sense of guilt. That uncontrollable urge to punish us that he seems to have is really our own unconscious urge to punish ourselves. This person has become our toy soldier.

4. Thus interpreted, we take this person as confirmation that our category of "external sinner" is true.

Once we project all that onto this person, something in us says, "See, I was right. There really are sinners out there in the world. Thank God the sin is not in me." And so we send out the dogs again, and the process starts over.

This is the defining perception of our world. The perception that sin is out there colors our world like the gray overcast of a cloudy day. It defines our world. We see ourselves literally surrounded by a hostile power that seems to animate all those bodies, making them dangerous and unpredictable, not to be trusted. Could it be that we're just seeing the face of our own ego projected onto a gigantic movie screen? Could it be that we're seeing reality through the distorted lens of one all-encompassing stereotype? Could it be that we made it all up?

The Course says that not only did we make up the world as we see it, it also says that the choice to see this world carries two devastating consequences:

1. It causes us to see a fearful world, constantly poised to attack us. Fear is the net result of false perception. Despite the little rewards we think we gain along the way, our general mood is one of fear.

2. It reinforces our view that we are a guilty ego, not a Son of God. Somewhere inside we realize that how we choose to see our world is more a statement about ourselves than about the world. We recognize that pasting the label "external sinner" onto everyone is a hateful act. And so our guilt just deepens.

These mechanics may seem depressing at first, yet it can also be quite liberating to see that the perception of sin is the result of such a bogus process. It can be like realizing that the Great and Powerful Oz is just a conjuring trick produced by the little man behind the curtain. Realizing this, we can see that the huge, menacing head that dominates our landscape is just an illusion, conjured by a crazy little thought hiding behind a curtain in our minds. Now, at last, we can let it all go; we can let go of the perception of sin. Now we will no longer see people possessed by the devilish power of sin, but instead shining with the holiness of God Himself. And that, says the Course, is salvation.

Forgiveness

Our great need is to let go of the perception of sin in the world. The Course's name for this letting go is *forgiveness*. Forgiveness is the Course's answer to the human condition.

Today, the benefits of forgiveness are being realized more than ever, thanks to research being done in the psychological community. Forgiveness, psychologists are discovering, can cleanse us of years of bitterness and anger that have been slowly poisoning us. I've heard it said that resentment—unforgiveness—is like swallowing poison and hoping the other guy will die. Forgiveness can also free us from the chains of feeling like a victim, and restore to us a sense of our own power. It can rescue us from living in the past, and give us hope for the future. It even has demonstrable health benefits: "A growing body of research reveals that those who are forgiving...have...fewer health problems and lower incidence of the most serious illnesses....Research also shows that people who receive training in forgiveness experience significant reduction in depression, and gain in self-confidence, vitality, and hope."[27]

From the Course's standpoint, the benefits of forgiveness that psychologists are discovering are just the tip of the iceberg. The benefits ultimately go far beyond what we have dreamed of, because forgiveness itself goes beyond how we have defined it. The Course gives forgiveness a significantly new definition, one that contains a whole different approach, and that consequently gives forgiveness both a broader scope and more transformative power.

The dictionary defines forgiveness as giving up the feeling of resentment, and the Course would agree. Yet what is the cause of that feeling? As we saw earlier, emotion comes from the meaning we perceive. In this case, the emotion of *resentment* comes from the perceived meaning of *sin*. We feel resentment when we perceive another as having sinned, as having done harm for the sake of selfish gain. To give up the feeling, we have to give up the perception that causes it. Unless we get rid of the cause, the effect will remain. The Course therefore defines forgiveness as *giving up the perception of sin*. When we do that, the feeling of resentment automatically vanishes with it.

As logical as this sounds, this is an unconventional definition of forgiveness. It stands, in fact, in stark contrast to forgiveness as usually understood. Forgiveness normally means that you really did sin against me, but I have decided to forgive you anyway. Let me expand on the two parts of this statement:

1. You really did sin against me

You intentionally harmed me for the sake of your own gain. This means that, as a result, I'm justified in resenting you; I have a right to resent you. It also means that I have a right to retaliate against you. I cherish these rights, for by exercising them, I somehow gain back some of the dignity that you took from me.

2. But I will forgive you anyway

You don't deserve it, but for the sake of being loving and repairing our relationship, I'm willing to give up my right to resentment and my right to retaliation.

This sounds noble, but both the Course and experience teach us that it is not actually possible. Remember, emotion follows from the meaning we perceive. The emotion of resentment follows automatically from perceiving that a sin has been perpetrated against us. To really believe that "In your sinfulness you have done me real harm" *is* to feel resentment. Conventional forgiveness tries to hang onto that belief while letting go of the feeling caused by it. How can we hang onto the cause yet get rid of its effect? This is why forgiveness feels like such a struggle. We're straining to give something we believe the other person does not deserve. We're laboring to do that which makes no mental sense. The Course puts it this way: "You conceive of pardon as a vain attempt to look past what is there; to overlook the truth, in an unfounded effort to deceive yourself by making an illusion [the other person's innocence] true."[28] Doesn't this quote describe exactly how trying to forgive usually feels?

As a result, we usually do not succeed in giving up that lump of resentment inside; we just store it in the cellar. We may indeed refrain from retaliating on the outside, but we still retain a smoldering inner retaliation. In short, we put on a show of forgiveness, a façade. And even this feels like a sacrifice; we feel that we've just given away our rights for nothing in return. But have we? The Course suggests that we have given them away in order to send a message that buys our ego something it wants. See if you can identify with the following messages. We may be sending a message of superiority: "My brother, you have injured me, and yet, because I am the better of the two, I pardon you my hurt."[29] We may be showing what a martyr we are: "Behold, how good am I who bear with patience and with saintliness the anger and the hurt you give, and do not show the bitter pain I feel."[30] We may just be trying to strike a deal: "I will forgive you if you meet my needs, for in your slavery is my release."[31] It is no wonder that the author of the Course calls this kind of forgiveness "forgiveness-to-destroy."[32]

To really forgive, to really let go of that resentment inside (the effect), we must let go of the perception underlying it (the cause). We must find a way to look on the exact same attack, and without denying or rationalizing, interpret it as something other than a sin. This means that we must interpret it as both *innocent* and *harmless*. It is not enough to just drop the word "sin," which most of us have done long ago; we must drop the concept.

I have tried to capture the contrast between forgiveness as conventionally defined and forgiveness as defined by the Course in the following table:

Conventional forgiveness	Course-based forgiveness
To forgive means that I let go of my resentment towards you, even though I keep the perception that you sinned against me and that I am justified in resenting you.	To forgive means that I let go of my false perception that you sinned against me and that I am justified in resenting you. Releasing this perception automatically releases my resentment.
To forgive is to give up the resentment.	*To forgive is to give up the perception that* ***causes*** *the resentment.*

Though this definition of forgiveness may be unique, I think the Course is putting into words an experience that happens to people everywhere. I believe that whenever someone truly forgives, truly releases all resentment, that person is experiencing what the Course is talking about. She may use the word "sin," yet the actual concept of sin is absent from her perception of what happened to her. For in her heart has arisen a deep, unspoken recognition that despite injury to her body or her property, her true wholeness remains unharmed. and that despite her attacker's callous actions, there is an inborn innocence in him that remains intact, making him still worthy of love. She may not be able to put it into words, but this recognition is what banishes the darkness of her anger and lights up her mind with love. It is the active ingredient that makes forgiveness happen.

A Course in Miracles aims to put this active ingredient into our hands by providing a picture of reality that supports it. Forgiveness as normally conceived feels so difficult because it does not make sense. Since we believe the person is unworthy of it, forgiveness becomes "a charitable whim, benevolent yet undeserved…Unmerited, withholding it is just."[33] The Course aims to remedy this state of affairs by giving us a picture of reality in which forgiveness makes perfect sense, in which it is anger that is senseless. Let's look at how the Course does this.

Forgiveness is normally an attempt to restore love and unity that have been damaged by attack. We can see this in a typical statement we might make to someone we are forgiving: "Hey, it's all right. What you did was no big deal. What really matters is our relationship and the love I feel for you." This statement says that what is really important is me continuing to love you and the two of us continuing to be together. Your attack on me has damaged both those things, but I don't want that to continue. I want to restore our love and unity. And so I'll simply let go of what you did.

The problem, of course, is that in our conventional view of reality, the love and unity I'm trying to restore are highly vulnerable, while the attacks are extremely powerful, easily able to damage the love and unity beyond repair. Your attack can be so heartless and harmful that it simply destroys my ability to love you, because it makes you unworthy of love. It can also shatter our unity, opening up a permanent rift between us. In short, it is like a missile launched at Humpty-Dumpty. In this case, those pieces are definitely not going to get put back together again.

In the Course's view of reality, this situation is completely reversed. To begin with, you are eternally worthy of love, because your nature as God's Son is forever changeless. Nothing you could possibly do could taint it. Moreover, our unity could never truly be shattered, for it is one of the pillars of Heaven, beyond the ravages of this world. As the Course says, "Whom God has joined no man can put asunder."[34] In this view, then, the love and the unity that forgiveness would restore is like the sun—too immense and permanent to be damaged by the little things of earth. In contrast, your attack on me was just a dream event, a tiny "fragment of a senseless dream."[35] Given that, how much power can it really have? Thus, instead of a missile launched at Humpty-Dumpty, it is really nothing but "mists before the sun."[36]

Think of how this transforms our understanding of forgiveness. It says that the love and unity forgiveness would restore could never actually be damaged. It says that the attack that forgiveness would release was never real in the first place. How could this fail to make forgiveness easier and more natural? For now, at last, it makes perfect sense; indeed, it is the only sensible thing.

Justifications for forgiveness

The thought system of *A Course in Miracles* amounts to an overall framework in which forgiveness is justified. Forgiveness is no longer an unmerited gift that flies in the face of justice. It *is* justice. One can see every idea in the Course as yet another support for the fairness and reasonableness of forgiveness. What follows are just four of the many rationales the Course gives for why forgiveness is always totally justified.

You cannot be hurt.

One of our most unquestioned assumptions is that we can be hurt. Yet can we really? If you had a dream in which someone shot you, you'd feel the pain, but would you actually be hurt? If you were playing a video game and your character died, you might experience it as a sort of little death, but did anything actually happen to you? Wouldn't it be wonderful if every one of our hurts was just like this? That is exactly what the Course teaches. It says that we are changeless beings, and changeless beings by definition cannot be hurt. When we feel hurt, it is because we identify with a dream figure—our body and personality—and so we feel *its* injury as if it were our own. Yet, if this is so, has anything really happened to us?

Therefore, when that person snubbed you, your image of yourself was hurt, but the changeless "you" that identifies with that image was not. You remained absolutely the same, eternally unchanged. "The changelessness of Heaven is in you, so deep within that nothing in this world but passes by, unnoticed and unseen....Nothing can intrude upon the sacred Son of God within."[37] If that person did not really hurt you, how can it make sense to resent her? It would be like Superman resenting someone who fired bullets that bounced off him.

To apply this insight I have used the following line from the Course (which I have changed into a first person statement). I think of the situation in which I feel resentment, and simply repeat this sentence to myself, slowly, while dwelling on its meaning:

> *I cannot be hurt, and do not want to show my brother anything except my wholeness.*[38]

"You are doing this unto yourself."[39]

We've actually already covered this point. In our discussion of perception, we said that our emotional experience of a situation is determined not by the outer form we see, but by the meaning we project onto that form. We also said that our perception of others as guilty sinners is simply the projection of our own buried sense of sinfulness.

As the Course says, "You never hate your brother for his sins, but only for your own."[40] The world is our inkblot; we're the ones who place the meaning on it. The world is our dream; all the figures we see reflect dynamics in our own mind.

Think of a situation in which someone you trusted stabbed you in the back. What this teaching means is that all the pain you experienced over that incident came from you. It came from the meaning *you* put on the situation. You saw her as a sinner only because you were trying to displace onto her your own guilt. You saw the "knife" she wielded as having such power over you only because it symbolized your own hidden wish to punish yourself. You did it all to yourself, which means *she* did nothing to you. How, therefore, can you resent her? You might find it helpful to call this situation to mind and repeat to yourself over and over, *"I am doing this unto myself,"* which means, "All the pain I'm experiencing here comes from the meaning *I* am projecting onto this situation." See if you don't feel lifted.

Attack is a call for help, a call for love.

One of the key aspects of the idea of sin is that the attacker gains from your loss. Think about when someone triumphs over you and humiliates you. Don't you picture him enjoying it, relishing the gain that came from your loss? He got what he wanted and now he celebrates. Yet what kind of person derives happiness from the unhappiness of others? Isn't that what we call evil? When you think to yourself, "He gained pleasure from someone else's pain," don't you feel something of the same revulsion that you feel toward those who delight in physically torturing people?

If this person really did get pleasure from your loss, then there would be evil in him, and he would deserve your anger. The Course, however, says that his pleasure is only superficial, and underneath it lies a disturbing thought: "What is wrong with me? Why would I seek to humiliate this person? I must be a bad person." He feels guilt, and this guilt causes the net effect of his attack on you to be unhappiness. He has not gained from your loss. It is in fact impossible for him to gain from the loss of others. This is a crucial fact; it is the evidence of an innate goodness in him. There is a goodness that lies at the base of his nature and that wants only love in all its purity. Love, in fact, is the only thing he is *capable* of wanting. And so in every attack, he is unconsciously

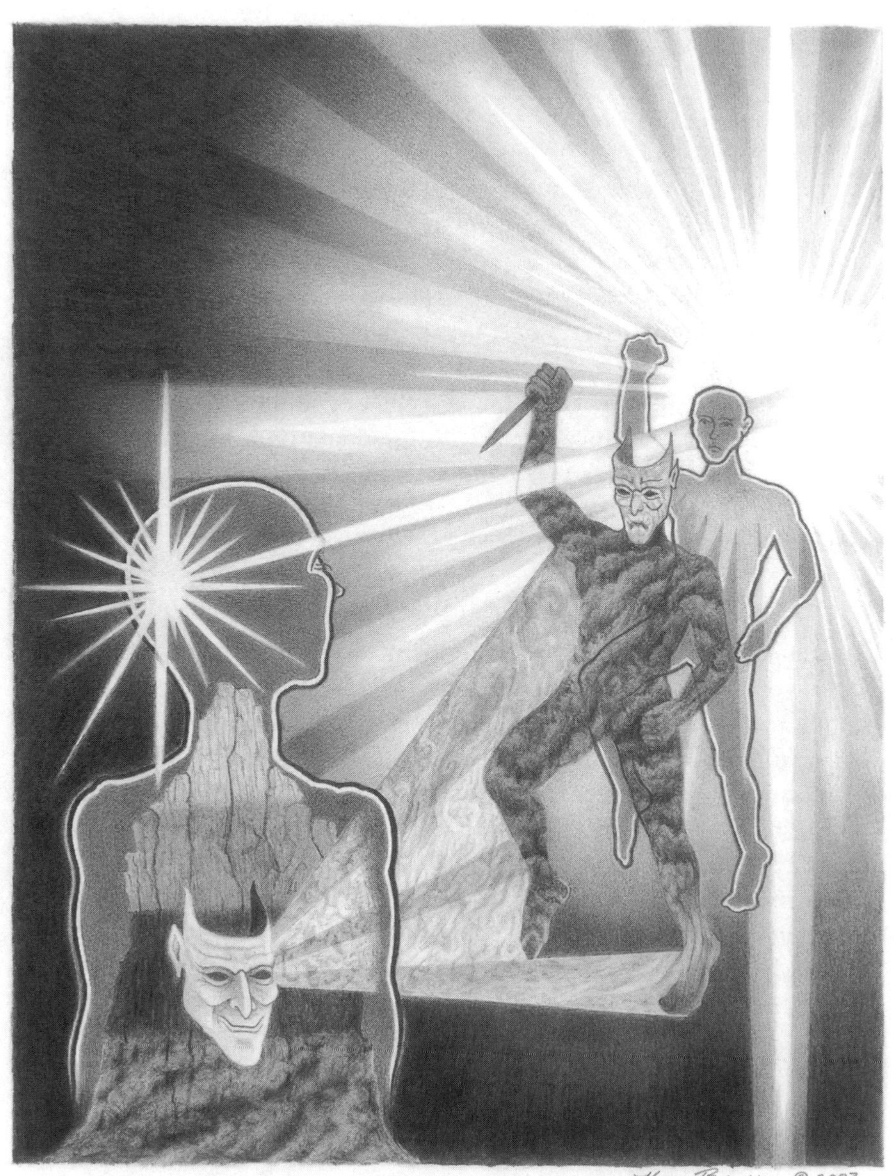

FORGIVENESS

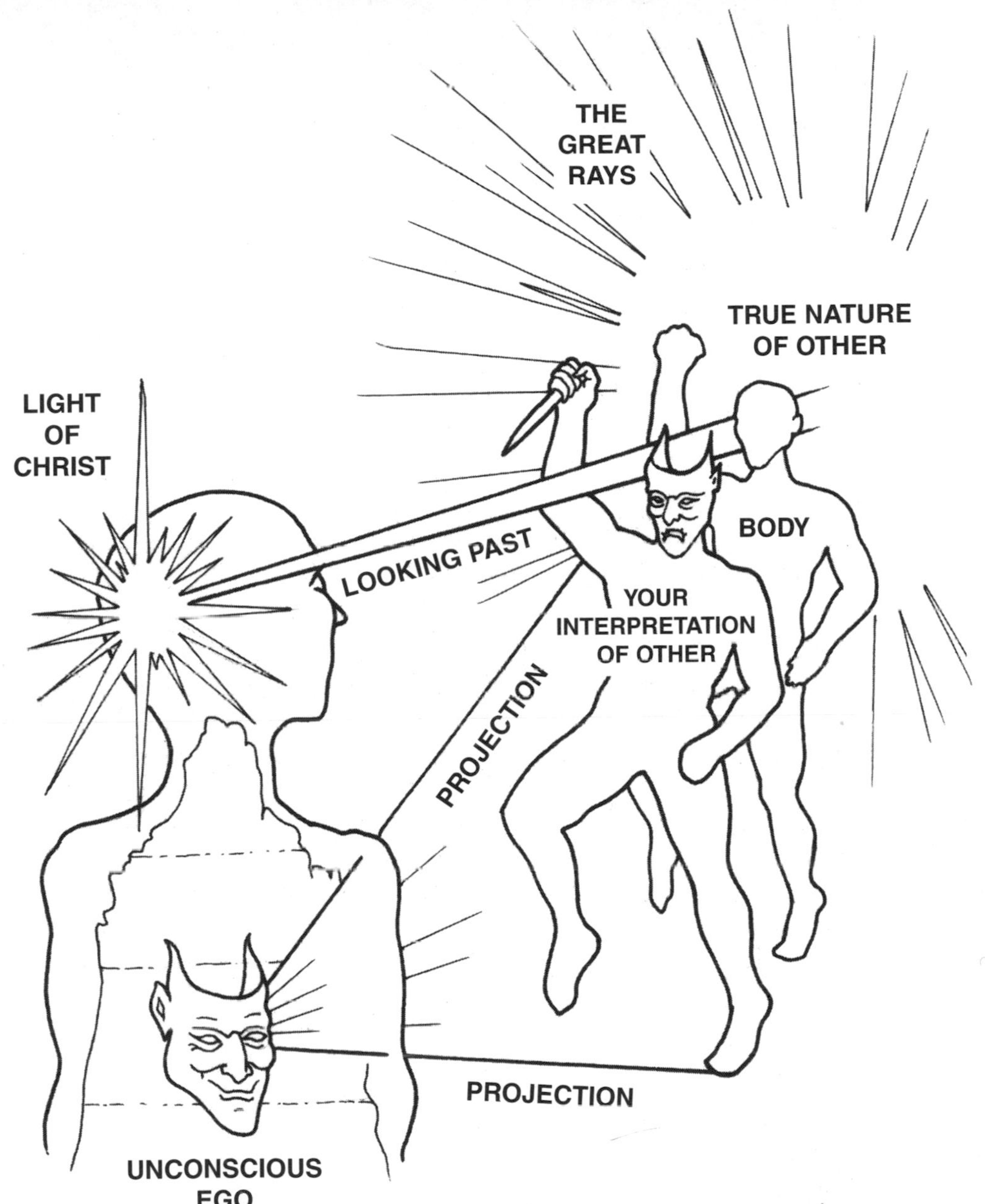

FORGIVENESS

When we see someone attacking us, we are seeing both that person's body and our interpretation of him or her as a sinful attacker. That interpretation is far more subjective than we realize. In reality, it is just the projection of our own unconscious ego. It is the externalized image of the "sinner" within. To forgive means to look past two things: the interpretation, in recognition that it is incorrect, and the body, in recognition that it is not that person's reality. We look past both to the holiness in the other person, to the radiant light of Who he really is. The Course calls this light the Great Rays.

reaching out for this pure love, and instead reaping a harvest of guilt.

He is not at all getting what he wants. He is stuck in a cycle of seeking love but only finding pain. He keeps reaching out for a rose, but all he gets is a handful of thorns. And the distress he feels is a call for help. It is a call for someone to give him what he is failing to find. It is a call for you to give him a rose. That is what forgiveness is: a gift of love to alleviate the guilt of those who seek love but instead find guilt. To help in the giving of this gift, I've used the following line, which is adapted from the Course, and in which I insert the name of the person I need to forgive:

> *Forgiving [name] is the natural reaction to distress that rests on error, and thus calls for help.*[41]

This person is a divine dreamer, not the dream figure you see.

Imagine for a moment that you are visiting Mahatma Gandhi in a mental hospital. It turns out that he has been exposed to some chemical that has affected his brain, and he is experiencing a brief psychotic break. It will clear up within a few days, but while it lasts, he honestly believes he is Adolf Hitler, and so he is ranting about exterminating the Jews and taking over the world. Would you see this encounter as a visit with Hitler, or a visit with Gandhi? After the encounter, would you tell your friends that you'd just seen Hitler, or that you'd just seen Gandhi?

Now imagine for a moment that this world really is a dream. There may be a person in your life who reminds you of Hitler, but what you see of that person—the body and personality—is simply a dream figure. The real question is: *who is the dreamer?* Who is the mind dreaming that it's that dream figure? Might it be possible that the dreamer is a being who is like Gandhi, only infinitely greater? Is it possible that he's a limitless spirit, at one with God, and holy beyond anything you can conceive? Could it be that one day in the distant future, he'll shake off his cloak of sleep and emerge as someone like Jesus or Buddha, in the brief time before he awakens from this world entirely? If you really knew all this to be true, would you be able to hold anything against him? To apply this idea, I've often practiced this line: *"You are the dreamer, [name], not the dream figure."*

The Course claims that if, even for an instant, you saw this person for Who he really is, "you could scarce refrain from kneeling at his feet."[42]

You would gaze on his holiness as one transfixed, forgetting the world around you, "unheeding of the body's witnesses before the rapture of Christ's holy face."[43] In this state of rapture, peace would descend on you and all your doubts about yourself would disappear. And you would know a happiness unlike anything this world can give.

These are just some of the ways in which the Course turns upside-down our perception that resentment is justified. Through the Course's gentle but compelling persuasion, our minds can realistically embrace a world in which there is no cause for anger. In this new world, a brutal murder is as easily forgiven as a minor slip of the tongue, for the principle behind all anger has been utterly negated. Anger and resentment are always a response to sin, and in the Course's view of reality there is no such thing as sin. This makes forgiveness much more than "a charitable whim." It makes it a simple acknowledgment of what is real.

The practice of forgiveness

How, though, do we actually forgive? The Course offers scores of practices which reveal exactly how it envisions the process. Based on these, we can distill the process into three steps:

1. Call to mind your current unforgiving perception.

Before we can let it go, we have to bring to mind our current perception of the other person. This requires self-honesty. It will do no good to hide our resentment behind a cloak of love and spirituality. Therefore, the Course will sometimes ask us to review in detail our negative perceptions of this person: "You will review his faults, the difficulties you have had with him, the pain he caused you, his neglect, and all the little and the larger hurts he gave…and you will think of his mistakes and even of his 'sins.'"[44] It also at times asks us to visualize the person's physical appearance, which, as it turns out, is an excellent way to bring to the surface the mass of resentments we carry toward that person.

2. Repeat and dwell on words that carry the new perception.

The Course's goal is to usher into our minds a new perception. To this end, it provides sentences that contain this new perception for us to repeat and dwell on. These sentences, rather than modifying the details of how we see this person, simply dismiss our entire current perception of him. They just wipe it clean, replacing it with something altogether different. Our job is to repeat these sentences not as mere words, but as gateways to a new universe of meaning. We focus our mind completely on these words, repeating them slowly and positively, and concentrating on what they mean. We apply them specifically to this situation, often naming the person we are trying to forgive. We may need to repeat them over and over again, and are even encouraged to add our own variations on their basic themes.

What follows is one of countless examples of such a practice in the Course. In this case, we silently address the person with whom we are angry as we would beseech an illumined master whose blessing has the power to awaken the divinity within us. Addressing him in this way pulls our mind toward actually *seeing* him in this way:

> *Give me your blessing, holy Son of God.*
> *I would behold you with the eyes of Christ,*
> *and see my perfect sinlessness in you.*[45]

3. The Holy Spirit will give you a miracle.

When we do this practice with sufficient focus and willingness, something happens. Resentments suddenly drop away, leaving our mind feeling clear and refreshed. A perception of the other person as innocent, majestic—even divine—comes into view, a perception which would have seemed impossible before. When this happens, it feels like a miracle, and it is. We often think of a miracle as the Spirit coming in and healing a sick body that is beyond our means to heal. In the Course, a miracle is the Spirit healing a sick *mind* that cannot heal itself. We cannot give ourselves the shift in perception we need, for our mind is much too divided about it. We need help from a totally undivided source: the Holy Spirit. He completes the process we began. The practice we did in the previous step was really a prayer to Him, a prayer that He lift our old, dark perception from our mind and instill in us a new perception. And, as the Course emphasizes, "all prayer is answered."[46] This is how the Love of God reaches down to meet our need in this world, for our greatest need is a change in perception.

This shift may happen in mere seconds, or it may take longer. When you are forgiving not just one event but the accumulated muck of an entire relationship, it will often take some time. In cases like this, I have found it helpful to set a daily time of fifteen to thirty minutes to sit down and do Course forgiveness practice until it feels like the muck has been cleaned out. This may take weeks or even months, yet in the long run this is a phenomenally short time to heal a resentment that can dominate one's entire life.

A new kind of interaction with others

Forgiveness allows us to enter into a whole new kind of interaction with other people. The Course says that every relationship, and even every encounter, has been arranged by the Holy Spirit because He sees the potential for salvation to pass between those two people. Normally, however, we are blind to this holy potential. We are caught up in our own little world, busy with our affairs, stuck in our judgments, living in the past—all of which keeps us from being fully present to the people we encounter. They pick up on this, of course. They sense that we have more important things on our mind, and we sense the same thing from them. As a result, the potential the Holy Spirit sees for the two of us usually just sits there, unused.

Forgiveness, however, clears your vision and allows you to truly see the one who is in front of you. You see past the person gaily chatting away, to someone burdened by a deep sense that she hasn't been treated right by the world, that she hasn't been loved by the right person, that her best efforts have gone unappreciated. You see past this, also, to a profound self-loathing. In a hidden vault in her mind, she is convinced that she is sinful beyond repair, that she has "made a devil of God's Son." The guilt that results from this is too much for her to face. It is the real source of her low self-esteem, and it is what attracts her to situations that punish and humiliate her. Yet you see past this dark cloud, too, and catch a glimpse of Who she truly is. You see an ancient purity in her, untouched by all that she has done. You see that she is a sun whose rays stretch to infinity, and whose incandescence can only briefly be obscured by the flimsy clouds of this world.

This vision cannot be contained; in one way or another, it finds expression through you. Perhaps with a kind word, or maybe through just the look on your face, you somehow convey to her that she is still as innocent as she was the instant God created her. And when she sees herself through your eyes, for a moment that unbearable burden of guilt slides off her shoulders. Your vision sets her free. It may even heal her body, for illness is just "guilt's shadow."[47] Take away the guilt, and its shadow goes with it. This is the main sense of the word "miracle" in the Course. It usually refers to the extension of healed perception from our mind to the mind of another, bringing healing to that person's mind, and sometimes her body as well.

If she really lets your gift in, what could she feel but the deepest gratitude? And how could she contain this? The Course speaks of her face shining with gratitude:

> The sick, who ask for love, are grateful for it, and in their joy they shine with holy thanks. And this they offer you who gave them joy. They are your guides to joy.[48]

Now she has become your guide. She is doing for you the same thing you did for her; she is seeing the light in you *for you*. The Course says, "And as [the light in you] shines your brothers see it, and realizing that this light is not what you have made, they see in you more than you see."[49] *She sees in you more than you see*, for she has been on the receiving end of the light in you. She has felt the full impact of it. She has been saved by it. How could you possibly appreciate it to the same extent that she does? Thus, she alone carries the secret of Who you really are. Let her gratitude show you that there is more to you than you thought. She is your savior. Let her teach you that you are not a miserable sinner, but rather the holy Son of God.

Finally, the two of you experience a sense of joining. Each one of you has seen a holy light in the other, a light that you love and want to join with. The walls of perceived sin that would keep you apart have come tumbling down. The Course proclaims, "And what has been forgiven must join, for nothing stands between to keep them separate and apart."[50] You realize, however dimly, that the light you see in her is the same light she sees in you. You realize that this other person is not an *other* at all.

Such encounters are what save us. The Course calls them *holy encounters*, and says that they are this path's unique means for speeding our homecoming, "the special means this course is using to save you time."[51] Indeed, it says that the holy encounter is the one holy thing that can happen in this dark and gloomy world. In the words of the Course, "This is the spark that shines within the dream":

> Within the dream of bodies and of death is yet one theme of truth; no more, perhaps, than just a tiny spark, a space of light created in the dark, where God still shines. You cannot wake yourself. Yet you can let yourself be wakened. You can overlook your brother's dreams. So perfectly can you forgive him his illusions he becomes your savior from your dreams....And now the light in you must be as bright as shines in him. This is the spark that shines within the dream: that you can help him waken, and be sure his waking eyes will rest on you.[52]

The Course also teaches a long-term version of such encounters, which it calls *holy relationships*. These are relationships that have been dedicated to a common purpose, one that transcends separate interests. Such relationships pass through a long developmental spiral, one that usually begins in what the Course somewhat charitably calls "the period of discomfort."[53] Yet as these relationships grow into maturity, the giving, receiving, and joining I described above reach ever-deeper levels, with profound transformative effects. The two people increasingly realize that the boundaries between them are illusory, that they are merely two parts of a single Self.

The concepts of the holy encounter and the holy relationship reflect a central emphasis in *A Course in Miracles*: we cannot get home alone. The above quote put it bluntly: "You cannot wake yourself." We are too trapped in the bubble of our separate ego. Yet there is a way out. Something happens to us when we give forgiveness, receive forgiveness, and join with another human being—some kind of grace enters us. We lose sight of our precious personal boundaries. We step out of our bubble, not by piercing its membrane with our own strength, but by taking the hand of another. This, says the author of the Course, is the one thing we must do to discover the boundlessness of our true Identity:

> Each one must share one goal with someone else, and in so doing, lose all sense of separate interests. Only by doing this is it possible to transcend the narrow boundaries the ego would impose upon the self.[54]

A new vision of the world; a new sense of self

Forgiveness is what makes these holy interactions possible. Forgiveness, in fact, is what makes everything possible. Its beauty undoes all the ugliness the ego has wrought. How do we move from feeling trapped on the ego's battleground to realizing that only Heaven is real? Forgiveness. In the end, forgiveness carries two global benefits that deposit us right at Heaven's gate, where God will come Himself to take us home. Those two benefits are 1) a new vision of the world, and 2) a new sense of self.

Forgiveness is what allows true perception, or vision, to dawn on our minds. What stands in the way of vision is not that our eyes are seeing physical forms out there. It is that we are wearing dark glasses which tint those forms with the murky shade of sin. All we need do is take off those glasses—which is what forgiveness is all about—and the light behind the forms will leap into view. The bodies will lose their significance as we gaze in rapture upon the radiant rays of holiness streaming from behind each one.

In the advanced stages of true perception, we truly live in a different world, even though we look on the same forms as everyone else. In this world, we constantly gaze upon "beauty that will enchant you, and will never cease to cause you wonderment at its perfection."[55] The same old ordinary things will be tinged with a divine radiance. "Each flower shines in light, and every bird sings of the joy of Heaven."[56] In this world, we will experience the crashing of the waves as those waves bowing down to the God in us, and we will experience the leaves at our feet as a royal carpet laid out before us.[57] In this world, "Everyone and everything I see will lean toward me to bless me. I will recognize in everyone my dearest Friend."[58] We will see no strangers, but rather see our own Self looking back at us from every pair of eyes we meet. Even when we are attacked, we will recognize the seeming attacker as the Christ sent to be our savior. He may be wearing a sinner's mask, but we will know that one glance from His holy eyes has the power to illumine us.

We will have stepped off the battleground of this world and will walk through a landscape washed clean of sin, through a land that is a pure reflection of Heaven. This is the promise the Course holds out to us: "To your tired eyes I bring a vision of a different world, so new and clean and fresh you will forget the pain and sorrow that you saw before."[59]

Forgiveness also instills in us a new sense of self. All of our self-seeking and attack, all the judgment and spite through which we look upon the world, have convinced us at a deep level that we are a sinful ego. Forgiveness has the power to reverse this, to teach us that our ego is just a flimsy mask worn by a being whose innocence is eternal. How does it do that? It really comes down to the three steps I outlined in the previous section: giving forgiveness, receiving forgiveness, and joining.

1. Giving forgiveness

In conventional thinking, the moment you are most justified in acting like an ego is the moment right after you have been attacked. At that moment, you seem to have the *right* to see the other person through angry eyes, the *right* to retaliate, and the *duty* to defend yourself. If in that moment, when your ego is seemingly most within its rights, you simply disregard it—you see the person through eyes of love, you release the person from any debt or retaliation, and you refuse to defend yourself—what does that say about you? It says that *you are not an ego*; you are something more. It sends a message we all understand, one that is captured in the words of the old saying, "To err is human, to forgive divine." This is the message your forgiveness sends to your astonished mind: "I must be divine."

2. Receiving forgiveness

As we saw in the previous section, when someone returns your forgiveness in the form of gratitude, this has the power to teach you the exact same message as above: that you are more than an ego, that you are divine.

3. Joining

Joining with another person provides you with experiential proof that the boundary the ego has drawn around you is just like those boundaries on a map: it is only ink on paper, it does not exist in reality. Joining proves to you that the ego never actually managed to fence in your limitlessness.

Forgiveness shows us that we are still God's immaculate Son, that our ancient holiness remains untouched, untainted. We discover that we never turned ourselves into that vile ego we saw in Chapter 3. And we realize that Heaven is still the only reality. We know, because we see its light shining behind all those inconsequential forms. Thus, we realize that the universe of suffering we saw arise in Chapter 4 never really arose at all. Through forgiveness, then, we finally come to understand that the separation never occurred, that nothing ever happened to cloud the radiant face of eternity. At this point, our long journey through time and space will come to an end. Our tour as a lonely creature wandering through an alien world will be done. Here, at the end of the road, we will find our Father waiting for us with open Arms. Speaking of this supreme moment, the Course has us say, "And all my sorrows end in Your embrace."[60] The sorrows of eons will melt away as we disappear into the embrace of the One we love above all things, and open our eyes in Heaven to discover that, in truth, we never left.

PART III

THE PROGRAM

We are therefore embarking on an organized, well-structured and carefully planned program.

Text, Chapter 12, Section II, Paragraph 10

Introduction to Part III

Thankfully, the Course doesn't just drop these radical teachings onto our heads and then expect us to go out and live them. How would we know how to apply these ideas? They represent the reversal of our whole frame of reference. In our attempts to apply them, surely we would mix them with our current frame of reference, and thus water them down and defuse their transformative power. Expecting us to figure out how to apply these lofty ideas would be like handing the legal code to hard-core criminals and saying, "Take this book and teach yourselves how to be law-abiding citizens." Or it would be like a cookbook telling us about a wonderful dish, how it looks, how it tastes, and then leaving us to figure out how to make it.

We need a program for applying these teachings, one that comes from the same high place as the teachings themselves. We need a program that teaches us, step by step, how to internalize these ideas, so that we eventually reach the condition where they are totally internalized, where they have become as natural to us as breathing.

Thankfully, the Course itself provides this program. The Course says that it has given us "an organized, well-structured and carefully planned program."[1] It has mapped out an entire educational journey that takes us from A to Z, from the depths of the ego to the Heart of God. The Course announces this, in fact, right on its cover. A "course" is an educational

THE PROGRAM

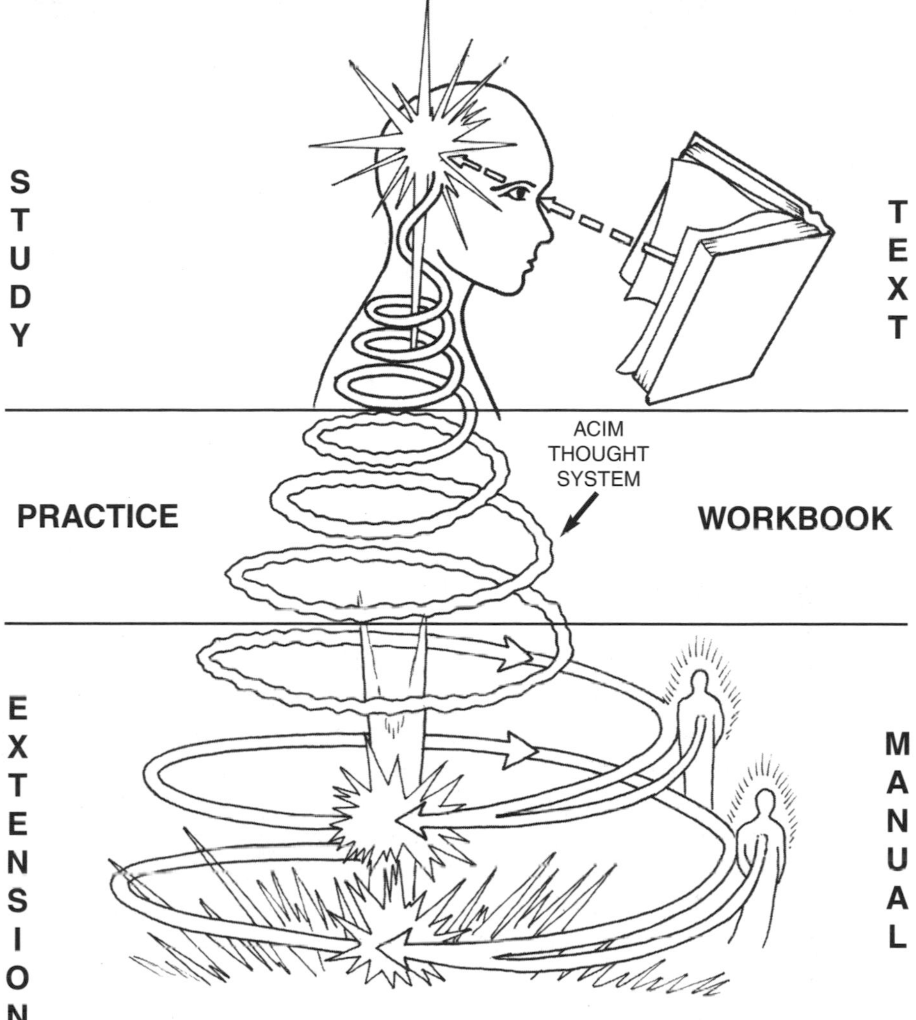

THE PROGRAM

The Course's program is really a single process in which the Course's thought system enters ever more deeply into our mind. This is represented in the illustration by the line of light that travels in from the book and spirals down into the depths of our mind. This process has three aspects or stages:

1. Study: As we study the Text, the Course's thought system leaves the pages of the book and enters our mind for the first time.

2. Practice: As we practice the Workbook, the Course's thought system penetrates more and more deeply into our mind. It becomes increasingly embraced as our own.

3. Extension: As we extend healed perception to others, we fulfill our function as teachers of God (as described in the Manual for Teachers). Through this extension, the Course's thought system receives its final reinforcement and becomes the sole foundation of our thoughts, perceptions, and emotions.

program. It is a series of lessons designed to teach us something. What is *this* course designed to teach us? Miracles, obviously. Right in its title, then, the Course announces that it is an educational program aimed at teaching us how to "do" miracles. As I said in this book's introduction, the Course does not present itself to us primarily as a teaching, but as a course, a program.

What does this program look like? This too is right there on the cover of the book, in the titles of the Course's three volumes: Text, Workbook for Students, and Manual for Teachers. In a normal educational course, the text is there to familiarize you with a body of ideas. You then do that course's workbook and learn how to apply those ideas in a more hands-on way. (You may, of course, do the text and workbook concurrently.) Finally, you have sufficiently mastered the ideas to teach them to others, which is what the teacher's manual helps you to do. In a conventional course, then, each volume represents a particular phase within a single process of increasingly internalizing that course's set of ideas.

The exact same curricular format is present in *A Course in Miracles*. Each of its volumes represents a particular aspect of its program, a particular phase in a single process. As with a conventional course, this process is all about internalizing this course's body of ideas, its thought system, its teaching. The teaching of *A Course in Miracles* is a lens through which we can see and experience reality, and the Course is trying to implant that lens in us. The process, therefore, is simply one in which that lens enters into us, at first superficially, and then ever more deeply, until it is established at the seat of our minds. There it becomes the foundation of our thoughts and feelings. It becomes the only lens through which we see, and thus the sole source of our experience of reality. At that point, we live in a different world, a world of safety, peace, and joy. At that point, we are saved.

As with a conventional course, this single process passes through three phases, represented by the Course's three volumes:

Text: studying the teaching

The Text is the first volume and represents the first aspect of the program. Through reading the Text, we allow the Course's teaching to enter our minds for the first time. At this stage, it enters primarily on an intellectual level, but that is enough for now. Before we can use the lens, we need to have it in our hands. Before we can truly internalize the teaching, we must simply become aware of it. It must leave the page and come into our consciousness. As it does, things begin to shift around inside us, as we ponder the radical possibility that these ideas just might be true.

Workbook for Students: doing the practice

In the Workbook, we take the same ideas taught to us in the Text and *practice* them. We place the lens in front of our eyes and look through it. This practice takes the form of dwelling on these new ideas, repeating them, and applying them to ourselves, the people we encounter, and all our upsets. We are also trained to drop to a place in our minds below all words and concepts, where we directly experience the meaning of which the Course speaks. The experiences that come through practice change us. They cause the teaching which entered through study to spiral deeper and deeper into our minds, bringing increasing amounts of peace and joy.

Manual for Teachers: extending to others

As the Course's teaching becomes a part of us through practice, it naturally begins to express itself in our behavior. We begin to extend the loving perceptions that are entering our minds. We do this not through preaching them on street corners, but through demonstrating them in our daily interactions. This benefits others, of course, but it also benefits us. It is a crucial part of our own educational process. It is, in fact, the final leg of our own journey of awakening. The Course says, "What you share you strengthen."[2] We all know from experience that when we share a thought with another person, that thought grows stronger within us. This is especially true if the other person then embraces the thought himself. "If the one to whom you give it accepts it as his, he reinforces it in your mind and thus increases it."[3] Thus, when we extend love to others, the thought of love grows stronger within us. When we give a sincere gift to another, "The thought [behind the gift] remains, and grows in strength as it is reinforced by giving."[4] This is how the Course's thought system becomes the real bedrock of our thinking. When love and giving become our habitual way of being, the thought system of love will become so reinforced and strengthened in us that it will fill our minds completely, chasing away all darkness and causing our minds to shine like the sun.

The Course's three volumes therefore represent three phases in a single progressively deepening process. The same light that enters us through study spirals deeper and deeper through practice. Then, as we extend this stream of light to others, it flows into us even more deeply, until it becomes our radiant foundation, until everything in us rests on it. And then we have reached the end of the road.

This doesn't mean that we have to go through the Course's volumes in order; the Course in fact says that we don't. Yet even if we don't, we'll most likely pass through the phases they represent in order. Early in our journey, our main focus will probably be on just taking in the ideas. That will be our study phase. We'll hopefully graduate from this into a practice phase in which our main focus is on doing the practice and receiving its benefits. And ideally, we'll eventually reach an extension phase, where our main focus will be on extending to others and on the fulfillment that comes through that.

Study, practice, and extension obviously involve work, and this is a stumbling block for many students. We are well aware that getting results in almost any area of endeavor—physical fitness, financial security, acquisition of skills—takes work. Yet we have a curious resistance to the idea that work is required in the spiritual arena. There, we expect results effortlessly and instantaneously. We know that getting stronger physically means lifting weights, yet we often hope to get stronger spiritually without lifting a finger. In the end, I think, this perspective actually takes more out of us than just going ahead and doing the work. For we generally don't get those effortless results, and we don't know why, and now we don't know what we can do *to* get results. On the other hand, there is nothing so energizing as doing the work and seeing the results.

Study, practice, extension—this is the formula for walking the path of the Course. I cannot emphasize this formula enough. Without it, the Course is merely a series of inspiring ideas that excite us but then leave us wondering how in the world we can make them practical, how we can live them. Without this formula, the Course's teachings become like the stars in the sky: beautiful, inspiring, but totally out of reach. However much we may yearn to rise to their heights, all we can do is look up, powerless to leave the earth.

With this formula, however, the Course becomes a genuine path in which each step of the way is mapped out for us. There is no mystery about how to get there. We're told quite clearly what to do to take a step forward, and we're told the results that will come from doing it. And when the next step comes, the same instruction is there for it. The Course often emphasizes the practical, step-by-step nature of its curriculum, for the last thing it wants to do is leave us wandering in circles in a trackless wilderness, unable to find our way home:

> This course offers a very direct and a very simple learning situation, and provides the Guide Who tells you what to do. If you do it, you will see that it works. Its results are more convincing than its words. They will convince you that the words are true.[5]

Each of the next three chapters will explore one of the aspects of this study-practice-extension formula. These chapters are extremely important, especially if you have reached a point where you are genuinely interested in walking this path.

SIX

The Text: Reconstructing Our Worldview

Since ancient times, the reading of a spiritual text has been a fundamental activity for serious seekers. This is not a superficial "head trip," but a deep-level reconstruction of one's worldview. Enlightenment involves untangling a knot in the mind, and study of spiritual truths is an essential part of the untangling process. This is why reading and study of the Text is the first leg in thc program of *A Course in Miracles*. Studying the Text may sound like the height of boredom, yet it is important to see the purpose of this text as different from that of the textbooks we studied in school. We must approach it not as if we are learning a new batch of information, but as if we are being taught a new way of thinking, a new way of seeing the world.

The Text

The Text is the first and longest of the Course's volumes. Containing over sixty percent of the Course's words, it provides the "theoretical foundation"[1] for the entire Course. The other two volumes also contain teaching, but the Text is where the Course's thought system is laid out in all its breadth and depth. The early Text lays down themes that are foundational for the rest of the Course, and as the Text proceeds, it explains key Course ideas—such as special and holy relationships, and the holy instant—that are barely mentioned in the other two volumes.

The Text is a masterpiece of spiritual thought. There is really no other book like it. It treats a dizzying array of themes—there are literally hundreds—yet manages to weave them together so masterfully that each theme, fully understood, contains within itself all the others. It sounds familiar notes which have been sounded by sages for thousands of years, yet has a habit of taking off in its own unique directions and making bold statements that no one has ever made.

All of its teachings are totally focused on one outcome: shifting our perception and thereby curing our suffering. Though the Text soars into very abstract realms (some of which we explored in Chapter 4), its ideas are not intended to be a spiritual version of a fantasy novel—an escape from life into an entrancing mental realm. Its whole intent is that we actually apply its ideas, rather than using them as mere intellectual playthings. It says, "This is not a course in the play of ideas, but in their practical application."[2]

The Course, in fact, claims to teach only ideas that contain transformative content, and to avoid ideas that are merely about form and thus are open to different contents, different meanings. As an example, let's look at the idea of reincarnation. This idea is really about form: Does my mind pass from body to body over time? Being about form, the idea is a kind of empty container that can be filled with different sorts of content. We can fill it with content of the ego: we can become preoccupied with our past lives, or prideful over the special personages we supposedly were, or feel as if we are the product of such a long chain of lives that there is no hope of change. All of which adds up to this: *who I am is the product of who I was*. Or we can fill it with content of the Holy Spirit: we can conclude that since there is an "I" that apparently remains unchanged no matter how many bodies come and go, who I am must be *spirit* and must be *eternal*. In sum: *who I am is totally unaffected by who I have appeared to be*.

The idea of reincarnation is therefore, in a sense, an empty form that is inherently neutral and that can easily be filled with the ego's content. This means that from the Course's standpoint, it has no inherent benefit *and* carries potential threat. For this reason, the Course purposefully avoids teaching reincarnation. It also avoids a long list of other common teachings that are also primarily about form: rituals, diet, exercise, chakras, past history, future predictions—the list could go on.

In their place, the Course focuses exclusively on ideas that are made purely of transformative content, ideas such as "who I am is totally unaffected by who I have appeared to be." That idea is not a form open to different meanings. It is pure meaning, meaning that *by its very nature* liberates the mind. It is inherently transformative. If you absorb such an idea, properly understood, into your mind, it changes things. It makes you feel different. It lets the light in. It *is* the light. That is the only kind of idea the Course teaches.

It is important to remember this while reading the Text. You are not being taught a series of irrelevant theories. You are not being given tantalizing concepts to engage your mind so that you can hide from your problems. You are being given the very stuff of salvation, ideas which will light your mind with peace and joy and open up a new perception of the world, if you let them in, if you apply them. The Course captures all of this in a single potent line:

> For the ideas are mighty forces, to be used and not held idly by.[3]

Beginning reading of the Text

Since *A Course in Miracles* is a spiritual path that is also a book, the fundamental activity on this path is *reading the book*. This, however, presents students with an immediate problem: the Course is written in a language all its own. As every student soon discovers, the Text is not an easy read. I've spoken to many students who have tried repeatedly to get past the first few chapters without managing to do so.

How does the new student navigate the waters of the Course's unusual language? For the majority of new students, the answer, I believe, is simple: *just keep reading*. Don't try to understand it all; you're not going to. Don't worry about how much of it sounds like gobbledygook or a foreign language—it has sounded that way to thousands of students who went before you. If you run into a sentence you don't understand, don't spend a long time trying to figure it out. Don't take voluminous notes and try to piece it all together. Just keep reading.

You really are learning a new language. For a toddler who is learning his native tongue, the important thing is not to deeply examine the meaning of each statement he hears, nor to be laboriously taught the rules of grammar and syntax. The important thing is just to be immersed in the language, to be surrounded by it. After enough time, from this jumble of sounds, a clear meaning will slowly begin to emerge. There is actually a place in the Course that likens us to infants learning a new language. It says that while we may think normal language is understandable and the Course is incoherent, the reverse is actually true: We will never be able to make sense of our world, yet one day the Course will make perfect sense to us. Its teaching is our *true* native tongue:

> Of all the messages you have received and failed to understand, this course alone is open to your understanding and can be understood. This is *your* language. You do not understand it yet only because your whole communication is like a baby's. The sounds a baby makes and what he hears are highly unreliable, meaning different things to him at different times....But what he hears and does not understand will be his native tongue, through which he will communicate with those around him, and they with him.[4]

In the face of this new language, remember that you are a baby. So just stick with it, just keep reading, and it will slowly begin to make sense.

How an experienced student should read

Once you feel more comfortable with the Course's language, how do you now approach the reading of the Text? In all such matters, I believe in taking our cue from the Course itself. What, then, does *it* say about how we should read it?

It advocates reading a passage slowly,[5] reading it carefully,[6] even reading it "several times if you wish,"[7] and then thinking about what you have read.[8] We can see this approach in these instructions for the "What Is?" sections in the Workbook:

> These [one-page sections] should be reviewed each day [for ten days]....They should be slowly read and thought about a little while.[9]

Here, then, is what we might call the Course's dictum for how to read it:

> Read slowly, carefully, even repeatedly, and think about what you read.

The word for this kind of reading is, of course, *study*. "Reading" is generally more passive. When we read, we simply *receive* or *take in* the meaning of the words we see. "Study," on the other hand, is more active. When we study, we come to our reading material with an intention to really learn it. This intention turns us into active readers. We bring our full attention to our reading, we ask questions and hunt for answers, we read over and over if need be, and we reflect on what we have read and try to grasp it as a whole. This is what the Course wants us to do with it, to *study* it. After all, when someone hands you a textbook, what *else* are you supposed to do with it? The author of the Course gave the following piece of guidance to his first students, Helen Schucman and Bill Thetford, and applied it to all future students as well:

> Bill has very intelligently suggested that you both should set yourself the goal of really studying for this course. There can be no doubt of the wisdom of this decision, for any student who wants to pass it.[10]

Why on earth would we want to do all this studying? We are so used to being passive recipients of information, to being fed a barrage of provocative images, music, and narration, all carefully coordinated to absorb our minds without any work on our part. So why *study* a *text*? Because, in the case of this text, it is just so rewarding. There are treasures in these words, treasures we will only lay hold of when we give these words our undivided attention. As with so many things in life, we must give our mind to *them* before they give their treasures to *us*. We can see this in the following instructions, which tell us how to approach the sentences we review at a certain point in the Workbook:

> Merely read each of the two ideas assigned to you to be reviewed that day. Then close your eyes, and say them slowly to yourself. There is no hurry now, for you are using time for its intended purpose. Let each word shine with the meaning God has given it, as it was given to you through His Voice. Let each idea which you review that day give you the gift that He has laid in it for you to have of Him.[11]

Here, we only receive the gifts laid for us in these words if we go over them slowly, without hurry, letting "each word shine with the meaning God has given it." In these instructions the line between study and practice is blurred, so that study becomes a spiritual practice; study becomes *experience*. Obviously, to study every line in the Text in this way would be impractical, but if we approached our study in this general spirit, think how much more we would get out of it! This is not just a text, it is a scripture. This is not just information, it is spiritual food, and as with all good food, we should savor every bite.

The rest of this chapter will discuss in more detail how we can approach the Text in this way. What I'll share with you is based on a system that Allen Watson, one of my fellow teachers at the Circle of Atonement, learned in his Bible study days, and which we've adapted to fit the Course. The system consists of three steps:

> **I. Observation**: What does it say? Here we simply notice the words and punctuation before us.
>
> **II. Interpretation**: What does it mean? Here we try to understand the meaning conveyed by the words.
>
> **III. Application**: What does it mean to me? Here we apply the meaning to ourselves and our lives.

Under each of these headings I'll also discuss some aspect of the Course's special language.

I. OBSERVATION

Paying attention to every word

I'm by nature a skim-reader; I can't stand having to read every word of anything. The Course, however, has wrestled me to the ground. I have been forced to concede that, at least in its case, reading every word is an absolute must. You can't skim-read the Course. It may seem as if the Course is repeating itself endlessly, using a hundred words to say what could have been said in ten. But that is a serious misperception. The truth is actually the reverse: as with poetry, the Course is saying in ten words what would take at least a hundred to explicitly make clear. To illustrate this point, I once wrote an article in which I tried to draw out the meaning contained in one paragraph of the Text. What the Text compressed into a hundred words it took me *forty-five* hundred to explain.

In the Course, every word counts. Every word has been carefully chosen.[12] The author of the Course mentioned this feature in a private aside to Helen Schucman. He said, "As long as you take accurate notes, every word is meaningful."[13] This is also implied in the passage I quoted above, which says that "each word" is shining with meaning from God.

Thus, the first step in reading the Course properly is to simply pay attention to everything you see. Notice every word and every punctuation mark. Do not skim. Be observant. *Notice.*

Filling familiar terms with new meaning

One reason it is important to notice each word is that the Course does something very unusual with its words. It takes familiar terms and fills them with new meaning, sometimes radically new meaning. We don't expect this; we quite reasonably assume that familiar terms will contain familiar meaning, and that if there is new meaning to express, new terms will be invented. Yet despite all the new meaning the Course wants to convey, it refuses to invent new words. This stems from its basic teaching that the Holy Spirit will take *any* one of our forms, no matter how unholy it may appear, and use it for His holy purpose.

That is what the Course does with words. It sees our words as carriers of the ego's virus, yet rather than discarding the carrier, the Course cleanses it of the virus and makes it a carrier of the vaccine. We can see this with the term "Son of God." Think of some of the painful associations around that term. Traditionally, it refers only to Jesus; by implication, it means that there is someone who is incredibly close to God, in both nature and relationship, and that *we are not that someone.* It means that God plays favorites, and that we mere mortals dare not hope to get into the real inner circle.

The Course radically redefines this term. It retains the notion of a divine being conceived by God as His beloved Son, yet it denies that God would play favorites. So, it sees everyone as raised up to that level. It says that we are *all* Sons of God—all equal parts of the one Son. We all stand in that wondrous relationship with God, in which He shares Himself completely with us. This includes Jesus, who is, by nature, our equal. In this view, he was simply the first Son to wake up to Who he was.

Getting used to this new meaning will take time, and may be a difficult process. Yet while the Course is slowly retraining our sense of this term, it is also changing our whole sense of our relationship to God. For this new meaning of "Son of God" takes all the sense of exaltation and grandeur that we associate with Jesus and applies that to *us*. And if we really take that to heart, we walk a little taller. We live out the Course's counsel: "Walk you in glory, with your head held high, and fear no evil."[14]

With "Son of God" as our example, we can see what the Course typically does with terms. It identifies some core meaning in a term and then carries that meaning to its purest, most logical extreme, pushing out other meanings in the process. We saw this in the last chapter with "forgiveness." At the core of forgiveness is the letting go of resentment. However, the Course then claims that to really let go of resentment, we must also relinquish the perception that someone sinned against us. Yet the idea that someone wronged us is part of the conventional definition of forgiveness, and so that part of the definition gets pushed out in this new definition.

The Course does not just do this with a few terms, but rather, to varying degrees, with *hundreds*. This is an essential part of its use of language. Into most words of any consequence, the Course places a small world of meaning that is part of the overall world of meaning the Course is trying to instill in us. This turns its words into a series of potent vehicles for its message. With each sentence, and each word in each sentence, this new world of meaning comes streaming into our minds.

This understanding of Course terminology has important implications for the step of *observation*. It means that, as we read, we need to take note of key terms. There are two kinds of key terms to watch out for:

1. Basic Course terms, such as miracle, forgiveness, Son of God, Atonement, etc.
2. Key terms in a particular section: In any given section, certain words will repeat which may not be basic Course terms, yet which are key for that section.

As an example, please read the following paragraph, trying to be observant. Try to notice every word and punctuation mark:

> There is a kind of justice in salvation of which the world knows nothing. To the world, justice and vengeance are the same, for sinners see justice only as their punishment, perhaps sustained by someone else, but not escaped. The

> laws of sin demand a victim. Who it may be makes little difference. But death must be the cost and must be paid. This is not justice, but insanity. Yet how could justice be defined without insanity where love means hate, and death is seen as victory and triumph over eternity and timelessness and life?[15]

In this paragraph, we should notice some basic Course terms: salvation, world, sin, death, insanity, love, eternity, life. Yet the key term in this paragraph is one that primarily occurs only in this chapter of the Text: *justice*. It occurs five times in this paragraph, which is where it is really introduced. Thankfully, this paragraph tells us that the Course's definition of justice is one "of which the world knows nothing," and that the world's definition is pure "insanity." This notifies us that from here on, whenever we see the word "justice," we should recognize that it is being used in an unconventional sense.[16] Otherwise, the passages in which it appears—such as "justice cannot punish"[17]—will sound like nonsense.

II. INTERPRETATION

The Course's symphonic style

What makes the Course so hard to understand? Course students often complain about long, convoluted sentences, but that is not the problem. There are surprisingly few of those. Most sentences are short (averaging about fifteen words)[18] and to the point, as you can see by looking at the paragraph quoted above. The Course's writing is generally a series of concise, clear statements. The difficulty lies not in the statements themselves, but in the connections *between* the statements. This is where a reader's comprehension breaks down.

In typical nonfiction writing, the author arranges his ideas in a linear string of points. Each sentence makes a point, and this point builds on the sentence before it, while also setting up the one after it. These points are strung together, one after another, like beads on a necklace. The Course, too, is a series of sentences, but the way it conveys meaning is only somewhat like a string of beads. In many ways it is more like a *web*. Invisible threads of meaning go out from each sentence, connecting with several, even dozens of sentences around it. The sentence draws its meaning from this entire web, and in turn, enriches the entire web. Now this is true of all writing *to some degree*, but it is true of the Course's writing to an extraordinary, perhaps unparalleled degree. And this is what makes it often hard to understand.

This means that, as we saw in Chapter 2's discussion of the Course as a work of art, the Course is written much like a symphony, where musical themes constantly weave in and out of one another. In the Course this interweaving reaches a phenomenal level. In a section of two or three pages there might be forty or fifty themes weaving in and out of one another.[19] All in all, the Course contains literally thousands of "leitmotifs" (a term for recurring themes in a piece of music or literature). These leitmotifs take the form of recurring ideas, terms, phrases, images, practices, and biblical allusions.

This may make the Course's writing initially hard to understand, but it also makes it saturated with depth upon depth of meaning, and crystal clear when you know how to read it. To understand how this makes for a depth of meaning, think again of the string of beads, and imagine that a particular statement is one of the beads on the string. In normal writing, that statement primarily connects with the statement right before it and the one right after it. Thus, it draws its meaning mainly from just those two statements. Now imagine that the string is transformed into a web, with, let's say, a bead of dew (a statement) at each node of the web. Now, instead of a bead being connected mainly to just two other beads, it is connected to the entire web. Now the meaning of that single statement is what it means *in relationship to* each and every one of those surrounding statements. Meaning travels to it from each and every bead, with the result that it draws its meaning from the whole web. By being placed in a richer context, its meaning and significance have been immeasurably enriched.

As I said, this also makes for incredible clarity, for if you misinterpret that statement, you wrench it from its place in the web and thereby snap a good many of the threads. The whole web gets stressed and torn. Conversely, when you interpret that statement correctly, all the threads stay intact, all the connections are honored. The Course thus provides, in its style of writing, an internal "auto-correction" device.

One of the wonderful side effects of this symphonic style is that quite often, clarity will spontaneously dawn on your mind without your knowing how it happened. The fact is that even if you don't see all the threads (and you won't), they're still there, and meaning is still traveling along them into your mind. This meaning will occasionally coalesce and burst into consciousness, in the form of an "aha" experience that *seems* to come from nowhere.

To see how this symphonic style works, let's examine the following sentence:

> Let us be glad that we can walk the world, and find so many chances to perceive another situation where God's gift can once again be recognized as ours![20]

By itself, this sounds rather vague and obscure, making us wonder why the author felt it worthy of an exclamation point. The sentences before it help some, but not enough: "To give this gift is how to make it yours. And God ordained, in loving kindness, that it be for you." And the sentence following it does not help at all: "And thus will all the vestiges of hell, the secret sins and hidden hates be gone." The clarity we need does not lie in the sentences immediately before and after. Instead, it lies in a web of connections that fan out from this sentence to earlier passages in its section. In the following table I track some of those connections. On the left I give a phrase from our sentence; on the right I discuss the earlier passages which that phrase connects to, as well as the meaning which those connections provide:

our sentence	**connections to preceding passages**
"so many chances to perceive another situation"	Much of this section is about difficult situations. It says that each one is a lesson "that you failed to learn presented once again,"[21] so that you have "another chance to choose again"[22] (notice the similarity with our "so many chances to perceive another situation"). These chances never run out. This whole idea is beautifully expressed in the image of Christ appearing to us: "In every difficulty, all distress, and each perplexity Christ calls to you and gently says, 'My brother, choose again.'"[23]

"Let us be glad"	In light of the above, "let us be glad" means, "Let us be glad when faced with an apparently difficult situation, because it gives us a chance to choose again." In fact, "let us be glad" has just been used in the same sense a few sections before: "Let us be glad that you will see what you believe [a world of sin and death], and that it has been given you to change what you believe."[24] In both cases, we should be glad when faced with the effects of our mistakes, because then we can undo them.
"walk the world"	Two paragraphs before, we were told that choosing again will give us power to bring the peace of God "to everyone who wanders in the world uncertain, lonely, and in constant fear."[25] Their wandering the world clearly parallels our walking the world. This suggests that our sentence has something to do with bringing the peace of God to all those wandering people.
"God's gift"	The previous paragraph told us what God's gift is: the vision of "a different world, so new and clean and fresh you will forget the pain and sorrow that you saw before."[26]
"where God's gift can…be recognized as ours"	The previous paragraph also told us that this gift is already ours: "And God ordained, in loving kindness, that it be for you."[27] This means we need only recognize that His gift is ours (as our sentence says). How do we recognize it is ours? That paragraph told us this as well: "To give this gift [to others] is how to make it yours."[28]

These connections endow our sentence with both depth and clarity. They make plain what the sentence is trying to convey, and reveal that its message is one of real relevance. Its joyous, upbeat tone is actually addressing situations we would consider painful, and giving us a positive way to view them. Below I will try to capture our sentence's real meaning in light of its connections with preceding passages, and then I will again quote the sentence. As you read it this time, you will be able to actually see in it the meaning the author placed there:

> Let us be glad that we can walk the world and find ourselves faced with so many trials! For these are wonderful opportunities to undo our past mistakes. In them, the lessons we failed to learn before are presented to us again, giving us yet another chance to learn them. In these trials, Christ is appearing to us in all His glory, asking us to choose again. These opportunities are everywhere; they will never go away. Yet if we can choose right this time, all the pain our past choices caused us will fall away. We will be given Christ's vision and imbued with power to bring that vision to others.
>
> Let us be glad that we can walk the world and see so many people wandering alone and afraid! For now we have the power to heal them. Through our vision, we can grant them a vision of the Christ in them. This is a joyous opportunity for us, for by giving them this vision, we will fully claim it as our own. We will look upon a new and clean and liberated world, and all our sorrows will melt away. In the end, we will recognize that this vision was ours all along, as a loving gift from God Himself.

> "Let us be glad that we can walk the world, and find so many chances to perceive another situation where God's gift can once again be recognized as ours!"

Perhaps now, you can see that this line is literally packed with meaning, bursting at the seams with it. Obviously, we cannot pay this kind of in-depth attention to every sentence in the Course. The point of this exercise is simply to demonstrate how the Course is written. If we realize that it is written more like a web and less like a string of beads, we can read it in a way that's appropriate to its construction, and our comprehension will dramatically increase.

Reading in light of the surrounding web versus reading by projection

How exactly can we read the Course in a way that fits its symphonic style? The answer is simple: *we must read each sentence in light of its surrounding web of meaning.* We must learn how to read with one eye on the sentence and one eye on its surrounding web, always seeing the sentence *within* that web. We need, in short, to become highly sensitive to *context*.

This way of reading stands in direct contrast to how students often read the Course. When confronted with a puzzling sentence, most students ask themselves, "Given what I know about the Course in general, what must this sentence mean?" They then reach into their fund of key Course ideas, find the one that seems most relevant, and then interpret the sentence in light of that idea. That sentence, in their eyes, now expresses that key Course idea. Indeed, all the sentences they read merely express the same set of perhaps four or five key themes. They're simply reading that set of themes into every sentence they encounter. As a result, those sentences lose their ability to say something novel to these students. The sentences become blank projection screens onto which the students project what they unconsciously assume *ought* to be there. I call this *reading by projection*. In my mind, this is the single biggest threat to really understanding the Course. It deprives the Course of its own voice, a voice that can teach us new things. Instead of the Course's pages bestowing on us their treasure of new meaning, we just paint them over with the whitewash of our prior assumptions.

The two styles of reading are so different that they even look *physically* different. If, when you find a confusing sentence, you lift your head from the page and ponder what this sentence must mean in light of what (you believe) the Course teaches, then you're almost certainly reading by projection. Instead, keep your head down. When you hit a puzzling sentence, your eyes should automatically be looking around in adjacent sentences and paragraphs. Your eyes should be exploring the surrounding web of meaning. You should be looking for *words* and *ideas* in the surrounding material that are *also* in the sentence in question. This one issue of lifting your head up or keeping it down will to a large degree determine how much you understand what the Course is really trying to tell you.

To illustrate the difference between reading by projection and reading in light of the surrounding web, let's use a well-known sentence from the Course as an example:

> *The sole responsibility of the miracle worker is to accept the Atonement for himself.*[29]

What does this mean? Don't try to answer that question—it was actually a trick question. Before you can know what this sentence means, you need its surrounding context. The whole point is that without the surrounding web *you do not know*. Your first impulse should be to *look to that web*. So let's do that. We'll look in the preceding paragraphs for words and ideas that are in our sentence, such as miracle, miracle worker, the miracle worker's responsibility, and accepting the Atonement. (Looking in *subsequent* material is also extremely helpful, although for this exercise, I will only draw upon preceding material.) As we scan for related material, we find a passage from two paragraphs before our sentence that is clearly relevant:

> The right-minded neither exalt nor depreciate the mind of the miracle worker or the miracle receiver. However, as a correction, the miracle need not await the right-mindedness of the receiver. In fact, its purpose is to restore him *to* his right mind. It is essential, however, that the miracle worker be in his right mind, however briefly, or he will be unable to re-establish right-mindedness in someone else.[30]

This passage contains almost everything we're looking for: miracle, miracle worker, the miracle worker's responsibility. It paints a fairly simple picture. We have a *miracle worker* who is giving the *miracle* to a *miracle receiver*. The miracle's purpose is to lift the receiver into a state of right-mindedness. Yet in order to give this state to someone else, the miracle worker must possess it himself. He thus has a responsibility to "be in his right mind, however briefly."

Perhaps the next clearly relevant passage is from the paragraph right before our sentence:

> All forms of not-right-mindedness are the result of refusal to accept the Atonement for yourself.[31]

This contains the remaining item we are looking for: accepting the Atonement. This passage says that *not*-right-mindedness equals *refusal* to accept the Atonement for yourself. This obviously means that *right-*mindedness equals *accepting* the Atonement.

With all of this context, we are now in a perfect position to understand what our target sentence means. As before, I'll give first the meaning of the sentence as revealed by its connections to previous material, and then once again quote the sentence itself:

> Working miracles means giving right-mindedness to others. Yet before the miracle worker can give right-mindedness to another, he must first accept it into his own mind. He must accept the Atonement for himself, however briefly. This is his responsibility; in fact, his *only* responsibility. Once he does this, the miracle will naturally go forth from him and heal others.[32]
>
> "*The sole responsibility of the miracle worker is to accept the Atonement for himself.*"[33]

In light of those previous passages, what this sentence means could not be clearer. Accepting the Atonement for yourself is the *precondition* for giving a miracle to another. This interpretation, however, is almost opposite to the meaning this sentence has been given by the majority of Course students. Seen apart from its surrounding web, and interpreted in light of a prevailing "it's all about me" attitude, this line has generally come to mean, "My sole responsibility is me; trying to help you is a trap of the ego." This sentence is therefore a classic example of the clash between reading by projection and reading in light of the surrounding web. In this case, as in many others, the two techniques yield virtually opposite meanings.

To read the Course in this way requires, above all, a certain attitude. You must be willing to let the Course tell you something new, something surprising, startling, even threatening. You need to assume that what it has to say is far more interesting than what you *expect* it to say. You have to trust that, in the end, its wisdom will uplift you, even when it's not what you want to hear.

III. APPLICATION

The importance of application in the Course's language

As I mentioned earlier, everything in the Course is geared toward practical change. This is reflected in the way its author writes. He addresses all of his writing very personally to "you," the reader. While he is schooling us in his thought system, he is constantly urging us to apply it. His writing, in fact, is peppered with statements whose only purpose is to urge us forward and move us to a decision. For example:

- He implores us: "My brothers in salvation, do not fail to hear my voice and listen to my words."[34]
- He encourages us: "Go on; clouds cannot stop you."[35]
- He asks us to reflect: "Think but an instant on this: God gave the Sonship to you, to ensure your perfect creation."[36]
- He makes promises: "And I will join you there, as long ago I promised and promise still."[37]
- He asks questions to provoke thought: "If you perceived the special relationship as a triumph over God, would you want it?"[38]
- Perhaps most of all, he urges us to apply his teaching: "Do this *one* thing, that everything be given you."[39]

This overriding emphasis on application is perfectly captured in the following personal guidance given to Helen Schucman by the author of the Course:

> Now take this personally, and listen to Divine logic: If, when you have been forgiven, you have everything else, and *if you have been forgiven*, then you *have* everything else.
>
> This happens to be the simplest of all [logical] propositions.
>
> If P then Q.
> P.
> Therefore, Q.
>
> The real question is, is P true? If you will review the evidence, I think you will find this inescapable. I went on very personal record to this effect....You have every right to examine *my* credentials—in fact, I urge you to do so. You haven't read the Bible in years.[40]

This is a classic Course blend of spiritual teaching and personal relevance. The author of the Course gives Helen a logical proposition, but she is not supposed to treat it as something apart from her. Its key premise consists of the author assuring her that she, Helen, is forgiven. He then gives her a way to believe him when he assures her of this: He urges her to read the Gospels as a way of examining his credentials. This way, she can decide for herself if she can trust him when he says, "You have been forgiven." All of this enables her to fulfill his initial injunction: "Take this personally." Think about that statement. So often, we take personally some insult that we really ought to distance ourselves from. Yet here is a message that we're tempted to keep at arm's length—it's just too incredible—but which we really *need* to take personally. That is the spirit in which we should read the Course.

Taking it personally

How can we take the Course personally? I think the key is to bring to the Course an overall attitude of "this applies to me." We have to *want* to take it personally. There are some concrete techniques we can use to express this attitude. I'll share three of them here.

Hear it speaking to you personally; insert your name

A simple technique, yet one that is surprisingly powerful, is to mentally insert your name at various points in a passage, especially after the word "you." Try it with the following passage. Whenever you see an asterisk, mentally fill in your name:

> You have the vision now * to look past all illusions. It has been given you * to see no thorns, no strangers and no obstacles to peace. The fear of God is nothing to you now *. Who is afraid to look upon illusions, knowing his savior stands beside him? With him, your vision * has become the greatest power for the undoing of illusion that God Himself could give. For what God gave the Holy Spirit, you * have received. The Son of God looks unto you * for his release.[41]

Hear these words as being from Jesus to you

It isn't required that a student believe the Course was written by Jesus; some students don't. However, if you do believe that he wrote it, this can add power to its words. I find that it helps to try to hear the words as being spoken by Jesus to me, especially in those places where he speaks in the first person. Let's try that with the following passage.

Insert your name at the asterisks as before, and consciously imagine that these words are being spoken to you personally by Jesus:

> Like you, * my faith and my belief are centered on what I treasure. The difference is that I love *only* what God loves with me, and because of this I treasure you beyond the value that you set on yourself, * even unto the worth that God has placed upon you. I love all that He created, and all my faith and my belief I offer unto it. My faith in you * is as strong as all the love I give my Father. My trust in you * is without limit, and without the fear that you will hear me not. I thank the Father for your loveliness, * and for the many gifts that you will let me offer to the Kingdom in honor of its wholeness that is of God.[42]

Apply any reference to "brother" to a specific person in your life

The Course is filled with teaching about how to see and treat others. There are over four hundred mentions of the phrase "your brother." This teaching, however, can sound rather vague and nondescript until we apply it to someone in particular. Then it comes to life. In fact, many of the references to "your brother" originally did refer to a specific person, since they were designed to help Helen and Bill see each other differently. In the spirit of this, I have found it helpful, whenever I see any reference to "brother," to read it as referring to some particular person in my life. So pick someone in your life, especially someone with whom you are having difficulties, and fill in his or her name wherever I have put a word in boldface below:

> What is within **your brother** still contains all of creation, everything created and creating, born and unborn as yet, still in the future or apparently gone by. What is in **him** is changeless, and your changelessness is recognized in its acknowledgment. The holiness in you belongs to **him**. And by your seeing it in **him**, returns to you. All of the tribute you have given [your] specialness belongs to **him**, and thus returns to you. All of the love and care, the strong protection, the thought by day and night, the deep concern, the powerful conviction this is you, belong to **him**.[43]

Application has really become the primary focus of my own study. After years of struggle with reading the Text, I finally settled into an approach that works for me. It can be broken down into four steps:

1. I take in the material slowly, focusing on one sentence at a time.
2. I take in each sentence very personally, treating it as transformative teaching meant just for me. I insert my name frequently, almost whenever I see the word "you."
3. When something is not clear to me, I consciously switch into detective mode, hunting in the surrounding context for clues to answer my question.
4. When I'm done, I return to my basic mode of taking in a sentence at a time, slowly and personally.

I find reading the Text in this way an extremely rich and rewarding experience.

CONCLUSION

Yes, studying the Text asks something of us. It's not a pill we pop, nor a television we turn on and passively absorb. It requires attention and focus. "It requires precisely what the untrained mind lacks. Yet this training must be accomplished if you are to see."[44] The Course speaks these words about meditation, yet the studying we are talking about *is* a kind of meditation. Like meditation, it can take your mind to places that nothing else can. Salvation is a journey of the mind. If you give your mind to the Text, you'll be amazed at how far it can take you on this greatest of all journeys.

SEVEN

The Workbook: The Practice of Salvation

Studying the teaching gives us the foundation, yet this is just the beginning. Atop this foundation, we need to build. We need to apply the ideas we have studied. After all, we don't just want to learn a bunch of concepts. We want to know the peace the Course talks about, to experience its promise of a liberated life. How do we do that? The answer given by *A Course in Miracles* is the answer given by paths of enlightenment for thousands of years: *spiritual practice*. Practice opens up a new world to us. Through practice, we experience the ideas of which the Course speaks. Through practice, those ideas leave the page and become living realities in our lives. The opening lines of the Workbook tell us plainly that only by adding practice onto the foundation of study will we achieve the lofty goal the Course holds out:

> A theoretical foundation such as the text provides is necessary as a framework to make the exercises in this workbook meaningful. Yet it is doing the exercises that will make the goal of the course possible.[1]

PRACTICE

What is practice?

When we think of spiritual practice, perhaps what first comes to mind is prayer and meditation. We think of people praying in church. We think of monks meditating in monasteries or caves. Prayer and meditation are practiced the world over, yet each tradition will shape these practices to reflect its own unique outlook. The same is true with the Course. It does include prayer and meditation, and many other practices, yet it shapes all of them to reflect its system, a system in which *meaning* occupies a central place. The whole purpose of the Course is to guide us into internalizing a different world of meaning. This is what its practice is about. In Course practice, we simply dwell on and apply transformative meaning. We apply it inwardly to ourselves and outwardly to the people and situations in our lives. By doing this, we invoke the *experience* of that meaning.

Since words are the main way we express meaning, most (though not all) Course practice involves concentrating on strings of words, on particular sentences. Repeating these sentences slowly and with intention is the Course's primary form of practice, and it is a powerful one indeed. The following passage spells out the focused, experiential way in which we are meant to repeat the words we practice:

> Then close your eyes and tell yourself again, slowly and thoughtfully, attempting to allow the meaning of the words to sink into your mind, replacing false ideas: *I am one Self.* Repeat this several times, and then attempt to feel the meaning that the words convey.[2]

That is what Course practice is about: letting the meaning of the words sink into your mind, trying to *feel the meaning* that the words convey.

Words get bad press these days from many spiritual seekers, yet we need only reflect on our experience to see that they carry immense psychological power. With a few words a hypnotist can lead a person into another state of consciousness. With mere words Hitler stirred his people to wage war on the world. With his words Jesus changed history. A single word can raise our emotions to the sky or dash them to the ground. Words can alter our state of mind. In Course practice, we harness this power of words and use it to usher us into a different world of meaning. We use it to transform our experience of reality.

Practice is absolutely central to the Course. From the very beginning, the Course's author was providing practices for his students. Even before the Course itself began coming through, he gave practice instructions to Bill Thetford. He suggested to Bill that he use

> a very short phrase like "Here I am Lord" and don't think of *anything* else. Just pull in your mind slowly from everywhere else and center it on these words.[3]

These are clearly meditation instructions. Bill is supposed to pull his attention inward, away from the world, and focus all of it on the repetition of a few words, words that are addressed to God. This is a classic meditation, one that, in fact, was used by the famous seventeenth-century monk Brother Lawrence, author of *The Practice of the Presence of God*. It is a potent practice which must be tried before it can be appreciated. If you will, then, please give it a try. Close your eyes, slowly pull your mind inward and focus it completely on these words: "Here I am, Lord." Say them slowly, again and again, for a minute or two.

What was the effect of doing that? I find that it gives me a sense of being immediately present to God, and of Him being immediately present to me. I feel as if He and I are face to face. This is exactly the effect intended by the author of the Course. He said that this practice was designed to convince Bill that he was a consciousness who was "capable of direct communication with the Creator of that consciousness."[4] The point of this practice, in other words, is to impart a sense of being in communication with God, directly present to God. By giving Bill this sense, this practice was specifically designed to overturn his emotional stance as the uninvolved observer, a stance that, according to the author of the Course, had made him feel alone, vulnerable, and even doubtful of his own reality. Much more than a mere ritual, this practice was designed to catalyze a profound psychological transformation.

The day after this practice was given to Bill, the dictation of the Text began. Though this may come as a surprise to many students, the Text contains quite a number of explicit practices, about thirty-five by my count. Some of them are very brief:

> When anything threatens your peace of mind, ask yourself, *"Has God changed His Mind about me?"* Then accept His decision [about you], for it is indeed changeless, and refuse to change your mind about yourself.[5]

Most are longer:

> Whenever you are not wholly joyous...say this to yourself as sincerely as you can, remembering that the Holy Spirit will respond fully to your slightest invitation:
>
> *I must have decided wrongly, because I am not at peace.*
> *I made the decision myself, but I can also decide otherwise.*
> *I want to decide otherwise, because I want to be at peace.*
> *I do not feel guilty, because the Holy Spirit will undo all the consequences of my wrong decision if I will let Him.*
> *I choose to let Him, by allowing Him to decide for God for me.*[6]

Even though they are in the Text, it is important not to treat these as just study material. They are practices. Indeed, I'd encourage you to try out at least one of the above two practices now. (This would require, in the first case, selecting a current threat to your peace of mind, and in the second, identifying a mood that is "not wholly joyous," before you repeat the words provided.) They have the power to reverse emotions that we might spend days wallowing in.

Practice as the engine of spiritual development

Surprisingly, the centrality of practice has so far gone unnoticed by most students of the Course. I have often called it the undiscovered key to *A Course in Miracles*—the word "undiscovered" being only a slight exaggeration. Students generally experience the Course as a series of powerful ideas. At first, simply reading those ideas can be enough to shake loose their current perceptions and propel them into radical openings. Yet after a while—perhaps as long as several years—that effect begins to wear off, and students start to wonder how these lofty ideas can be applied in their lives. At this point, most begin drifting away from the Course, either by exploring new paths or simply by opening their books less often. All of this, in my opinion, is the inevitable result of not delving into the inexhaustible goldmine of Course practice.

To understand the crucial importance of this practice, we must conceive of spiritual development in a certain way. Spiritual seekers often think of inner development as a process like this: Life presents you with a series of challenges that contain lessons. In each challenge you try to understand what the lesson is, and then you try to learn it. Through this process, you grow. The Course is not averse to this perspective—shades of it can be found in its pages—but it is not the primary way in which the Course envisions spiritual development. Rather, the Course mainly portrays development as *internalizing true meaning by training your attention on it.* Development, in its eyes, is the result not so much of learning the lessons contained in life's challenges (though that is included), but of our *disciplined interaction with the teaching*. Indeed, this is *how* we learn the lessons our lives present to us. In this overriding focus on a disciplined interaction with the teaching, *A Course in Miracles* is very much like a classical path of enlightenment.

Workbook Lesson 284 captures perfectly this way of seeing progress on the path. Its central idea is "I can elect to change all thoughts that hurt," and it delineates five stages in the gradual realization of this idea. For convenience, I have numbered the five stages:

1. This [idea] is the truth, at first to be but said
2. and then repeated many times;
3. and next to be accepted as but partly true, with many reservations.
4. Then to be considered seriously more and more,
5. and finally accepted as the truth.[7]

These five steps span the distance between the very beginning of the spiritual journey and the very end. At the start, we merely mouth some seemingly empty words. As we keep repeating these words, however, their meaning begins to emerge, and we increasingly accept that meaning into our minds. That meaning looms larger and larger for us, until it fills our minds. Finally, it becomes everything; it becomes the whole truth for us. And then we are home. The entire journey, therefore, amounts simply to this: *internalizing true meaning by training our attention on it.* This single process has power to carry us all the way to total awakening in Heaven. As the Course says: "To be in the Kingdom is merely to focus your full attention on it."[8]

The promises attached to practice in the Course's pages are

phenomenal. Indeed, they are limitless, because the whole purpose of practice is to deliver the Limitless. To get a sense of the untold importance the Course places on practice, take a look at the following quotes:

> Each [practice period today] will be a giant stride toward your release.[9]

> Each time you practice, awareness is brought a little nearer at least; sometimes a thousand years or more are saved.[10]

> Is it not worth five minutes of your time each hour to be able to accept the happiness that God has given you?[11]

> [Your worldly goals] gave you nothing. But your practicing can offer everything to you.[12]

The claims made for practice in these passages are stunning, and I don't think they are merely hyperbole. Speaking personally, I've never found anything that improves the quality of my life like the practice taught me by the Workbook. Nothing else comes close to its ability to heal my upsets and uplift my state of mind. Many years ago, I realized that the Course was resting all of its promises on this practice, and so I began, clumsily at first, to try to do the practice as instructed. The benefits I received spurred me onward, until now this practice has become a constant in my life. I'm nowhere near mastering it—I still feel like something of a novice—but I've come to rely on it like I rely on the ground beneath my feet. It's where I turn daily for healing and answers, for peace in the midst of life's storms, and for meaning in an insane world.

THE WORKBOOK

The Course considers practice so central to the path that it devotes its second volume to it. The Workbook for Students is a one-year training program in Course-based spiritual practice. At first glance, it may appear to be a simple book of daily devotions, which provides a special thought and some inspirational teaching for each day. In reality, though, the Workbook is a highly sophisticated program in which many processes are going forward all at once. It is teaching us to internalize a variety of ideas as well as training us in an impressive array of spiritual practices. It is slowly assembling these practices into an overall structure, which will eventually enclose our day, from start to finish, in the practice of salvation. And at the same time, the Workbook is preparing us to eventually set it aside and continue under our own steam.

One of the beauties of the Workbook is how gently it leads us. It never twists our arm. It asks for no prior experience from us in spiritual practice. It requires no heavy upfront commitment of time. It does not even ask that we believe the ideas we will practice. It takes us exactly as we are, as skeptical beginners, and lays out a program in which everything we need is provided. As the Course says: "You need offer only undivided attention."[13] The Workbook tells us exactly what to do and when, and even tells us what to do when we fail to follow its instructions. It can afford to be gentle because it plans to hook us through the benefits we experience, to convince us through the peace we find in our lives that this practice is worthy of our time and effort. It hopes to convince us so thoroughly that for the rest of our lives, we will continue to enter ever more deeply into the practice that it taught us.

To achieve this goal, the Workbook starts out asking almost nothing of us. For the first three weeks we practice only a few minutes a day. However, as the benefits of practice start to reveal themselves, the Workbook asks more and more of us. By Part II (which begins on Lesson 221), it wants us to practice morning and evening, every hour on the hour, several times during each hour, and in response to even minor upsets throughout the day. Yet even while it is asking us to practice more, it is giving us fewer and fewer instructions for what to do *during* those practice periods. Increasingly, we are given the freedom to decide how to spend these periods, based on what works for us and on the Holy Spirit's guidance within us. In the end, the Workbook's goal is to produce a student who practices regularly and sincerely, fueled entirely by her own motivation and guided by her own inner direction. She no longer needs the book; her practice flows completely from within.

A day enclosed in practice

The spiritual journey can seem interminable. Who knows how many decades or centuries or even millennia it will be until we have reached our goal. Goal-setting on this kind of grand scale is difficult for us, to say the least. Working up the motivation for a journey of a thousand miles is one thing, but a journey of thousands of *years*? The very thought can take the wind out of our sails. The Workbook, therefore, narrows the scale down to a single day. It trains us to have just one day in which we remember God all throughout the day, in which no matter what storms rage around us, we walk in peace and end up in the Arms of God. In a sense, then, this day becomes a miniature version of the entire journey home. If we can learn to have one day after another like this, we cannot be far from the gate of Heaven.

The Workbook's basic unit, therefore, is a single day. It guides us to enclose that day, and every hour of the day, in a finely woven net of spiritual practice. On the simplest level, its pattern is for us to practice morning and evening and throughout the day. The complete pattern, however, is more involved than this. I will attempt to sketch that complete pattern in the following six categories:

1. Morning quiet time
2. Hourly remembrance
3. Frequent reminders
4. Response to temptation
5. Asking for guidance
6. Evening quiet time

1. Morning quiet time

The Workbook places great significance on how we begin the day. How we do so is a statement of what we think the day is for. Hence, if we want our day to be about God, we must begin it with God. This is what the Workbook trains us to do. Ideally, it says, we should rise with holy words upon our lips. Then, as soon as feasible, we should take our morning quiet time. The purpose of this time is to anchor a mindset that will carry us through a different sort of day, a day "when echoes of eternity are heard."[14]

We begin the quiet time, of course, by reading the lesson for the day, and from there move into the main part: doing the first practice period. This practice varies from day to day, but perhaps the most frequent pattern is an *active phase* followed by a *receptive phase*. The active phase will often consist of applying that day's idea to specific things in our lives. For instance, Lesson 46 asks us to select people we have not forgiven and say silently to each one, *"God is the Love in which I forgive you, [name].*"[15] The receptive phase most frequently consists of Course-based meditation, which I will discuss later in this chapter. These practice periods can be truly transformative. One lesson says that this quiet time will be a mirror, framed in gold and set with diamonds, in which you see the face of your true Self.[16]

2. Hourly remembrance

Many of us are familiar with the following pattern: We experience a deep, peaceful meditation in the morning, and then, by lunchtime, we've turned into a ball of anxiety and frustration. The key to keeping the morning's peace is to renew it all through the day. This is the purpose of the hourly remembrances. We take a couple of minutes as the hour strikes, repeating the idea for the day, then perhaps having a brief meditation—the instructions vary. For instance, for a bank of nearly fifty lessons, we thank God for His gifts in the previous hour and ask for His guidance for the coming hour. In another series of lessons, we bring to mind any lingering negativity from the preceding hour and then let it go through forgiveness. The promises attached to really doing this are astonishing:

> Let no one hour cast its shadow on the one that follows, and when that one goes, let everything that happened in its course go with it. Thus will you remain unbound, in peace eternal in the world of time.[17]

3. Frequent reminders

Ultimately, it is not enough to practice on the hour. The Workbook will eventually train us to practice several times during the hour. These times consist of spending a brief moment repeating the lesson slowly and positively, while dwelling on its meaning. For example:

> Throughout the day use today's idea often ["God goes with me wherever I go"], repeating it very slowly, preferably with eyes closed. Think of what you are saying; what the words mean. Concentrate on the holiness that they imply about you; on the unfailing companionship that is yours; on the complete protection that surrounds you.[18]

Notice how we are supposed to repeat this idea: slowly, with eyes closed, concentrating on the rich, personal meaning it contains. I call these practices "frequent reminders." Their effect really adds up. Over the course of a day, they can uplift your entire state of mind. The Workbook says that they will "help to make the day as happy for you as God wants you to be."[19] Elsewhere, it says that each frequent reminder will add to the gifts you received in the morning quiet time, adding "further jewels to the golden frame that holds the mirror"[20] in which you see your true Self.

4. Response to temptation

Throughout a normal day, there are many threats to our peace of mind. Each one has the potential to start a chain reaction that can cast its shadow over our entire day. If we are going to have a day with God, we need a method for protecting our peace. The Course calls its method "response to temptation"—which means responding with practice to the temptation to give in to egoic thinking. It involves remaining constantly vigilant for any kind of disturbance of our peace, even seemingly minor ones (such as thinking a difficult decision is facing us[21]). Then, when we notice one, we respond by repeating the idea for the day with confidence, applying it specifically to this particular upset. Here is one such practice:

> The idea for today should also be applied immediately to any situation that may distress you. Apply the idea by telling yourself:
>
> *I have invented this situation as I see it.*[22]

It is truly remarkable how instantly a practice such as this can turn your feelings around. The Workbook says, "These are words which give you power over all events that seem to have been given power over you."[23] After experiencing the truth of this again and again, you finally come to believe the Workbook when it says, "There is a way to look on everything that lets it be to you another step to [God], and to salvation of the world."[24]

5. Asking for guidance

We are used to being in the driver's seat of our lives. Even if we drive in an erratic way, or occasionally lose control and crash into a tree, at least we can say we did it *our* way. Our decisions, however, just end up reproducing the thought system out of which they were made—the thought system of the ego. There is a whole other way to make decisions, and part of the Workbook's purpose is to train us in it. This other way involves learning how to turn within, quiet our mind, and ask the Holy Spirit for guidance. Lesson 71 says, "Ask Him very specifically:"

What would You have me do?
Where would You have me go?
What would You have me say, and to whom?[25]

My own experience when I ask is that, more often than not, I "hear" something. For me, it doesn't come as words, but rather as a sense, some idea surrounded by a feeling of rightness. This "sense" quite often doesn't fit my preconceptions of what I should do, and so it will often lead me to make decisions that don't fit my habitual patterns—which is a real blessing, for those are the very patterns that get me into trouble.

6. Evening quiet time

Finally, the Workbook trains us to end our day the way we began it. After all of the day's busy activity, we close our day in quiet with God. Ideally, we even bring words of practice with us into our sleep. This ending puts the final affirmation on the decision we made in the morning and reinforced all day long. It affirms that the words we practiced really *were* what we wanted. It says that our day really was about God.

Just as the morning quiet time set us up for a different kind of day, so the evening time sets us up for a different kind of *sleep*. The Course says, "It sets your mind into a pattern of rest, and orients you away from fear [fearful dreams]."[26] It carries us into a night of sleeping peacefully in God's Arms, resting in His Love. And if we sleep in this different way, we will surely waken to a different day. "And when you wake again, [your practice] offers you another day of happiness and peace."[27] We sleep with words of practice on our mind, "to waken once again with these same words upon our lips, to greet another day."[28] And the cycle begins again—another day of peace, another day with God.

It takes time to train us in these six aspects of Workbook practice. They do not become a consistent part of our lives overnight. We are simply not accustomed to the kind of mental discipline they require. So if you look at these six items and think, "I am so far from that," that's natural; it's to be expected. The author of the Course knows that we need someone to take us by the hand and train us, step by step, in this new way of using our minds. That is what the Workbook is for. If we'll simply focus on carrying out each day's instructions, it will take us where we want to go.

When you don't do it right

Of course, there are many days when we come nowhere near carrying out that day's instructions. What do we do then? There seem to be two options available to Course students:

1. Keep doing that lesson, day after day, until you have done it right. This is usually accompanied by pangs of guilt until you get it right.
2. Just forgive yourself. Realize that the point all along was not to do it "right," but to screw it up and forgive yourself.

Which option is the best? The Workbook itself repeatedly speaks to the issue of missed practice periods, and it does not endorse *either* option. It always gives the same clear message: When you notice you have been missing practice periods, do not be upset, do not feel guilty, and do not give up; just return immediately to your practicing. Here's an example:

> You will probably miss several applications [practice periods], and perhaps quite a number. Do not be disturbed by this, but do try to keep on your schedule from then on.[29]

The Workbook's main concern here is not a few missed practice periods; it is that we'll give up, either for the day or for good. That, ironically, is where both of those two options tend to lead. The first option—repeating the lesson until you have done it "right"—usually leads to feelings of "I'll never do it right. I'm hopeless. Why try?" The second option—just screw it up and forgive yourself—makes not practicing into a kind of virtue, the sign that you really "get it." The Workbook, however, labels all our missed practice periods as "mistakes" and says, "Let all these errors go by recognizing them for what they are. They are attempts to keep you unaware you are one Self."[30] Our ego is deeply threatened by our practice, for this practice has the power to unveil our true Self and expose the ego as an imposter. Our lapses in practice, therefore, are really attempts by our ego to keep us unaware of our Self by stopping us from practicing. We need to face that fact, and then, rather than giving power to the ego (by feeling guilty *or* by giving up), simply shrug it off and get back to practicing.

What if you read the lesson in the morning but don't do any of the practice at all? Should you go on to the next lesson or repeat that lesson? In this case, I would suggest doing the lesson over, since, in fact, you're not really doing it over. You haven't done it yet. Reading the lesson is not the same as *doing* the lesson.

Practice aids and support

In my experience, most people do not do the Workbook very well without help. They need the support of others, and also need the benefit provided by a variety of practice aids. There are a few kinds of support that I have found to be helpful. Students have found assistance in the *Workbook Companions* (Volumes I, II, and III), written by Allen Watson and myself. Another form of support is going through the Workbook with your study group. It helps if everyone is on the same lesson and can come together weekly to share their experiences. It's even better if there can be a kind of "buddy system," where each person in the group has a practice partner they can talk with daily on the phone.

I believe that the best kind of support is a mentor, someone who is proficient in Workbook practice and can guide you through its unfamiliar terrain. One form this can take is a weekly meeting with the mentor, perhaps with phone or e-mail consultations as needed between meetings. As I'll explain in Chapter 8, I believe that having a personal teacher is the primary form of support envisioned by the Course itself. Unfortunately, there are not many students who are, at this point, proficient enough in Workbook practice to be qualified to offer this kind of help. Yet even if someone is only a step or two ahead of you, having the benefit of that person's experience and support can be a great blessing.

In terms of aids, students have used all sorts of ways to help them remember the practice: beeping watches, egg timers, notes stuck to mirrors, lessons written on their palms, checklists, hand-held counters. I think all of these can be helpful, as long as they don't become gods in their own right. There should be no pride in using them—and no shame, either.

The most helpful aids I have found are these:

- Want to practice because you want the benefits
- Have a clock in plain view

- Do a practice period whenever you think of it

Prayer and meditation

For thousands of years, prayer and meditation have been considered the royal road to the Divine by seekers all over the world. Prayer and meditation are difficult terms to define, but I will attempt a definition of each. I think what we generally mean by prayer is *actively communicating with God in word or thought.* I think what we usually mean by meditation is *clearing the mind and focusing its attention in order to allow higher states to arise in us*. Defined in these ways, both prayer and meditation play an important role in the Workbook.

Prayer

In a sense, all of the Workbook lessons are prayers, though only a fraction of them are directly addressed to God. However, the Workbook contains 145 prayers (most of them in Part II) that are clearly recognizable as prayers. For example:

> *Father, my thanks to You for what I am; for keeping my Identity untouched and sinless, in the midst of all the thoughts of sin my foolish mind made up. And thanks to You for saving me from them. Amen.*[31]

The Workbook prayers ultimately contain a whole different approach to prayer. Conventional prayer is mostly about our outer journey; we normally pray for events and situations to go better. The Workbook prayers, however, are almost entirely about our *inner* journey. We express thanks for the progress we have made, and we pray for the inner shifts that will carry us even farther along the path. In conventional prayer, we do a lot of praising of God, as if we're there to fill some need of His, and as if this will coax Him into doing our bidding. The Workbook prayers, however, are devoid of flowery praise and magnificent titles. In these prayers, rather than trying to fill God's need, we let Him fill ours. We are His children, and so our job is just to *receive*. Moreover, the point of these prayers is not to change God's Mind, to persuade Him to do something He would not otherwise do. We speak to Him, yes, but we do so for the sake of changing our *own* minds. Thus, rather than saying "please" and doing lots of asking, we spend our time stating our intention, acknowledging the truth, and asking ourselves rhetorical questions—all methods for bringing *our own minds* to a new resolve. God is always giving; our job in these prayers is to strengthen our willingness and motivation to receive—not so much to receive outer gifts, but the inner gifts that will speed us along the way to Him.

Actually praying these prayers has a remarkable psychological effect (you may, in fact, want to try praying the above-quoted prayer). They induce a wonderful feeling of closeness with God. They also reshape our whole sense of God. Under the influence of these prayers, we see God more and more as a Father of lavish Love and generosity. We come to the point where we can join with the Course in saying, "He covers me with kindness and with care, and holds in love the Son He shines upon."[32]

The prayers are also an excellent preparation for meditation, for they pull in our scattered thoughts and desires, and focus them on God. This, in fact, is the purpose the Workbook gives to them. They are meant to introduce our times of quiet communion with God. As one of the lessons states, "And with this prayer we enter silently into a state where conflict cannot come."[33]

Meditation

The Workbook's approach to meditation is more traditional. In my view, there are three basic methods of meditation in the Workbook, all of which have parallels in other paths. In what I call Standard Workbook Meditation (which is taught beginning in Lesson 41), you focus your mind on the raw intent to sink down and inward, past the cloud of thoughts that chokes the surface of your mind. You sink toward the quiet center in you, the core of your mind, where God dwells. While doing this, you occasionally repeat the idea for the day, but primarily focus on sinking down and inward, filled with confidence and desire. Whenever you wander from your focus, you repeat the idea for the day to draw your mind back.

The second approach I call the Name of God Meditation. It is taught primarily in Lesson 183. Here you simply repeat God's Name over and over (no particular name is specified, so it can be a name of your selection). You repeat it not as a mere word, but as an act of calling on God to come and reveal Himself to you in direct experience. You focus all your attention and desire on this call, treating it as the only wish you have. When any other thought comes in, you dispel it by repeating the Name again, treating the Name as everything, and the wandering thought as nothing.

The Workbook's crowning method is what I call Open Mind Meditation. It is what we are asked to practice for the last 165 lessons of the Workbook. Being the crowning method, it is also the most difficult. Here, we consciously try to empty our mind of all words, all thoughts, and all beliefs. Our mind becomes like a vacuum, filled with nothing but silent, wordless expectancy. In complete stillness, we wait for the experience of God with the same silent anticipation with which one waits for the sunrise. We hold this intent *wordlessly*; we do not repeat words to maintain it (although we are allowed to use words to draw our mind back when it wanders). Ironically, although we all like to *talk* about going beyond words, when it actually comes to doing without them, we tend to find it quite difficult.

Going beyond words, however, is a huge part of the Workbook's goal. As I said, it wants to carry us into a new world of meaning. Since words convey meaning, it uses them as tools for getting our minds in touch with this meaning. Words, however, only point to this meaning. They are only symbols, not the thing in itself. Thus, after they introduce us to it, they must eventually step aside so that we can have a direct encounter with pure meaning; after a certain point, chaperones only get in the way. We can see all this in the following discussion of Open Mind Meditation:

> Yet are the words but aids, and to be used, except at the beginning and the end of practice periods, but to recall the mind, as needed, to its purpose [to draw the mind back from wandering]. We place faith in the experience that comes from practice, not the means [the words] we use. We wait for the experience, and recognize that it is only here conviction lies. We use the words, and try and try again to go beyond them to their meaning, which is far beyond their sound. The sound grows dim and disappears, as we approach the Source of meaning. It is Here that we find rest.[34]

Graduating from the Workbook

One of the main questions students have about the Workbook is:

When am I finished? Again, there seem to be two overall schools of thought on this:

1. You are never finished. The Workbook is meant to be done over and over again each year.
2. The Workbook is meant to be done only once. Repeating it probably signifies an unhealthy desire to gain God's approval by performing better.

Unfortunately, both these opinions miss the whole point of the Workbook. The Workbook is a training. When do you stop training? When you are trained. If you are trained, what point is there in taking the training again? And if you are not, why would you stop now? Can you imagine a piano teacher saying, "Well, you haven't learned the piece, but you must stop practicing it now. Any further practicing will be an unhealthy attempt to earn self-worth"?

The Course actually gives us a clear sketch of someone who has graduated from the Workbook.[35] It portrays him as someone who can practice morning and evening, all through the day, and in response to whatever upsets come along, *without the Workbook telling him to do so*. He has internalized the practice. It has become part of him, and he no longer needs a book outside of him to tell him to do it. He has become trained.

This is the goal the Workbook is shooting for. In the first half of the year, it does enclose us in a firm structure, telling us exactly what to do, how often, and when. It explains that this is not the ideal, although it is valuable for the student at this point:

> Structure, then, is necessary for you at this time, planned to include frequent reminders of your goal and regular attempts to reach it. Regularity in terms of time is not the ideal requirement for the most beneficial form of practice in salvation. It is advantageous, however, for those whose motivation is inconsistent, and who remain heavily defended against learning.[36]

The "most beneficial form of practice in salvation" is not to have a structure imposed on you from without. It is to have your practice flow from within, from your own genuine desire to reach the end of the journey. When the inner motivation isn't there, however, you *need* an external voice giving you an external structure. Otherwise, let's face it—

you'll probably not practice at all.

The Workbook hopes that by placing you in this structure, you will learn the benefits of practice so thoroughly that you begin to practice because you *want* to, not because you *have* to. It therefore starts withdrawing the structure over the second half of the year (starting, actually, in Lesson 124). Fewer and fewer specifics are given about what to practice, when to practice, and for how long. You are left increasingly on your own.

For most students, this means that their practice falls apart. The Workbook is hoping, though, that just the opposite will happen, that "your practicing will now begin to take the earnestness of love."[37] When you reach the end of the Workbook and your practice is fuller, deeper, and more heartfelt than ever, then you are probably ready to graduate from the Workbook.

It will almost certainly take more than one pass through the Workbook to reach this place. As you start the Workbook again, feel free to carry into the early lessons the practice you learned on your previous passes through. That could mean maintaining your morning and evening quiet time as well as doing more frequent practice during the day (elements that are not present at the beginning of the Workbook). Most important of all, try to keep your goal in front of you. Determine to do better this year. Never forget that you're shooting for the point where you can remove the training wheels and take off on your own.

What exactly do you do for your practice once you finally set the Workbook down? This topic is addressed in Section 16 of the Manual, "How Should the Teacher of God Spend His Day?" The short answer is that you keep practicing within the general structure you were taught by the Workbook. You spend morning and evening quiet time with God, you remember a thought frequently throughout the day (frequent reminders), and you respond to your upsets with practice (response to temptation). Within this loose structure, you're flying on your own, guided by your experience with the Workbook, by your "individual need,"[38] and by the Holy Spirit.[39]

In all of this, it is important to not get ahead of yourself. There is a very common temptation to believe that you're so far along that it is time to set the structure aside, dispense with formal practice, and just "be," just "live it." I think this is almost certainly the voice of the ego feeling threatened by where practice is taking you. Instead, be glad to submit to whatever training you need at your current stage, for as the Workbook says in its opening paragraph, "An untrained mind can accomplish nothing."[40]

CONCLUSION

As I hope is clear by now, the Workbook is not simply a book of daily devotions. It is far, far more than that. It is a masterful training manual in a different way of using our minds. It guides us into a different "mental lifestyle," and thus into a different way of journeying through life. As we saw in that last quote, without this training of our minds, we will not get very far on the path. Lesson 20 tells us:

> You want salvation. You want to be happy. You want peace. You do not have them now, because your mind is totally undisciplined.[41]

If you want peace and happiness, if you want the Course to be more than a "head trip," if you want to get past the starting gate on this path and see its lofty promises come true in your life, learn the practice. Do the Workbook.

EIGHT

The Manual for Teachers: Teach Only Love

The Text and the Workbook have been leading us through a process of maturation. As we study the Text, new concepts come into our mind, shaking loose our foundational assumptions about life. A new world of meaning enters in, opening up the possibility for a new way of experiencing reality. As we practice the Workbook, this new meaning begins to work miracles in us. We feel it releasing us from the grip of fear and lifting us into a world of light. We begin to taste this new way of experiencing reality. Occasionally, we stumble into moments of pure joy and liberation.

This, however, is not the end of the process. In a way, it is just the beginning. All along, the Course has had larger designs for us. It tells us quite plainly, "It is more than just our happiness alone we came to gain."[1] Perhaps without our realizing it, the Text and Workbook have been readying us to assume our true function as miracle workers. Like parents, they have been raising us to adulthood, so that we would finally be mature enough to take our place in the greater plan. To help us fulfill our role in this plan—a role of selflessly extending to others—the Course gives us a third volume, the Manual for Teachers.

Our calling: to be the instruments of salvation

The world is in trouble; it has *always* been in trouble. That golden age where everyone lived in harmony—it never happened. The world has always been a place of corruption, competition, and death. It has always been in need of salvation—not through belief in Jesus or some other doctrine, but through relinquishment of the source of all the trouble: the ego.

We are the instruments of this salvation. The Course says, "It is through *us* that peace will come."[2] God does not just step in, overturn the current order, and install living saints as heads of state. This is *our* world, and so the Holy Spirit must wait at the door until we let Him in. He must work through individuals who have allowed His light into their minds. They become His hands and feet in this world. It is not their belief in Him that qualifies them for this job; rather, it is their ability to forgive. They need to show with their lives that they stand for love in a world of hate. The choice to let love into our minds is thus the choice to take our place as saviors of the world.

All of us are saddened by what goes on in the world, but, we ask, what can we do? What difference can we make? The voices of those who stand for love and forgiveness seem so weak. Yet that is an illusion, says the Course, for they are the vehicles for a much greater Power. Therefore, they will succeed. "They will redeem the world, for they are joined in all the power of the Will of God."[3] The Course teaches that the length of time until the whole world awakens to Heaven "is in their hands,"[4] and each one shaves a thousand years off this total span.[5] It staggers the mind to think that each one of us can save the entire world a thousand years.

For this reason, the Course is constantly urging us to take our "rightful place among the saviors of the world."[6] In these comments, you can feel the author's concern for the bigger picture:

> There is much to do, and we have been long delayed....Take your place, so long left unfulfilled, in the Great Awakening.[7]

At times, he virtually pleads with us:

> Do not withhold salvation longer. Look about the world, and see the suffering there. Is not your heart willing to bring your weary brothers rest?[8]

In the end, he leaves us to ponder a single question, the question he says the Holy Spirit is continually asking each one of us:

> God's Voice...asks of everyone one question only: "Are you ready yet to help Me save the world?"[9]

EXTENSION

What do we do as saviors of the world? We extend. We give to others the new perception that we have accepted through study of the Text and practice of the Workbook. More specifically, we give them a new perception of *themselves*. We see them as something more than fallible humans, weighed down by sins. We see them as holy Sons of God, shining with God's glory. If this vision truly fills our minds, everything we say and do will convey this to them. We will not need to say, "You are the holy Son of God." The tone in our voice will say it. The kindness and respect we show them will say it. Even the silence between our words will say it.

This does not mean, however, that what we *do* is irrelevant. We are in the business of having a psychological effect on people, and anyone in that business knows that specific gestures, choice of words, and even timing make all the difference. For this reason, we need to check in frequently with our inner Teacher, the Holy Spirit. Only He knows the ideal form in which another can receive news of his holiness. And only He knows the form in which we ourselves can best *give* that news. He therefore designs, for each one of us, a special function (which I discussed in Chapter 1), our strong suit when it comes to extending miracles. This special function is tailored so minutely to our special strengths that it would not fit anyone else like it fits us. For Helen Schucman, it was scribing the Course. For others (such as myself), it might be teaching the Course. For still others, it might consist of being a therapist, or a spiritual healer, or a writer, or even an insurance salesman who leaves his clients feeling as though they have received more than just insurance. Each one of us has been assigned our special part in the overall plan, and if we keep in touch with the Holy Spirit, He will reveal it to us. I will discuss this topic in greater depth later in the chapter.

The final phase of our own development

To devote our lives to the salvation of the world sounds like such a sacrifice, like a surefire recipe for burnout. Most of us, I think, got on the spiritual path out of a deep concern for our own inner states. We see the path as a way of exchanging fearful and depressed inner states for peaceful and blissful ones. The whole presumption under which we are operating is, "It's about my inner states." Thus, when we hear that we are called to dedicate our lives to the welfare of others, we may understandably respond, "This isn't what I signed up for."

Yet the Course does not want to strap us to the altar and make us a human sacrifice to the cause of global salvation. On the contrary, it continually reminds us that devoting our lives to the salvation of all is how *we* get saved.

How does this work? According to the Course (as we have seen in previous chapters), the true underlying cause of our suffering is guilt. Deep down, we hate ourselves for the selfish creatures we think we have become. This guilt is the ultimate cause of our depression and low self-esteem, the hidden cause of all the calamities we experience—which we dream into our lives as punishment for our "sins"—and even the cause of our experience of being cut off from God. Everyone knows that only the holy deserve to be with God.

To awaken to our true estate as Sons of God, therefore, we will have to become absolutely convinced of our inherent holiness. And will we gain that conviction through pursuing the salvation of ourselves alone? The thought of "myself alone" is the cause of this whole mess. That thought is the ego. Trying to gain liberation from the ego for *ourselves alone* is what the Course calls "undertaking an ego-alien journey with the ego as guide."[10] And where do we think this guide will take us?

There is only one way, says the Course, to shed your guilt and fully awaken to your holiness: you have "to live so as to demonstrate that you are not an ego."[11] You have to prove to your own skeptical mind that you are something more. How? By seeing effects come forth from you that would only come from a Son of God. By living in a way that egos don't live. When you expand your tight ball of self-concern to include everyone you meet, you bring a breath of Heaven to this stale world. The author of the Course declares:

> Nothing in the world is holier than helping one who asks for help. And two come very close to God in this attempt, however limited, however lacking in sincerity.[12]

We do not have to do it perfectly. If, in the midst of our imperfections, we see holy effects emerge from us—we see kind thoughts, we see people helped, we watch these people "shine with holy thanks"[13]—our concept of ourselves begins to transform. We start to consider that maybe God did plant a spark of Himself in us when He created us, that maybe we haven't succeeded in entirely corrupting that holy light, that maybe, just maybe, it shines there undimmed. In other words, by continually giving love, we eventually awaken to our nature *as* love. The Course puts it beautifully: "Teach only love, and learn that love is yours and you are love."[14]

The psychological principle behind this is something we all experience. When you give a gift out of pure, unselfish love, how do you feel? You not only feel good, you feel better about yourself. Somewhere inside, you think, "If that came out of me, that says something about me. Maybe I am a good person after all." We've all felt this at different times. We call it the joy of giving. The Course takes this familiar altruistic principle and makes it a central plank in the plan to wake us up. The importance given it by the Course implies that we have no idea of its real power. The Course is saying that true giving has power far beyond occasionally lifting our low opinion of ourselves; it has power to prove to us, permanently and beyond a shadow of a doubt, that we are holy, that we are more than merely human, that we are God's Son.

To get a sense of this, try thinking of the best feeling you ever had after giving a gift. Take a moment and think of a specific instance if you can. Once you have thought of one, notice how good you feel about yourself, how upright and clean you feel. Now imagine that you give in this way more often, so that this good feeling about yourself intensifies and deepens. Could that feeling intensify to the point where you felt that you were a good person, through and through? Could it intensify to the point where you felt that you were a holy being? If selfless giving became your natural way of being, as natural to you as breathing, could it possibly convince you that you were divine?

The author of the Course would answer an emphatic "*of course.*" He declares, "There is no other way to find your Self."[15] This is why extension is the final phase in the Course's process of awakening. Study and practice take us far, but by themselves they are not enough. We can study the Course until we know it backwards and forwards, we can have the most mind-altering experiences in practice, but to make it all the way home, we must take the next step and devote ourselves completely to extension. Extension is the crowning phase of the path. Only through it will we fully embrace the guiltlessness that is the truth in us. Only through it do we truly enter the spiritual life and experience its benefits: being effortlessly carried along, knowing that we are the instrument of a greater plan and are living for a useful purpose, seeing that we are genuinely contributing to the happiness of others, and feeling the guilt and fear fall off our shoulders as we approach "the glorious surprise"[16] of discovering Who we really are.

THE MANUAL FOR TEACHERS

Students are generally confused about the Manual for Teachers. What is it for? Most probably take their cue from what was written by Helen Schucman in the Course's Preface: "The Manual for Teachers, which is written in question and answer form, provides answers to some of the more likely questions a student might ask."[17] According to this, the Manual is a kind question-and-answer clarification of the Course's teaching. Yet if this is so, why is it called a manual *for teachers*?

The Manual itself mentions its role as clarifier of the teaching,[18] but clearly gives this second priority, placing its main emphasis elsewhere. In its Introduction, it announces itself as a handbook for the teachers of God:

> This is a manual for the teachers of God....Who are they? How are they chosen? What do they do? How can they work out their own salvation and the salvation of the world? This manual attempts to answer these questions.[19]

Teachers of God are those who, by virtue of their progress on the path, are ready to embark on their function of extension. They are teachers in a much deeper sense of the word than, say, a school teacher. They "teach" people a new way of looking at reality, and do so primarily through the love and forgiveness they extend. In other words, "teaching" here is a synonym for "extension." Teachers of God are "extenders."

Though teachers of God come from all different paths, the Manual explains that *it* was written for teachers on this path—*A Course in*

Miracles. "This is a manual for a special curriculum [*A Course in Miracles*], intended for teachers of a special form [again, the Course] of the universal course."[20] The Manual was written for those students who, having studied the Text and graduated from the Workbook, are ready to assume their role as teachers of God.

The Manual, therefore, represents the third and final phase of the Course's program: extension. Its purpose is to familiarize teachers with their newfound role: what that role is, how they can carry it out, how to handle problems that arise in trying to do so, and how to deal with various other issues on this new journey.

The first third of the Manual discusses two important forms that the role of teacher of God may take. The first form (discussed in Sections 1–4) is that of the *teacher of pupils*. This person fills something like the traditional role of the spiritual teacher. He enters into relationship with particular pupils and shepherds them along his way or path. The second form (discussed in Sections 5–8) is that of the *healer of patients*. This is a teacher of God who has acquired healing abilities and goes to sick people as a spiritual healer. I'll discuss both of these forms in greater detail below.

Many of the Manual's remaining sections address typical concerns that will arise once one has stepped into the role of teacher of God. Here are some of the concerns addressed:

- Whether to change one's life situation, now that one is a teacher of God (Section 9)
- How to make decisions in one's life (Section 10)
- How to spend one's day as a teacher of God (Section 16)
- How to practice, now that one is done with the Workbook (Section 16)
- How to deal with pupils' resistance to learning (Section 17 and 18)
- Whether and how to use words in one's teaching and healing (Section 21)
- How to make up for one's limitations as a teacher by calling on Jesus' help (Section 23)
- How to represent the Course to pupils on issues like reincarnation (Section 24)
- How to deal with the psychic powers that may arise as one advances (Section 25)

- How to regard the pursuit of the direct experience of God (Section 26)

As I mentioned above, the Manual also has a function of answering general questions to clarify the Course's teaching. It "is...intended to answer [some of the] questions that both teacher and pupil may raise...in terms of a brief summary of some of the major concepts in the text and workbook."[21] Many of its sections, therefore, deal with general concerns such as God, the world, peace, justice, sacrifice, death, etc. Even many of these, though, conclude by applying what they have said to the role of the teacher. For example, the section "What Is Death?" concludes with this remark: "Teacher of God, your one assignment could be stated thus: Accept no compromise in which death plays a part."[22]

Students generally love the Manual for its role as clarifier of the teaching. There's no question that it is easier to read than the Text. Unfortunately, though, this role has almost completely eclipsed its primary purpose: to be a *manual* for *teachers*, a handbook for those in the third phase of the Course's program. Appreciating the importance of this third phase is crucial. Our inner work with the Course—our study and practice—is meant to flower into our becoming a blessing to everyone we meet. As I pointed out in Chapter 2, the main sense of the title *A Course in Miracles* is not that this course will teach us to *experience* miracles (although that is part of it), but that it will teach us to *extend* miracles. Given this, it would be fair to retitle the Course in this way: *A Course in Becoming a Miracle Worker.*

OUR SPECIAL FUNCTION

As I mentioned earlier, each one of us is given a special function. This is our own particular way of extending forgiveness and healing. The content of everyone's function is exactly the same—we extend to others a vision of themselves as blameless and clean, as God's Son. Yet the form in which we do this is different for each one of us, tailored to fit our unique strengths, as well as our particular culture and life situation.

This idea inevitably raises a number of questions: Is there really a specific function waiting for me? If so, what is it? Why haven't I found it yet? How can I find it and start doing it? This subject has been a major focus in my own life, both in terms of my own special function and in terms of helping people I know find theirs. Seeing myself and others go through this process has taught me a great deal, and I would like to share some of what I've learned about it.

In my experience, the special function is absolutely for real (that is, as real as anything is in this unreal world). There really *is* a specific role that has been assigned to each one of us. This role lies there silently waiting for us, almost like some kind of electronic mechanism in sleep mode, waiting for a signal to set it in motion. That signal is usually sent by some critical shift or breakthrough in our inner development, some new plateau we've reached in our journey up the mountain.

At that point, the mechanism comes to life, and starts to exert a pressure on our lives, pushing us to take certain paths instead of others, nudging us into meeting certain people, awakening new interests in us. All the while, it is sending us hints about what our function will be. Some of these hints will be actual snapshots of that function, though even while looking directly at them, we'll probably not appreciate their significance. The time will come, though, when we begin to mentally link one snapshot to another. It then occurs to us that Someone has been sending us a series of pictures of the same thing, and that this thing is no small matter; it is our destiny. Now we can start to actively pursue this destiny. Part of what spurs us on is our recognition that the function we're glimpsing suits us perfectly. It is as if some Mind that knows us better than we know ourselves has looked into us and unerringly seen the best in us—our talents and abilities, our buried aspirations and dreams, our deepest yearnings for the sublime—and wrapped it all into a package that is the perfect vehicle for expressing the best in us.

It may take years, however, until we are actually ready to unwrap this package. For entering into our function is not just a matter of making changes on the outside. The outer form of our function is just a vehicle for the inner content, and we only gain this content through progress on the path. That is why study and practice are so important. Without that inner content, we'll either be too afraid to carry out our function, or our attempts to do so will be hollow. Usually, there is a great deal of the former—the fear. There is a battle that is waged on the way to our special function, for in the end, this function is not just a hobby (although it may start as one); it is a whole different life, and it is not the life we planned for ourselves. Along the way to it, therefore, we usually experience deep resistance. We feel as if we're giving up the life that has grown so comfortable and familiar, forgetting that the misery of this life is what caused us to want our special function in the first place! Thankfully, though, we'll be led gradually, with time enough to see that this new direction is in our best interests, that it really is our heart's desire. Each step in the process will go forward only as we give it our consent.

Actually starting to carry out our function represents the end of a long journey, and the beginning of another, for even at this point, we're still relatively immature along the path. We still have all of our human foibles and anxieties, and we carry them right into our function. Yet, however imperfectly we carry it out, there is a deep satisfaction that comes from knowing that a light has entered our lives and we've set our hand to its work. Despite our worries and self-doubt, we know that we're filling a useful purpose, we're playing our part in a larger plan, and this gives our lives a meaning that nothing else could. It gives us something to live for.

Though we may not realize it at the time, we start out incredibly green. As in any endeavor in life, we grow through experience. That mechanism that brought us this far is not done with us. It is still guiding us along, constantly placing situations on our path that spur us onward. It is always asking things of us that we cannot quite do yet, and as we stretch to do them, we slowly ascend the mountain. It sends us people who need what we have to give, and their presence is a powerful force in pulling us upward. The gratitude they show us and the change we see in them cause us to reevaluate our dim view of ourselves, continually revising it until we accept that we are not sinners at all, but holy Sons of God. And when the day comes that we fully accept that, we stand at the top of the mountain. Our journey is over. Whether we realize it or not, the force that brought us to that pinnacle was none other than our special function.

A personal example

As a concrete example of at least the early stages of this journey, I'll briefly share some of my own story. In my late teens I knew where my life was headed. I was preparing myself for a career as a kind of philosopher/theoretical psychologist. I was trying to fashion a system aimed at explaining the nature of mind, both its fundamental nature and how it works on the surface in terms of thought, emotion, memory, and will. I felt that the foundation for this system was an original insight that had great promise. I loved seeking truth, and I could think of nothing I'd rather do than put together a grand system of truth and communicate it to the world.

In my early twenties, however, I had a series of highly synchronistic occurrences. In hindsight, these occurrences contained a clear message: I was being called out of an academic career and into a life of serving God outside conventional structures. It took some time, though, before I really saw that message, and even longer before I accepted it.

For example, on my twenty-first birthday, I spent part of the day making plans about what I intended to be my magnum opus, a massive book in which I would lay out my philosophical system in its entirety. On that day, I felt I was inwardly "given" a title for the book, one that emphasized Jesus as a symbol for the true nature of us all. Later that same day, I was given *A Course in Miracles* as a birthday present. As I looked back on this later, I was amazed by the commonalities between these two books. Both were massive tomes setting forth intellectual systems that were philosophical, psychological, and ultimately spiritual. Both claimed to reveal how our minds and emotions work and to reveal what we fundamentally are. And both held up Jesus as a symbol for the rest of us, human in appearance but divine in truth.

I found this fascinating but didn't have a clue as to what it really meant. I assumed, of course, that I would devote my intellectual energies to my book, and that the Course showed up that day as a sort of symbol for my book. I didn't realize that *my* book was the symbol; that on that day I was being shown what I would *really* devote my intellectual abilities to. It didn't occur to me that I would spend my life championing a system devised by someone else—a "someone else" who was not even in a body. Had it occurred to me, this idea would have made my intellectual career seem like a joke.

Yet events had their way with me. My wife and best friend both started working for a local Course center, which subsequently asked me to teach there, and later, to write. I wrote a popular introductory booklet, which led to my being asked to travel and speak. I turned around one day and found I had a career as a teacher of *A Course in Miracles*. Ten years after I received the Course, I finally caved in. I realized that the author of the Course was an immeasurably better thinker than I, or anyone else I had encountered. I realized that it was a worthy calling to devote my life to his system, even though it meant giving up *my* system. And I realized that interpreting his system made use of the exact same abilities and love for truth that had been the impetus for my system. I finally understood that this was what I had been hired to do from the beginning. This is what Someone was trying to tell me the day I got the Course. I had simply been blinded by my own ambitions.

Another dozen years have passed since then, and I marvel at how perfectly my function has been designed for me. It really does make use of the best in me. I get the opportunity to research the Course and pull out the massive and multifaceted system that underlies its long train of beautiful words. I absolutely love exploring it, discovering the intricacies of the author's mind, and sharing those discoveries with others. I would pay for the privilege of doing this, yet instead I get paid to do it. My function, however, has required me to stretch far beyond what I feel I do best. Public speaking, leading groups, working with people one-on-one, leading an organization—I have had to stretch into all of these arenas (not without a good deal of grumbling), but I feel I'm the better for it. Finally, being a Course teacher has made me three times the Course *student* I would have been otherwise. If I hadn't been a teacher, I might easily have been little more than a dabbler. As it is, I'm far more serious about spiritual awakening and have received far more benefits from the Course. All in all, I am deeply grateful that the choice of my function was *not* left up to me.

Each person's special function will be different, because each one is tailor-made. The Manual, however, focuses on two overall forms that these functions might take. Although they are only two forms among many, they seem to have particular significance, for the Manual, as I said earlier, devotes its first third to setting them out. The first four sections introduce us to the role of the teacher of pupils, and the second four sections discuss the role of the healer of patients. Not every experienced Course student will be called to fulfill one of these roles, but judging by their importance in the Manual, we can assume that a great many will.

The teacher of pupils

One of the most universal and time-honored roles in the world's spiritual traditions is that of the teacher or guide, someone who takes aspirants by the hand and leads them along the way. This role seems particularly crucial on those paths that aim for profound internal change. On such paths, it would be foolish to go it alone. The road is too unfamiliar, the danger of being led astray by one's ego too great.

The Course is one such path. It does aim for profound inner change. It views the ego leading us astray as the *norm*, rather than the exception. Moreover, it is a highly sophisticated system of thought and practice with its own unique terminology. On a path such as this, you would *want* a teacher. You would probably feel lost without one. Indeed, new students of the Course are often desperate for guidance. They feel as if they have touched down on an alien landscape. They don't know how to get around, and they certainly don't speak the language. They need a local who can show them around. They show up at study groups hoping to get directions, yet they often leave empty-handed, feeling that the group was a case of the blind leading the blind.

There is thus a tremendous need for guides who know the way, and the Course openly acknowledges this need. The Manual speaks repeatedly of teachers who will shepherd pupils along the path of the Course. Indeed, this role is clearly implied in the volume's title. By definition, a manual for teachers is written for teachers who will guide students through the particular course of which that manual is a part, guiding them through that course's text and workbook. The same is true with this manual for teachers. It frames itself as a handbook for teachers who will lead pupils through this particular course, *A Course in Miracles.*[23]

This goes against the conventional wisdom about the Course, which asserts that it is a self-study course. Yet the Course never says that it is a self-study course—not once. Early on, someone applied that term to the Course and it stuck. The Course, however, sees itself quite differently. It seems to assume that people will begin its path under the guidance of a mentor. I say this because whenever it discusses new students of *A Course in Miracles* (which it does in two sections in the Manual), it does not call them "students," but "pupils," and depicts them as pupils *of* a Course teacher.[24] Whereas you can be a student of a book, you can be a pupil only of a *person*. This, it seems, is how the author of the Course pictured new students, as being led along this path by another person who is their guide.

We live in a culture in which the role of spiritual guide is viewed with intense suspicion. Yet when you think about it, such a role is perfectly natural. Yes, it can be abused, but it cannot be avoided, for the role of the teacher (in the broadest sense of the word) is part of the fabric of human life. We are all faced with the issue of making our way in life. We have to decide what it's all about, what direction to take, where happiness lies and how to get there. We need to resolve huge questions and pick our way through impossible mazes. Most of us don't sit alone in our rooms and design our own way through this minefield. Rather, we turn to particular people in our lives, individuals in whom we see something we respect. We decide to learn their "way," and so they in essence become our guides, our teachers, however informal the relationship may be. They pass on to us the way they have learned to walk themselves. If you reflect on your life, you'll probably find that this has been a major theme. Indeed, this is how we mainly proceed in life. It is how we grow up (following the lead of parents and teachers and friends); it is how we generally learn skills, crafts and professions; it is how we learn most anything.[25]

And it is how we learn spiritual awakening. The author of the Course teaches that true religion is not the formal religion of church, ritual, and ceremony. True religion, he says, is actually indistinguishable from true psychotherapy: It is the holy relationship between a guide to sanity and his pupil.[26] One of them knows the way to sanity, the other follows. In this sacred joining, something indefinable passes from one to the other. There is a light that shines in the teacher's way of being, and this light is slowly absorbed into the pupil. Now, it shines in him too. Thus, when you ask why, in the Course's eyes, new students should walk this path under the guidance of a teacher, the answer is simple: This is the way it has been done for millions of years. This is the way it has *always* been done.

In the Course's view, the benefits are just as great for the teacher. For through the pupil's gratitude and appreciation, the teacher learns that he is not the person he thought he was. He is a holy Son of God. His pupil is quite literally his savior, pulling him out of the pit of self-condemnation. Thus, he needs the pupil just as much as the pupil needs him.

The Course seems to assume that this will be a natural role for many experienced students of its path. They will have spent untold hours studying the Course. They will have practiced Workbook lessons daily for perhaps years. They will have learned how to apply this teaching to all of their situations and relationships. They will have learned how to live it. After all that, they have so much to give, and what is worse than spending years acquiring a gift and having no one to give it to? Giving it away is a blessing for *them*. Indeed, their work with the Course will not reach its maturity until they do so.

What does this role look like concretely? It will look different for every teacher and pupil, but it does require an actual relationship between the teacher and pupil. They need to meet one-on-one, at least occasionally. This does not mean that the teacher cannot lead groups; it just means that he must also meet privately with at least certain students, if he wants to tap the full potential of the teacher-pupil relationship. For what mainly passes between teacher and pupil is not simply intellectual concepts, but something much deeper, something which will only pass in the context of a genuine, deep relationship.

The teacher, as you can see, is really a mentor. It is vital not to think of him as primarily a *conceptual* teacher. To capture this role in its fullness, I have designed a list of six aspects, all of which are drawn from the Course's own descriptions of the teacher-pupil relationship. The list begins at the surface of the teacher's role and moves its way toward the depths.

1. Conceptual teacher

Your pupils will invariably ask you to clarify the Course's concepts. They need that clarification, for those concepts are the foundation for their whole journey with the Course. However, this is only the topmost layer of your function as a teacher.

2. Guide through the program

The Course's program takes the student through an educational process. It begins with study of the Text, moves into practice of the Workbook, and culminates with extension as a teacher of God. Your job is to guide your pupils through this program as a Sherpa would guide them up a mountain. You need to make clear to them what the program is, help them decide which aspects to focus on at a given time, motivate and encourage them, and help them over the various obstacles they encounter.

3. Belief doctor

The role of the teacher has some of the role of the counselor in it. Your pupils will naturally bring personal problems and issues to you. Your job is to uncover the beliefs that are the real cause of their pain, and help them let go of those beliefs through forgiveness.

4. Forgiver

Your job goes beyond skillfully navigating through the concepts, the program, and your pupils' personal issues. You are called to be a true healer, to heal your pupils' deep-seated guilt with the balm of your forgiveness. On a general level, this means constantly looking past their bodies and personalities to Who they really are. More specifically, it means viewing their moments of resistance to the Course (and to you) as a precious opportunity to teach them that no matter what they do, they are still God's blameless Son.

5. Exemplar

The most powerful way of teaching, says the Course, is by example.[27] As teachers, we need to be living demonstrations—in our demeanor, our behavior, and our life—of the Course's way. This doesn't mean that our words are useless in communicating our message, but, as the Course says, these words will only carry real power "if we exemplify the words in us."[28]

6. Holy relationship partner

So much of the transformative power in the teacher-pupil relationship is in the relationship itself. Even though one is the teacher and the other the pupil, real joining can still take place—as many of us know who have established a deep bond with a teacher figure in our lives. This joining has power to change the two participants forever, for it proves to them experientially that they are not separate selves. The Manual speaks movingly of this:

> The demarcations they have drawn between their roles, their minds, their bodies, their needs, their interests, and all the differences they thought separated them from one another, fade and grow dim and disappear.[29]

Can you imagine how blessed you would feel to have a teacher who embodied all six of these aspects? How much faster you would travel along the path? Can you imagine how blessed you would feel to *become* such a teacher? If *A Course in Miracles* is your path, it is quite likely that you are called to become exactly that.

The healer of patients

The other major role described by the Manual is the healer of patients. This, too, is a very ancient role. Long before modern medicine, there was the shaman, the tribal healer. Spiritual healers no longer occupy a central place in our culture, but they are still present in our society. One naturally thinks of Christian Science practitioners, charismatic Christian healers, Reiki healers, and New Age spiritual healers.

On an outward level, the Course-based healer looks very much like the traditional spiritual healer. She comes to a physically ill patient,[30] or perhaps to someone struggling with depression or some other emotional issue, and attempts to be "a channel for healing."[31] She appears to be a person of special power and virtue, qualities that the patient, by comparison, seems to lack. She approaches this specific malady, with its particular level of severity. She uses words, perhaps even her hands. She invokes the name of Jesus. Something seems to pass from her to the patient. And the patient is healed.

Yet while engaging in this very traditional set of appearances, something entirely different is going on in her mind. Her whole focus is on overlooking the apparent reality of every single thing I just described. That, in fact, is how she heals.

Rather than trying to heal the body by aiming healing energy at it, she completely ignores the body, overlooking its importance and even its very existence. The specific disease, being part of the body, means nothing to her, even if it is life threatening. She knows that, despite appearances, the real problem is the patient's mind. She knows that his sick body is merely a visible picture of his sick thoughts.

She understands that she is not the true healer, but only a channel for the Holy Spirit. She is only a catalyst who sets in motion the real Healer within the patient. She therefore does not see herself as in charge of the process. This does not mean, however, that she is filled with self-doubt. Because she is not relying on herself, she does not worry about her inadequacies. She rests upon a Power in her that can never fail.

She may use her hands, words, gestures, and may feel energy moving around, yet she knows that these are not what heals. What heals is simply her vision of the patient as forgiven, guiltless, healed, and whole (we discussed the topic of vision or true perception in Chapter 5). Since she cannot give this vision without having it in her own mind, she focuses on fulfilling her one responsibility: accepting true perception for herself. With this perception comes joy, and so she heals not by feeling the burden of the situation, but by being happy and carefree. She does not experience her giving as a sacrifice, but rather as a gift to herself. She therefore does not need to be compensated for being drained of her time and energy, for by healing she was only filled. However, she may accept remuneration from her patients as an expression of their gratitude and their caring about her material well-being.

Above all, she does not see herself as the superior being coming to the inferior sick person. She knows that in reality, they are both equal Sons of God, equal in power and in holiness. Indeed, her healing rests on her ability to see past the patient's appearance as a malfunctioning body and maladjusted mind. She overlooks his body *and* mind and humbly gazes on the holy light of Who he really is.[32] She stands before this light in silent rapture, seeing nothing to change, nothing to forgive, and nothing that could possibly need healing. She also sees nothing separate from her, for she is not looking on this person's *special* light, but on the infinite light in which everyone abides. Caught up in this light, she does not see herself and the patient as two beings having an exchange, but simply as One Mind experiencing Its oneness.

On the outward level, what she does will look very much like what other spiritual healers do. Yet on the inside, despite many parallels, it will probably be quite different. In my experience, most healers see themselves as channeling some kind of spiritual energy to the body. This energy is apparently semi-physical, for it can interact with the body and heal it. The energy is often invoked through quite specific techniques, such as when a Reiki master visualizes particular symbols. The Course-based healer, rather than channeling a certain energy to the patient's body, is channeling a certain *perception* to the patient's *mind*, a perception of the patient as the holy Son of God. And she does so simply by being absorbed in this perception herself. This holy perception may engender physical effects: the healer's hands might become hot and she might give off some sort of quasi-physical energy. But these are merely byproducts of the real healing agent: the true perception in the mind of the healer.

The Course clearly expects to unleash multitudes of healers into the world. To be a Course-based healer, however, you must first go through the Course's program. It's not enough to have paranormal abilities. You must, first and foremost, be a faithful student, steadfastly pursuing your own awakening. Your healing must flow from a genuine depth of personal study and practice, from your sincere commitment to see the world differently. Only on this foundation can you enter the world as a true miracle worker.

CONCLUSION

A life of extension may sound like foolishly draining ourselves dry for the sake of being good. Yet that misses the whole point: extension is a blessing to *us*. It gives us the power to make a difference, and who has not felt the ache of wanting to help but feeling powerless to do so? It provides us with a meaningful life, in which we give ourselves to a larger purpose, in which we make our own unique contribution to the whole. Finally, it awakens us to our hidden divinity, for only a divine being would just extend, purely and ceaselessly, without any hooks or strings. According to the Course, extension will one day awaken us so completely that we will disappear from this dream world altogether, just as Jesus did.

At present, we are so very far from that goal. Even those of us who are teachers of God are shot through with imperfection. That is why we need a manual. Its job is to help us teach perfection so well that we ourselves finally get it, and awaken from the realm of imperfection forever:

> This is a manual for the teachers of God. They are not perfect, or they would not be here. Yet it is their mission to become perfect here, and so they teach perfection over and over, in many, many ways, until they have learned it. And then they are seen no more, although their thoughts remain a source of strength and truth forever.[33]

PART IV

LIVING THE COURSE

The path becomes quite different as one goes along.
Nor could all the magnificence, the grandeur of the scene
and the enormous opening vistas that rise to meet one as
the journey continues, be foretold from the outset.
Yet even these, whose splendor reaches indescribable
heights as one proceeds, fall short indeed of all that wait
when the pathway ceases and time ends with it.
But somewhere one must start.

Manual, Section 19, Paragraph 2

Introduction to Part IV

We have familiarized ourselves with how the Course came and what it is, and most important, with its teaching and its program. Now that we have a sense of the broad contours of the path, we can address specific issues about actually walking this path. Quite naturally, the questions that one faces when just starting out are different than the questions that arise farther down the road. We'll discuss many of these key issues in Chapter 9, "Setting out and Continuing on the Path." Finally, we'll discuss *why* one would walk this path—what are the benefits? What makes this path worth traveling? That is the subject of Chapter 10, "The Promise of *A Course in Miracles*." That chapter concludes by answering a final, crucial question: What kind of person are we aspiring to become? What sort of human being does this path aim to produce?

NINE

Setting out and Continuing on the Path

As with any path, there are issues to be addressed about traveling on this one. How do you get started? What kind of aids are needed along the way? What about when the going gets tough? How do you decide that you are going to stay on this path? And once you do, how do you make sure you keep moving? This chapter will address some of the many issues around walking the path of *A Course in Miracles*.

Which volume should you start with?

While you can gain a great deal from the Course by attending meetings or reading books based on it, real work with the Course means using the book itself. This raises the question: Which of the three volumes should you start with?

The most logical answer, of course, is to begin with Volume I, the Text. This makes sense, because the Text lays the foundation for the other two volumes. Indeed, the Course seems to assume that you are going through its volumes in order, starting with the first. There are many places where a later volume will make reference to an earlier volume, clearly assuming that you have read the earlier one. The Workbook, for instance, says, "Bodies attack, but minds do not. This thought is surely reminiscent of our text, where it is often emphasized."[1]

Many students, however, find the Text to be rough going, especially its early chapters. They feel more at home in the Workbook or Manual. Is it all right, then, to begin with one of those? The last section of the Manual says that yes, the new student can begin with *any* of the three volumes. However, there are a few things to bear in mind about this:

- If you don't start with the Text, you'll eventually need to return to it and study it (that is, if you decide to stay with the Course).
- Even if you don't progress through the volumes in order, you'll probably still progress through the stages they represent in order—the stages of study, practice, and extension. This means that in your early work with the Course you'll probably be in a "study phase," in which you'll be primarily absorbed in ingesting the concepts. That is where you'll get your "juice"—from reading those transformative ideas. If you do the Workbook while in this phase, then, you'll probably be most engrossed in reading the Workbook's teachings, rather than in doing its practices. If you keep progressing, however, you'll probably eventually transit into a "practice phase," where your main focus will be on doing the practice. At this point, the practice is where you'll get your "juice." Finally, you'll hopefully reach an "extension phase," where, even though you still study and practice, your real joy will come from extending love and forgiveness to others, and so that is where your main focus will be.
- This means that if you start the Course by going through the Workbook or Manual (rather than the Text), you'll almost certainly need to return to those volumes again later on. The reason is that at that stage in your work with the Course, you'll probably experience them mainly as communicators of the teaching, as "little Texts." And that is part of their purpose. Yet each one has another purpose that is its real focus. The primary purpose of the Workbook is to guide you in doing the practice, and the primary purpose of the Manual is to provide instruction for teachers of God—mature students on this path. Therefore, you should return to each of those volumes later, when you are ready for what they are really about.

The question of a teacher

I said earlier (in Chapter 8) that the Course portrays new students walking this path under the guidance of a personal teacher or mentor. This makes total sense when you reflect on the world of difference a good mentor can make in any area of life. As a new student of the Course, therefore, should you look for a personal teacher?

The immediate problem with this is that at this stage in the Course's history, there are very few who meet the Course's qualifications for assuming that role. The Manual portrays the qualified teacher as one who has studied the Text, and is so established in Workbook practice that he can put the Workbook down and maintain his practice every day and all through the day. Unfortunately, very few Course students are at this stage.

On the other hand, a good teacher could transform your whole experience of the Course. Rather than a book you read for a few months, the Course could become a roadmap to God that changed your life forever. I would recommend, therefore, that you simply be open to the possibility that you are meant to have a teacher, and trust that if you are, you'll be brought into contact with this person.[2] Keep your eyes peeled for someone who has the kind of relationship with the Course that you want to have. Look for someone who does the study, who is sincere and diligent in the practice, and who demonstrates Course principles in his or her relationships with others. Look for someone who is still learning and is open about his or her mistakes and shortcomings. Beware of someone who is a good talker but who does not "walk the walk," and also steer clear of someone who tries to hire himself as your teacher. Listen, instead, to a quiet voice within you that recognizes your teacher when he or she shows up. Then approach this person and ask if he or she would meet with you regularly as your Course mentor.

Study groups

Currently, the main support for students is probably weekly study groups. They come in all shapes and sizes, ranging from groups that simply read aloud from the Course to groups that discuss personal issues and never touch the Course; from taught groups to facilitated groups to leaderless groups. Attending a group is not an inherent part of doing the Course, but, depending on the group, it can be helpful. If you feel drawn to find a group, I would recommend the following:

- Look for a group that is led by someone you respect
- Look for a group that involves opening your book, that directly engages material from the Course itself
- Look for a group that is focused on the Course, rather than one that mixes it with other teachings
- Make sure that the group is not the extent of your involvement with the Course, that you spend private time with the Course on a daily basis
- Take in what the group says, but be willing to form your own views of the Course based on what it says

How much upfront commitment is required?

One of the wonderful things about the Course is that it asks so little upfront. It does not ask for a great deal of time. The Workbook's early lessons, for instance, ask for about two minutes of practice a day. And it does not ask that you believe all its radical ideas. In speaking of the new student, the Course says, "He need merely accept the idea that what he knows is not necessarily all there is to learn. His journey has begun."[3]

All the Course asks from the beginner, therefore, is a slightly open mind and a little willingness to experiment. Out of this small investment, the Course hopes to prove itself to you. It hopes to show you from the benefits you receive that it deserves your effort and your trust. As it says, "If you do it, you will see that it works."[4]

In this way, the Course hopes to escape the tug-of-war with God that almost everyone alive falls into. We think that He is trying to yank us over to His side, and so we stand our ground and pull back. This can stop the spiritual journey dead in its tracks, since, of course, the whole point of the journey is to go over to God's side. The Workbook refers to this: "You will not [gain true perception] if you regard yourself as being coerced, and if you give in to resentment and opposition."[5] To relax the tug-of-war, the Course hopes to gradually win our trust, so that when it pulls on the rope, we experience it as someone pulling us out of a dark pit, and we do everything we can to cooperate. "This works against the sense of opposition," it says, "and reminds you that help is not being thrust upon you but is something that you want and that you need."[6]

Give yourself time to learn the language

Chances are that when you first pick up the Course, its language will be virtually impenetrable. My advice is this: Just be patient and keep reading, and the mist will slowly clear.[7] With time, the Course's language and thought will begin to seem quite natural and familiar. The Course seems to be fully aware of this. As I mentioned earlier (in Chapter 6), it likens our learning of it to an infant learning language.[8] It says that what at first sounds like mishmash to us will eventually be recognized as our native tongue.

Expect that your ego will have difficulty with the Course

The Course makes a pregnant comment while explaining why reincarnation should not be taught as part of its system. Referring to the new student, it says, "His ego will be enough for him to cope with, and it is not the part of wisdom to add sectarian controversies [like reincarnation] to his burdens."[9] The picture this paints, though brief, is quite clear. The new student's ego will be challenged to the core as it encounters the Course. As a result, it will be having seizures, giving its owner a lot "to cope with," loading him with "burdens." During this time, what wisdom is there in piling even more burdens onto him, especially useless ones like sectarian controversies?

Other comments throughout the Course echo this same theme. The Course clearly expects that its students will feel challenged by it, and in response, will resist it. It assumes that students will complain that the Course is too hard,[10] that it is impossible to learn,[11] that its goals are simply too different from theirs.[12] The Course sees these complaints, however, not as honest assessments, but as the frantic projections of a frightened ego. Quite simply, the ego feels attacked by the coming of the light. It is threatened by our impending liberation from its chains. It is afraid, not that the Course will not work, but that it *will*.

For this reason, the ego's volatile reactions to the Course are legendary among students. There are countless stories of students throwing their book across the room, tossing it in the trash, or flushing it down the toilet (one page at a time). It seems that few students escape feeling intensely threatened by the Course at one time or another.

This is simply part of the process. The Course openly aims at turning our minds upside-down. Its goal is the relinquishment of everything we hold dear.[13] Of course we'll resist. When we do, rather than feeling guilty, we can take it as a sign that the Course is having the effect it expects to have, and that the more positive effects it expects—joy and peace—must be on their way.

Give yourself time to fully accept the Course

After the line I quoted above—"his ego will be enough for him to cope with"—comes this one: "Nor would there be an advantage in his premature acceptance of the course merely because it advocates a long-held belief of his own."[14] The two lines put together provide a revealing window onto the beginning of one's journey with the Course.

The first sentence, as we saw, says that the Course will be challenging the student's ego so severely that it is not wise "to add sectarian controversies [like reincarnation] to his burdens."[15] The second sentence cautions that one should not rush a student into a "premature acceptance of the course" by telling him that it teaches a favorite belief of his (like reincarnation). Rushing him into premature acceptance clearly means rushing him *past* that phase in which his ego feels so burdened by the Course. This implies that he actually needs to go through that phase. Apparently, only by doing so will he come to a *mature* acceptance of the Course.

An analogy would be answering a proposal of marriage. Before you say yes, you want to come to a mature acceptance of being married to this person. If you have doubts or questions, you want time to resolve them. You don't want to be rushed past them by unrealistic fantasies you have about him. You want to walk down the aisle having accepted him for who he is and having realistically and wholeheartedly committed to marriage with him.

The same is true with the Course. Before you really commit to it, you want to be able to resolve your issues with it. You want to be able to wholeheartedly embrace it, based not on some superficial misconception of what it is, but based on what it really is. You want to come to a mature acceptance of it.

And this will take time. On the way there, you will have to come to terms with some very radical ideas, as we can see from this passage:

> There is no world! This is the central thought the course attempts to teach. Not everyone is ready to accept it....[But for those who are,] their readiness will bring the lesson to

> them in some form which they can understand and recognize. Some see it suddenly on point of death....Others will find it in experience that is not of this world....And some will find it in this course.[16]

This implies that if the Course has been sent to you, it has been sent precisely because you are ready for its central thought: "There is no world!" It also implies that maturely accepting the Course is *synonymous* with truly accepting that central thought. And that is a tall order. Embracing the idea that the world is not the only reality, that it is not even a lower or lesser reality, but that there is no such thing as a world, can take some time. So be patient with yourself in the process. Give yourself the time you need.

Deciding whether or not the Course is your path

I believe that accepting the Course as your path is a crucial step, if the Course is indeed meant for you. Up until you make that decision, it is perfectly fine to consider the Course to be one of many valued spiritual teachings in your life, to dip into it at random, and to jump sporadically around in the Workbook. However, once you decide that it is your path, it is time to roll up your sleeves and get down to work. It is time to really take this course. Up until now, you've been auditing. Now you're enrolled. Now it is time to study the Text in earnest, to do the Workbook lessons consecutively and with discipline, and to consider the Course's teachings to be the lens through which you will see the world.

This may sound like voluntarily putting on a straitjacket, yet we all know that until you fully commit to something, you are to some extent standing on the outside, and therefore do not have full access to the gifts it offers you. The point at which you truly commit to the Course is the moment all its gifts become available to you. That is when its potential is really within your grasp. It is logical to assume that you can get farther on the spiritual journey by focusing yourself on a single path than by dabbling in many. As an old adage asks: Would you rather dig six wells of ten feet each or one well of sixty?

However, before you dig that single sixty-foot well, you want to make sure you are digging in the right place. In this case, you want to make sure that the Course really is your path. How can you tell?

In answer to that question, I'd like to tell some of my own story. In my case, I was incredibly resistant to having a single path. As a result, it took me years to decide that the Course was it for me. I finally did so under the pressure of at least six reasons. Somewhere among these reasons there may be something of relevance for you.

1. The Course gave me more benefit than other paths.

When I first got involved with the Course, I was passionately eclectic. I believed then (and still believe) that the truth was like light streaming in through many windows and cracks in the wall. The idea of having a single path, quite frankly, struck me as narrow and bigoted. For many years, therefore, the Course was just one of my many cherished teachings. As the years went by, however, the Course gradually devoured my spiritual life, until it was virtually the only thing I used. The reason for this was simple: I derived more benefit from it than from anything else. It seemed to have a unique gift for penetrating to the heart of the matter. It unveiled the core thought patterns behind my daily upsets and gave me transformative insights that shifted those patterns. It seemed at the same time more challenging, more uplifting, and yet more practical than anything else. Therefore, slowly and without my noticing, like a weed in the garden, it simply took over my spiritual life. Eventually I had to admit that my ideal of drawing on many sources had become just an ideal, one that was not reflected in my life.

2. The Course eventually made the most sense to me.

In the beginning, there were many elements of the Course that felt alien and vaguely distasteful to me. I didn't like the strong Eastern flavor in the Course. Its central focus on forgiveness rather than love didn't feel appropriate. I didn't appreciate how harshly it spoke about the world and how emphatically it proclaimed the world's unreality. Its insistence that we are already perfect, rather than evolving toward perfection, struck me as rather nitpicky. Over time, however, the Course seemed to rewire my brain, so that ideas I initially didn't relate to began to make sense to me. Gradually, my conscious belief system experienced a revolution. That which had initially felt alien, weird, or uncomfortable now seemed to be the most sensible, sublime, and even obvious truth.

I didn't feel I was abandoning my reason or caving in to some cultish program of brainwashing. I felt I was simply being convinced by the

Course's reason and logic. There is an immense power of persuasion in the Course, and this power had an even greater effect on me when I started teaching its thought system. At that point, five years into my relationship with the Course, I still didn't consider it my path. Now, however, I had to become an instrument of the Course's persuasion. I had to draw out its logic and make plain its arguments. And as these arguments rolled off my lips, they sounded pretty good to me, too. In trying to persuade others, I ended up persuading myself.

3. I came to believe that the Course chose me.

Choosing a path can be an incredibly difficult process. What can relieve this pressure is realizing that the choice is not up to us. The Course says, "You are not free to choose the curriculum, or even the form [the particular path] in which you will learn it."[17] Your true path is not yours to decide. It has already been assigned to you, not arbitrarily, but based on a total consideration of all of your needs. Thus, it's a done deal. There's nothing you can do about it. You can either live in denial or accept the truth.

This was absolutely my experience. When I received the Course, it never occurred to me that this was to be my lifelong spiritual path. I remember reading an interview with Judith Skutch Whitson, publisher of the Course, in which she said that the Course was not meant to be everyone's path. I breathed a conscious sigh of relief, because I knew it was not mine. Yet my early encounters with it were accompanied by some highly synchronistic occurrences that should have made me sit up and take notice. After that, the Course started literally invading my life. Friends of mine began getting involved with it. My best friend began working for a local Course center. Then my wife started working there. This center then asked me to do projects for them, then teach classes there. Then they asked me to write an introductory booklet on the Course. Once this was published, I began receiving invitations from other centers to travel to other areas and speak about the Course. Then I received requests to write for various Course newsletters and magazines. The Course was gobbling up more and more of my life, until, as I sit here today, it *is* my life. Somewhere in the middle of this process I finally faced the obvious. Some sort of plan had barged into my life and taken over, and at the center of this plan was *A Course in Miracles*. The fact that I hadn't chosen it didn't seem to matter; it had already chosen me.

4. I eventually just "knew" that the Course was my path.

I believe that if the Course is your path, sooner or later you'll just know. That is what eventually happened to me. I can't tell you how I know; I just know, as certainly as I know that I'm right-handed. Planted inside the student is the recognition of who his teacher is. Yet, as you can see from what I've shared, it was a long time before I "just knew." A great many changes had to take place in my mind and in my life before this knowing could surface. Consider yourself fortunate, therefore, if you pick up the Course, and along with it comes a flash of supernatural insight telling you that this book is for you. Instead, you'll probably go through a longer process, in which you spend weeks, months, or even years wondering if the Course really is your path. Then finally, one day, you look within and realize that you just know.

5. I made a bet that truth would lie in the direction of the noblest vision of reality.

When I first got on the spiritual path, perhaps my main standard for truth was that if a number of respected voices said it, then it must be true. An idea qualified as truth if this mystic and that channel and that great teacher all said it. In matters of the spirit, where nothing could be proven, I found safety in numbers.

The Course, however, threw a monkey wrench into that system. True, it did contain many of the ideas that I had encountered elsewhere. On the other hand, many of its core teachings were ideas that I could literally find nowhere else. That the world didn't come from God but was our *attack* on God, that my way home is to see *guiltlessness* in my brothers, that guilt is the source of all human suffering—I was unable to find these ideas anywhere outside the Course. Yet they were *central* to the Course.

Since these ideas had only one voice behind them, they didn't pass my test for truth. Yet they were at the heart of the Course, which even at that time was a very important teaching for me. What should I do? I finally resolved my dilemma by dispensing with the standard of multiple voices and adopting a different standard for spiritual truth. I realized that of all the teachings I had come across, the Course's vision stirred in me such a sense of grandeur, beauty, and perfection that I could only characterize it as the noblest vision of reality that I had encountered. The Course's vision was so ultimately affirming as to seem too good to be true. Yet something in me said that rather than being evidence that the Course was wrong, this was actually a sign that it was right. In response to a deep voice in me, I made a faith assumption that truth simply must lie in this direction. It must lie in the direction of the noblest vision, rather than the basest. Somehow, reality must, simply must, be perfect. This was definitely a gamble, and a huge one at that. Yet in the end, we all must stake our lives on a particular voice in us, a voice that tells us what is genuine and what is not, and I was willing to bet that this voice in me was the truest one. I decided, therefore, that the Course's vision was simply too good to be *false*. And, as risky as such a decision may be, it has satisfied me ever since.

6. I came to believe that the author is Jesus and to trust that he knows what he is talking about.

It took me a number of years to feel really settled about the Course's claim to be authored by Jesus. After all, that is not a claim to take lightly. How I reached this acceptance was primarily due to two factors. The first was what I saw as remarkable parallels between the Jesus of history and the author of the Course.[18] The second was that the more familiar I became with the Course, the more a recognition in me grew. Something in me recognized something in its author. It is difficult to describe this recognition, yet part of it is quite simple: I know that he knows. I see in him a truth that is so pure, so sublime, and so certain, that I know I can place myself and my awakening safely in his hands.

Such a statement probably sets off a chorus of warning bells. In a society suspicious of authorities, this can sound dangerously gullible. Such a stance also went distinctly against my intellectual grain, which told me to place my trust in objective evidence and logic, not in the views of a particular individual. Consequently, it took me many years to come to peace with this idea of following a single person. Now, however, this approach makes perfect sense to me. After all, there must be those who grasp the truth more accurately and completely than I do, and if the deepest sense of truth in me tells me that a greater truth lives in them, it would simply be pettiness and egotism not to give them my trust. As the Course's author puts it in the Manual, appealing to those who truly know is wisdom, not gullibility:

> No one on earth can grasp what Heaven is, or what its one Creator really means. Yet we have witnesses. It is to

> them that wisdom should appeal. There have been those whose learning far exceeds what we can learn....Then turn to one who laid all limits by [Jesus], and went beyond the farthest reach of learning.[19]

All six of these realizations grew in me slowly—*very* slowly—until a full seven years after I got the Course, I finally realized, "The Course is my way home. Whether I like it or not, it's the path that has been assigned to me." It took me a long time, but once I was truly certain, there was no going back.

I have two points I want to make with this story. First, everyone will have his or her own way of deciding whether the Course is his or her path. Second, there is no need to rush this decision. As I mentioned in the previous category, there is no "advantage in...premature acceptance of the course."[20] The Course is not about forcing us into a commitment to it. Rather, it wants to teach us through lengthy experience to associate our freedom with it. It wants to teach us this so fully that committing to it becomes the most logical and natural thing to do, "as simple as opening your eyes to daylight when you have no more need of sleep."[21]

Do I use it alone or in combination with other teachings?

Once you finally settle on the Course being your path, should you do it by itself or in combination with other paths? When you think about it, the answer to this question is almost too obvious to mention. If the Course is your path, then it is the path you should walk.

In today's eclectic spiritual climate, this can sound like having the doors of the One True Church closed on you, trapping you inside. Let me, therefore, take some time to explain this idea. It does not mean that you cannot read other spiritual teachings. It just means that they are not the path you walk. They are not your guide on the journey, the Course is. Its teachings are the lens through which you look out onto the world. Its practices are your methods for communing with God, seeking guidance from the Holy Spirit, and healing your daily upsets. It is as if you are traveling up a mountainside. You may read about other people who took different routes up that mountain. You may gain inspiration from their success. You may even understand your journey better by reading about the way by which *they* made it to the summit. But you still have to take *your* route. You cannot ascend the mountain from two different angles at once. The Course echoes these sentiments in four important passages, which I will comment on in the following four points.

1. Using other practices keeps you from receiving the benefit of what was made for you.

> This is the special means this course is using to save you time. You are not making use of the course if you insist on using means which have served others well, neglecting what was made for *you*.[22]

The "means which have served others well" are long periods of meditation,[23] and fighting against the temptation to give in to sin. These are time-honored methods in world spirituality, and they work; they have gotten people up the mountain. Yet they are not the Course's means, which (in this context) is experiencing holy instants in moments of joining with another person. You may feel deprived if you are told that you should not use those traditional means. Yet, ironically, you are deprived *by* using them. For if the Course is your path, then its means were made especially for you. They are tailor-made to get you up the mountain as fast as possible. Thus, by using those traditional means instead of the Course's, you are actually lengthening your journey.

2. Mixing the Course with other things will very likely introduce fearful elements into it.

> As you read the teachings of the Apostles, remember that I told them myself that there was much they would understand later, because they were not wholly ready to follow me at the time. I do not want you to allow any fear to enter into the thought system toward which I am guiding you.[24]

The Course is trying to lead us into a way of looking at reality that is totally free of fear. Human minds, however, are soaked with fear. Consequently, elements of fear manage to seep into almost every thought system in this world. A good example is the New Testament, which carries a message of love, yet also speaks of a wrathful God dividing the saved from the damned on the day of judgment and sending

His Son to be crucified as a blood sacrifice. For this reason, we need to read the New Testament (and all other teachings) with discernment. We cannot just take it in uncritically. For, as the above passage says, it was written by men who at that time "were not wholly ready to follow" Jesus into the complete freedom from fear that he held out.

3. Mixing it with other teachings may introduce ideas that waste time by detracting from the Course's radical, practical focus.

> It cannot be too strongly emphasized that this course aims at a complete reversal of thought. When this is finally accomplished, issues such as the validity of reincarnation become meaningless. Until then, they are likely to be merely controversial. The teacher of God is, therefore, wise to step away from all such questions, for he has much to teach and learn apart from them. He should both learn and teach that theoretical issues but waste time, draining it away from its appointed purpose.[25]

Our minds want answers to a thousand fascinating questions. Do we live once or many times? Were there highly advanced ancient civilizations? Was Noah's ark a historical reality? Where do we go when we die? On what date will the world end? Little do we realize that our search for these answers is unconsciously propelled by our need to avoid the central issue of our existence: the "complete reversal of thought" that will liberate us from all suffering and limitation. Most teachings to some degree indulge this need; they emphasize various form-related issues that do not shift our mind toward this complete reversal. Therefore, mixing those teachings with the Course will provide us with a series of backdoors through which we can escape into juicy side issues, allowing us to comfortably ignore the one central issue.

4. The Course is a complete path; there is no need to mix in anything else.

> You are studying a unified thought system in which nothing is lacking that is needed, and nothing is included that is contradictory or irrelevant.[26]

This passage represents a bold claim on the part of the Course. It says that the Course contains everything we need on the journey to God.

There is no reason to turn elsewhere. The very needs we try to meet by looking elsewhere are actually met right there in its pages, if we pay attention. This claim might be seen as egotistical, but in my view, it reflects a tremendous compassion on the part of the Course. It wants to take care of us along the way. Walking to God means following a path that our eyes cannot see, and this leaves us wondering if we are on the path or have wandered off, if we are progressing quickly or dragging our feet. The Course wants us to know that with it as our guide, we are in safe hands.

Should we read material about the Course?

It would be rather odd for a book about the Course to say, "Don't read books about the Course." Writings about the Course can be extremely helpful. I would just add two qualifiers. First, don't let secondary material become a substitute for the Course itself. Reading the Course regularly, ideally on a daily basis, is a crucial habit for the serious student. Second, always be willing to measure secondary material against the Course itself. Writings on the Course have come from some purportedly very high sources, including Jesus (speaking through other channels) and ascended masters. Yet, in my view, no matter whom it purportedly comes from, you should still consider it nothing more than an interpretation of the Course. It is an artistic rendering, not a photograph. As such, it will not reflect the Course with full accuracy. I've never seen an exception to this, and I include my own writings in that observation. You, as the reader, are therefore left with the responsibility of deciding what you accept and what seems to you to be out of accord with the Course. Nothing can take that responsibility from you.

Is there a Course lifestyle?

Yes, there is, but not of the sort that you might expect. In addressing this issue, the Course first contrasts two traditional lifestyles, that of the spiritual renunciant, who is engaged in ascetic self-denial, and that of the conventional person in society, who is doing his best to indulge himself:

> Many have chosen to renounce the world while still believing its reality. And they have suffered from a sense of

> loss, and have not been released accordingly. Others have chosen nothing but the world, and they have suffered from a sense of loss still deeper, which they did not understand.[27]

The Course then goes on to lay out a lifestyle that lies "between these paths":

> Between these paths there is another road that leads away from loss of every kind, for sacrifice [the way of the renunciant, where you sacrifice the world] and deprivation [the way of conventional living, where you feel deprived of God] both are quickly left behind. This is the way appointed for you now. You walk this path as others walk, nor do you seem to be distinct from them, although you are indeed. Thus can you serve them while you serve yourself, and set their footsteps on the way that God has opened up to you, and them through you.
>
> Illusion still appears to cling to you, that you may reach them.[28]

In this lifestyle, then, the outer form of your life looks like everyone else's ("nor do you seem to be distinct from them"), yet beneath the conventional form is a completely different content ("although you are indeed"). This middle way thus has the *form* of the conventional lifestyle and the *content* of the renunciant's. You are really a monk, but with a briefcase, a family, and a lawn to mow. You clothe yourself in these conventional forms not because you believe in them, but so "that you may reach them"—your brothers. You want to lead them by example into another way. Consequently, you don't want them to be distanced from you by your special robes. You don't want them to be daunted by your heroic sacrifice and self-denial. You want to send the message, "I'm just like you, only happier." When you dress in the same clothes, eat the same food, and shoulder the same burdens as they do, yet pass through it all with more peace and forgiveness, they are much more likely to silently look to you as their guide along the way.

Be patient with the journey and with yourself

Many Course students get the wrong impression about the process of awakening. They assume that because in reality we are already home, waking up to that fact must happen more or less instantaneously, perhaps in a single powerful enlightenment experience. While in theory this is possible, the Course has a different way of imaging the process. It always characterizes it as a foot-journey along a path or road, in which we take one step after another. Along this path, we may experience dramatic jumps ahead—that is what miracles are—but these are still jumps "within the larger temporal sequence."[29] The Course says that these jumps forward can save a thousand years at a crack. If that is so, just imagine how vast "the larger temporal sequence" must be.

Therefore, see yourself as being on a journey. The journey may be an illusion, but it is a journey nonetheless. And because it is, you don't sit down and wait to be catapulted to the end in one big blowout experience. Instead, you focus on putting one foot in front of the other, each day, each hour, even each minute. The journey begins with a single step, and it is moved forward by additional single steps. Be patient with yourself and with the process, for unless you are, you might fall into despair and give up altogether. The following quote captures the ideal attitude to hold in mind on the path:

> You have agreed to cooperate in the effort to become both harmless and helpful....Your attitudes even toward this are necessarily conflicted, because all attitudes are ego-based. This will not last. Be patient a while and remember that the outcome is as certain as God.[30]

This passage points out a fundamental irony on the path: Even while we have dedicated ourselves to getting beyond our egos (to becoming "both harmless and helpful"), we are clearly ambivalent about the whole project. We are torn between what we are heading toward and what we are leaving behind. This inner conflict can be extremely discouraging. It can—and often does—make us feel like failures as spiritual seekers. Yet we have good reason to be patient with our inner split. We can relax in the confidence that "this will not last," because "the outcome is as certain as God."

Signs of progress

Along the way, we do need signs of progress, so that we can be sure we're not just spinning our wheels. However, I think we should look for these not so much in unusual inner experiences—though such experiences *can* be helpful indicators—but more in how we respond to life. Do we respond with peace in the face of difficult circumstances? And do we respond with love in the face of "difficult" people? If you can look at a recent situation and honestly say, "I responded to this in a higher way than I would have a year ago," then I think you're making fast progress indeed.

The Course provides an even more down-to-earth measure: how do *others* respond to *us*?

> It is easy to distinguish grandeur from grandiosity [in yourself], because love is returned and pride is not.[31]

> And you will recognize which you have chosen [the ego or the Holy Spirit] by *their* reactions.[32]

It is so easy to fool ourselves into thinking that we're fast outpacing the rest of humanity when, in fact, we may be just getting more abrasive and weird. How can we tell if our progress is genuine? If we're truly awakening to the love within us, others will see and they will respond. The love we gave will be returned. This is how we recognize our progress on the path—"by *their* reactions." It may feel threatening to submit ourselves to this measure, but when we do, we might be surprised. We might discover that others indeed are responding to us with more love, which means they are simply returning the love that *we* gave *them*.

A day in the life of the mature Course student

After we have been on this path for some years, we want to get to the place where the path as a whole is at work in our lives, where all pistons are firing, so to speak. We want to be actively working with each of the different aspects of the Course's program, so they can all blend together into a beautiful whole. Concretely, this means that each day ideally ought to include study, practice, and extension.

To make this possible, we will need to begin the day with God. We will need a chunk of time in the morning that is devoted to starting the day off on the right foot. Establishing this time is a must. We all begin our day in some kind of preparation for the day as we see it. The question is this: Based on how we get ready for the day, what do we think the day is for?

1. Daily study

Students who have been with the Course for many years often read it less and less with time. They have read it so much that the sharp edges of its teaching have worn smooth for them. Unfortunately, they do not realize how much those words still have to give them. There is an inexhaustible richness in the words of the Course; there are always further depths to mine. Moreover, at this more advanced stage in the journey, we do not read mainly to gain new insights. We read because encoded in those words is a certain state of mind, and contact with them pulls us toward that state. We read to momentarily take into ourselves the endpoint toward which the Course is drawing us. Reading now is more than learning ideas; it is spiritual food.

I find that two or three pages a day is enough. At this rate, you can cover the entire Text in a year (though "daily study," of course, can also include the Workbook or Manual). It can help, in fact, to follow a schedule. On the Circle of Atonement's website (www.circleofa.com), there is a Text reading schedule that gets you through the Text in one year by having you read about two and a half pages every weekday.

2. Daily practice

Doing the practice is crucial, even more so than doing the study, in my view. The Course in fact equates doing a practice period with taking a step forward on the journey. It tells us, "Each one you do will be a giant stride toward your release."[33] There is a beautiful prayer in the Workbook, in which we say to God: "Quicken our footsteps now, that we may walk more certainly and quickly unto You."[34] We ask Him to "steady our feet,"[35] to correct our stumbling and our wandering off the path. Yet all of this talk about Him leading us along the path specifically refers to Him *leading our practicing*: "Lead our practicing as does a father lead a little child along a way he does not understand."[36] The implication is clear: Doing the practice and walking along the path are somehow *one and the same*. Doing a practice period is an act of moving our foot forward on the path.

Therefore, rather than doing the Workbook and then laying the practice down—as so many students do—we need to keep practicing in the manner in which the Workbook taught us. Our goal is to continually grow in the practice, to become strong in all the various kinds of practice we learned from the Workbook:

- *Morning and evening quiet time*: at least fifteen minutes of practice to begin the day and close the day; primarily receptive practice, such as meditation
- *Hourly remembrance*: two or three minutes of practice as the hour strikes
- *Frequent reminders*: dwelling on the lesson for the day as often as possible
- *Response to temptation*: responding to upsets by repeating the idea for the day

The purpose of being strong in all these areas is not to fulfill some spiritual quota; it is to learn how to tap into the source of happiness within us. The Course says that you experience yourself as far from home only because "you do not remember how to look within."[37] In a sense, we are like brain-damaged patients. In the same way that they need to laboriously relearn skills that used to come naturally, we have to painstakingly relearn how to look within. It takes a lot of practice.

3. Daily extension

Just as showering and dressing ready us to go to work, so our morning quiet time readies us to go out and perform our real job as miracle workers. We are sent out into the world to visibly uplift the people we encounter. We do this when our thoughts, our smile, our kind words convey to them the heartfelt message: "Awake and be glad, for all your sins have been forgiven you."[38] The Course expects that we will consciously devote each day to this function of giving miracles. This, in our eyes, will be what the day is for.[39] Hence, we will be actively on the lookout for situations in which miracles are called for. The Course assures us, "You will recognize these situations."[40]

To facilitate this, I find it very helpful to remind myself that every interaction is meant to be a holy encounter. As we saw in Chapter 5, the Course teaches that literally every human encounter has been arranged by the Holy Spirit, because in that meeting He sees a holy potential, a potential for the giving and receiving of salvation. So He brings the two people together, and once He does, it is up to them to actualize this potential. For this reason, I try (emphasis on "try") to remember this while I'm with a person. I might repeat to myself a line such as "let this be a holy encounter," or "we share the same interests." Or I might think of these lines from the Course:

> When you meet anyone, remember it is a holy encounter.
> As you see him you will see yourself.
> As you treat him you will treat yourself.
> As you think of him you will think of yourself.
> Never forget this, for in him you will find yourself or lose yourself.[41]

One final component is asking for guidance all through the day. Workers need a boss, and miracle workers are no exception. How do we know where someone waits in need of our help? How do we know what that person's real need is, what words or gestures will be just the right ones? Without Help, we do *not* know. This is why the Workbook trains us extensively in the habit of asking the Holy Spirit for guidance all through the day. There is a bank of nearly fifty lessons (153–200) in which we are told to come to God each hour "and learn what He would have us do the hour that is yet to come."[42] If we actually follow those instructions, we'll end up asking for guidance over seven hundred times. The purpose of this guidance is not to help us buy winning lottery tickets; it's not there to give us a divine edge over the competition. Its purpose is to guide us in our function as miracle workers. It's there to make us the loving instruments of "a larger plan we cannot see in its entirety."[43]

Getting to the place where all these pistons—study, practice, and extension—are firing will probably take us a number of years. Yet once they are, our days and our hours will be framed in God, our thoughts will be filled with light, and our lives will be imbued with purpose. At this point, we can be sure that we are moving quickly on toward the end of the path, where God awaits us with open Arms.

TEN

The Promise of *A Course in Miracles*

A Course in Miracles is really all about laying hold of gifts, about claiming what it calls our "natural inheritance."[1] One of the Course's repeating images is that of the treasure house, a vast storehouse filled with "a limitless supply"[2] of treasures. These riches are not gold and silver, but rather the miracles that lift our mind out of despair, and that we can carry into the world to lift the minds of others. As the Course depicts this treasury, its doors are always open wide, welcoming us, silently declaring that all the riches inside are ours. Once we start carrying them out, we would naturally expect the store to be depleted, yet somehow, it miraculously increases. Hence, there is no reason to be shy about carting out all the treasures we can bear.

This image is the key to what *A Course in Miracles* really is. The Course is merely a detailed set of instructions on how to find that treasure house. It is a path to the storehouse's front doors. Its only purpose is to put our feet on the right road, keep us moving along it, and get us *through those doors*. Actually, we don't have to wait until the end of the path to enjoy these riches; the Course expects us to visit the treasure house at many points along the way. However, the final goal is to enter it and never leave, to make it our home. This is why we walk the path and do the work, not because some authoritative book told us to, but because we want to abide in the treasure house.

Thus, in order to put the Course in final, proper perspective, this chapter will explore some of the Course's benefits, some of the gifts it promises to those who walk this path. We already covered some of the major gifts in Chapter 5: a new kind of interaction with others, a new vision of the world, a new sense of self. Thus, the list that follows is by no means exhaustive, yet I hope it will help convey a sense of the treasures that await us on this journey.

Holy instants

We generally experience ourselves locked into a particular state of mind. In this state, life looks rather drab and mean, problems can appear hopeless, and sources of fear dot the landscape like small fires springing up. In this state, there is no solution to the basic human dilemma. We are stuck. "Therefore," says the Course, "God must have given you a way of reaching to another state of mind in which the answer is already there. Such is the holy instant."[3] A holy instant is similar to Maslow's concept of a peak experience. It is an instant in which we are momentarily lifted out of the prison of our usual dull, anxious state of mind. Suddenly everything is bright with hope and washed of all the stain we saw before. It is as if a divine shower has swept through the area, putting out all the fires and making everything new and clean and fresh.

In the Course's view, moments such as these are not meant to be rare gifts. Rather, they represent a basic, daily need. "What you need are intervals each day in which the learning of the world becomes a transitory phase; a prison house from which you go into the sunlight and forget the darkness."[4] For this reason, the Course provides extensive instruction in how to enter holy instants. Here is one such instruction, which I have laid out on separate lines so you can treat each line as its own separate step:

> Take this very instant, now,
> and think of it as all there is of time.
> [Imagine that] nothing can reach you here out of the past,
> and [that] it is here that you are completely absolved,
> completely free
> and wholly without condemnation....
> Learn to separate out this single second,
> and to experience it as timeless.[5]

A friend of mine tells the story of a profound holy instant he experienced. He used to attend a Course study group and would typically judge the leader for her long visualizations, which he felt had almost nothing to do with the Course. One time, however, he came to the meeting determined to forgive her with no strings attached. To his complete surprise, as soon as the visualization began, he found himself inwardly experiencing a holy encounter between him and the leader, in which both were in a bodiless, spiritual state. He says:

> The thing that struck me right away is that I felt more love/joy in being in [her] presence than I have ever felt before....It was an experience of pure absolute bliss in coming into contact with someone....I felt a love, a sense of love, that surpassed any concept of love that I have experienced on a conscious level. I have been in love, I've had many male/female relationships, and in looking back it was no comparison, because it was so much greater than anything that I had ever experienced. And I said, "this is love."[6]

Remarkably, this is exactly what the Course claims about the holy instant. Love is such an elusive concept, and so often associated with what in the end amounts to using someone else. The Course says that after all of our unloving attempts at love, we will finally learn the true meaning of love in the holy instant.[7]

Finding your function

I have already shared that each one of us is assigned a special function, our particular form of extending miracles to others. In Chapter 1, I related the story of Helen Schucman's discovery of her function as scribe of *A Course in Miracles*. In Chapter 8, I shared my own story of moving into my function as a teacher of the Course. Both of those stories were meant to underscore the point that the special function is *for real*. The Holy Spirit really does design for each person a function that is perfectly suited to his or her special abilities and unique situation in time and space.

The special function answers a deep hunger in us. How many of us have spent years wondering what we are here to do, what our purpose is? How many of us have longed to make a difference, to make our own unique contribution to the whole? Most of us funnel this urge into spending our lives carving out our special niche on the societal totem pole. Yet the Holy Spirit takes this same impulse and channels it in a different direction. "To each He gives a special function in [the global plan for] salvation he alone can fill; a part for only him."[8] The following story comes from Helen Schucman, from when she first started having the visions that would culminate in her scribing of the Course. It has always struck me as a beautiful example of just how deeply we yearn to find our function:

> I was suddenly swept away by a sense of joy so intense I could hardly breathe. Aloud I asked, "Does this mean I can have my function back?" The answer, silent but perfectly clear, was, "Of course!" At that I began to dance around the room in an intense surge of happiness I had never felt before. I would not have believed it was possible to experience such happiness as that answer brought with it, and for a little while I kept repeating, "How wonderful! Oh, how wonderful!" There seemed to be no doubt that there was a part of me I did not know, but which understood exactly what all this meant.[9]

This function is there waiting for us. One of the Course's central goals is to lead us to it, by guiding us in the inner development that makes us ready to carry it out, and by teaching us how to listen to the Holy Spirit so we can find out what it is.

Being truly helpful

There is within each of us a yearning to be truly helpful. It is frustrating to sit by, powerless to do anything, while a loved one is suffering. And who of us does not feel better about ourselves when we help another? The Course tells us that if we could take the limits off our helpfulness, we would also take the limits off our joy. And it aims to teach us how to do just that.

In walking this path, therefore, we often find an ability to be helpful that we did not know was there. Some of us find an inner wisdom that can help others in either formal or informal counseling. Some of us find the ability to send healing from our mind to the minds of others, sparking both inner experiences and physical healings. Others find other gifts of helpfulness.

We also find ourselves reaching out to people whom we previously would have ignored or avoided. As an example of this, Bill Thetford, co-scribe of the Course, was directed by the author of the Course to attend a professional conference on rehabilitation. His purpose for going was to get over his fear of those who need rehabilitation, those with broken bodies, damaged brains, and weakened egos. He was given this beautiful prayer, a favorite among Course students, to repeat while he was there:

> *I am here only to be truly helpful.*
> *I am here to represent Him Who sent me.*
> *I do not have to worry about what to say or what to do, because He Who sent me will direct me.*
> *I am content to be wherever He wishes, knowing He goes there with me.*
> *I will be healed as I let Him teach me to heal.*[10]

Another story from the early days of the Course combines all of the elements I've mentioned above. The story involves Helen Schucman and Bill Thetford and takes place in 1965, just before the scribing of the Course began. Helen at this time was at the height of her "magic phase," in which she was experiencing paranormal abilities and, while frightened by them, was also feeling rather inflated by them.

She and Bill were sent by their hospital on a research visit to the Mayo Clinic in Rochester, Minnesota. The night before they left, Helen received in her mind a detailed picture of a Lutheran church, which she felt sure they would see when they arrived. Yet after an exhaustive search of most of the city's churches, they came up empty-handed. Finally, the next day, while at the airport waiting to return home, Bill found a guidebook with a picture of the very church Helen had "seen." Ironically, it had occupied the very site of the Mayo Clinic, having been torn down to make way for the clinic. This, however, was not the end of the story.

On the way home, they had a layover in Chicago. In the airport, Helen saw a young woman sitting by herself against a wall. Bill noticed nothing special about her, but Helen, apparently by way of the same abilities that had shown her the church, "could feel waves and waves of misery going through her."[11] She simply had to go over and talk to her. Once she did, Helen insisted that the woman sit between her and Bill on the plane, while Helen held her hand.

Her name was Charlotte. She had felt like her life was "closing in" on her, and so, without any planning, she had left her husband and three children. With nothing but a small suitcase and a little money, she was heading off to New York City to make a new life, with no specific plans of where to stay. Helen related:

> She was a Lutheran, and she was sure all she had to do was find a Lutheran church in New York and they would take care of her there. Bill and I exchanged glances. The message was not hard to grasp. "And this," I seemed to hear, "is my true church...helping another; not the edifice you saw before."[12]

Helen and Bill proved extremely helpful to Charlotte during her brief stay in New York City, after which she returned to her family. But that was not the end of the story either. For it was through reaching out to this complete stranger, someone that many people might have wished to avoid (given that she was abandoning her three children), that Helen learned the real purpose of her psychic gifts. They were not there to glorify her ego. Their real purpose was to equip her with a newfound ability to help others. This realization led directly to her decision (in the scroll cave vision described in Chapter 1) to turn them over entirely to God's use. And this is what made possible her function of using those gifts to scribe *A Course in Miracles*, which in turn would help thousands upon thousands of people. In retrospect, the entire episode was a process of Helen being shown exactly how she could become "truly helpful."

Benefiting others across the world

We can especially feel powerless to help when we watch crises in distant parts of the world—either collective disasters or personal tragedies. What can we possibly do, sitting there in our living room? Perhaps more than we realize. The Course claims that when we experience what appears to be a private holy instant, it affects people literally across the globe.

A number of Workbook lessons point this out, and for a very practical reason: the Workbook wants us to do its practice. When we sit down to do spiritual practice, there is a great temptation to feel that we are being self-indulgent and irresponsible, that we are lavishing attention on ourselves and ignoring the needs of others. And this causes us, quite simply, to sit down and practice *less often*. Again and again, therefore, the Workbook reminds us that our practice directly benefits others, that "healing comes to many brothers far across the world, as well as to the ones you see nearby, as you send out these thoughts to bless the world."[13] This healing is not so much like a uniform force field that radiates out from us; rather, it is doled out intelligently, based on the openness of the receiver. The Holy Spirit, we are told, will carry our gifts "around this aching world...and He will lay them everywhere He knows they will be welcome."[14]

It is very difficult to prove that healing in our minds can affect people at a distance. However, there is a story of Helen and Bill's that is at the least highly suggestive. Helen tells it in her unpublished autobiography:

> Bill and I were working on a research report and I was concentrating on the statistical treatment of the data. Suddenly and very unexpectedly I laid the papers down and said, with great urgency, "Quick, Bill! Joe, your friend from Chicago, is thinking about suicide. We must send him a message right away." Bill sat down next to me as I "sent" an earnest mental message to Joe. The words I used were: "The answer is life, not death." Afterwards, I said to Bill, "I bet there was nothing to it," but I was wrong. Bill called his friend that evening to ask him if he was all right. Joe was glad he had called; he had been very depressed, and had actually picked up a gun that afternoon, but something held him back. He put the gun down.[15]

We may be tempted to see this as a story about someone with unusual abilities. Yet the Course would have us consider that all of us have the ability to heal people at a distance, and that we do so every time we sink into the peace of a deep meditation or feel the relief that comes from giving up a grievance.

Happy days

The desire for a happy day goes very deep in the human psyche. We tell each other, "Have a nice day." We look forward to special days. Each day when we arise offers us a fresh start, giving us the hope that perhaps, just perhaps, today will be one of those days we have always dreamed about.

The Course is actually on our side in this. It, too, wants us to have happy days. It even encourages us to have *special* days. The key, it tells us, lies in aiming for a whole different kind of day. To us, the day is good when all the players and props on the stage of our lives behave the way we want; when, instead of treating us like a convict, they treat us like a king. In the Course's view, however, a truly happy day comes from peering into a gracious reality that is always there, irrespective of how things go on the outside. The happiness comes not from gorging ourselves on the feast of the world, but from tasting timelessness. A Workbook prayer captures this perfectly: "And what I will experience is not of time at all. The joy that comes to me is not of days nor hours."[16]

How do we have such a day? By constantly drinking from the well of that timeless reality. That is what the Workbook trains us to do. As I mentioned in Chapter 7, it trains us to start the day with God, end the day with God, and meet with Him briefly every hour and even frequently in between. This represents one of the Course's major learning goals. The Course therefore regards our ability to enjoy "a day of undisturbed tranquility"[17] as an important indicator of progress on its path, a sign "that we have found the way, and traveled far along it to a wholly certain goal."[18]

One of my favorite prayers in the Course speaks beautifully of this perfect, happy day. Again, I'll lay out its sentences on separate lines. This makes it easier to actually pray, which I would encourage you to do:

> *Be in my mind, my Father, when I wake, and shine on me throughout the day today.*
> *Let every minute be a time in which I dwell with You.*
> *And let me not forget my hourly thanksgiving that You have remained with me, and always will be there to hear my call to You and answer me.*
> *As evening comes, let all my thoughts be still of You and of Your Love.*
> *And let me sleep sure of my safety, certain of Your care, and happily aware I am Your Son.*[19]

In this prayer, God is depicted as a Presence of pure Love. All He does is shine on you, love you, care for you, keep you safe, and cherish you as His beloved Son. He does not in any way hold Himself apart. Every minute He is there, keeping you company and listening for your slightest call. In the face of this Love, you cannot help but respond. You make Him the center and the circumference of your day. You awaken in the morning with your mind only on Him. You spend every minute just dwelling with Him, basking in the sunshine of His Love. Even while your body is busily engaged, something in your mind is still, resting with Him. You take time each hour to thank Him for always being there for you. As the sun sets on this day of peace, this dwelling with Him still goes on. All you want to think about is your Father and how much He loves you. Finally, when you lie down to bed, you are really laying yourself in the cradle of His care and safety. You are resting on the ocean of His Love. You drift off to sleep in happiness, your mind absorbed in the one fact that means everything to you: that you are His Son.

What could compare to a day like this? Is getting the raise or the promotion really as good as this? Even when everything goes wrong on the outside, we can still have this. Training in how to have such a day would surely be priceless, and that is exactly what the Course offers.

Receiving guidance

When you think about it, it's absolutely amazing that we try to chart our own course through life. We like to believe we make one sound decision after another. Yet our decisions are so arbitrary, based on such a scarcity of information, and so warped by our personal desires that we simply have to be kidding ourselves. The Course lists three requirements for making a sound decision: 1) having all the relevant facts, which would ultimately include knowing "an inconceivably wide range of things; past, present and to come";[20] 2) being able to predict all the effects your decision would have on anyone even remotely affected by it; and 3) having a totally unbiased perception of the situation, so that your decision "would be wholly fair to everyone on whom it rests now and in the future."[21] The Course concludes by asking, "Who is in a position to do this? Who except in grandiose fantasies would claim this for himself?"[22] Indeed, who? It then goes on to say the following:

> There is Someone with you Whose judgment is perfect. He does know all the facts; past, present and to come. He does know all the effects of His judgment on everyone and everything involved in any way. And He is wholly fair to everyone, for there is no distortion in His perception.[23]

To really consider that this Someone—the Holy Spirit—is there and is available can be a massive relief, for somewhere inside we know that our decisions are just shots in the dark. For this reason, the Course's instruction in how to hear the Holy Spirit and how to turn to Him throughout the day is incredibly practical and useful. It is one of the most valuable things I have learned from the Course.

I spoke briefly about my own experience of inner guidance in Chapter 7, but I'll share a bit more here. I feel my experience is widely applicable because I do *not* hear an inner voice. I know people who hear very wise and helpful inner voices, but I never have. Instead, when I ask, I get little shots of intuition. Rather than a series of words, I generally get a single "sense." You could say that it's the nonverbal essence of an idea, to which I then put my own words. This sense is often completely different than what I was thinking before I asked, and when it differs, it is invariably wiser; it heads me in a better direction. It is always more loving and patient, more considerate of others, more in keeping with the lofty principles in which I believe. And it has countless times told me things that I didn't know beforehand, but which subsequently proved to be correct. It is definitely wrong at times[24]—I believe it's healthy to face that and admit that—but the stronger and the more surprising the sense is, the greater the likelihood that it will turn out to be right. I honestly can't tell you where it comes from. All I know is that it is far superior to my normal, unaided thoughts. Its sheer usefulness has caused me to ingrain in myself the habit of turning to it many times a day, which has made it one of the staples of my life.

I could share so many stories of my guidance telling me things I couldn't have known, but I'll confine myself to one. Several years ago, I and my colleagues at the Circle of Atonement, the Course-based organization that I head, went through several months of clarifying our mission. At the end of this process, we planned to release a newsletter in which we described this mission and then invited people to join us and lend us their support. It was to be a watershed event for us. There was just one problem: We didn't have the money to print and mail the newsletter. I asked for guidance about how to get the newsletter out, given our lack of money. The sense I received was: "Leave it to me." I asked again, not sure if I was hearing correctly. I got: "This newsletter is in my will. I will see to it." Finally, since it seemed we were being told not to take any action, I asked if there were any attitudes we should hold. The answer was unswerving: "That of loving servants who are waiting for their master to act."

So, according to this guidance, we weren't supposed to lift a finger. We were just supposed to sit there and wait for manna to fall from the sky. In a way, I liked this message, because it meant I didn't have to do anything. The last thing I wanted to do was run around trying to drum up funds. On the other hand, what if we sat there waiting like good servants, all filled with faith, and the money never came? I expect you can guess where the story is heading. Within about a week someone who knew nothing of our plight, and who had never before given a significant amount to the Circle, felt guided to donate several thousand dollars, more than enough to cover our printing and mailing expenses. It was hard not to conclude that the voice that told us to just sit there, waiting for our master to act, knew exactly what it was talking about.

This is a typical story. I have heard, and experienced, countless ones like it. It is amazing to me that this gift of higher wisdom is available to us and yet is not more utilized in the world. True, seekers of many faiths turn within for guidance, but why don't governments? Why don't corporations? Perhaps someday they will.

TEN CHARACTER TRAITS OF THE SPIRITUALLY ADVANCED

At one point, the Course itself (in Section 4 of the Manual, "What Are the Characteristics of God's Teachers?") provides an extended discussion of the gifts that come to those who become truly advanced on this path—or any path, for that matter. It calls these individuals advanced teachers of God, and says about them: "God gives special gifts to His teachers, because they have a special role in His plan for Atonement."[25] When we think of those who are highly spiritually advanced, two kinds of gifts generally come to mind: paranormal powers and powerful inner experiences. We think of the saint as someone who can heal the sick or read minds or perhaps levitate, someone who slips easily into rapturous visions and ecstatic mystical states. Significantly, however, neither supernatural powers nor blissful inner states are included in the gifts the Course speaks of here. The gifts we normally think of seem to have been intentionally left off the list. What, then, are the gifts the Course speaks of? They are *character traits*. The special gifts God gives to those who come near to Him are gifts of character.

I find something exquisitely appropriate in this. Who of us has not heard of the spiritual master who can drop into *samadhi* at will, yet who in his worldly dealings displays the kind of character traits we have come to expect from dirty politicians? I think we all assume that something is really amiss there. True, we all long for mystical experiences. Yet just as fundamental is the longing to be *good*, to be a person of true and uncommon goodness. In a culture in which so many people feel they have suppressed their real feelings in the attempt to be good, I almost feel as if I'm speaking blasphemy. But the yearning is there, and it's so powerful that we'll do almost anything under its pressure—even twisted things like suppressing our feelings. We want to be good, and that desire is unquenchable. As I have said many times in this book, the Course claims that all of our pain comes from our deep-seated belief that we have permanently stained our original goodness, that we have corrupted ourselves beyond all repair. A moment's ecstasy is wonderful, but if afterwards we are faced with the same person we detest—ourselves—then that belief in our corruption has not been undone, and that overpowering urge to be good has not been satisfied.

The following ten characteristics—drawn from "What Are the Characteristics of God's Teachers?"—paint a portrait of a person who is pure goodness, a person who in any land, at any time, would be considered a saint, a person whom any tradition would be honored to call its own. This is the person the Course is leading us to become.

1. Trust

We look out and see a world that can't be trusted. People are scurrying about focused on their needs and heedless of ours. Random winds are blowing that swirl about us, thoughtlessly disrupting our affairs as though we don't exist. In this general chaos, if we want to survive, it seems we have to exercise some sort of control. We can turn our patch of wilderness into a garden, but only if we can tame all those wild forces: put fences up to keep out the rabbits, post signs to keep out all those trampling feet, and—just in case—keep our shotgun loaded and ready.

In contrast, the advanced teacher of God looks on the world with total trust. He has learned that "all things, events, encounters and circumstances are helpful."[26] He knows that there is no such thing as randomness, that even the wild winds blow with his best interests in mind. For he trusts that, despite appearances, the world is governed by an unseen Power, a Power that is in love with him. Thus, he has no need to push the flow. He does act; he decides to go right instead of left, he decides to do this instead of that. But his actions flow from his connection with that unseen Power. Thus, if this Power so directs him, he too will plant a garden, but once he does, he will make sure that he invites everyone into it, because he trusts them.

2. Honesty

Because we don't trust the world, we all, to one degree or another, become career magicians. We present to our audience a carefully constructed illusion. A little misdirection, a little sleight of hand, and we have them believing in something that's not actually real. Our signature trick, however, is not making tigers appear; it's conjuring an illusion of ourselves—as wonderful, attractive, intelligent, caring, and sincere. If we're really skilled, we have our audiences believing in an image of ourselves that is no more than a bit of stage magic. Who would love us, we wonder, if we showed them the truth?

Because the advanced teacher of God implicitly trusts the world, he can afford to be completely honest. He is not afraid of what will ensue, for he is not protecting a false image of himself. He's not trying to be something that he's not. His honesty, in fact, is rooted in self-honesty. He has admitted to himself what he knows, deep down, to be the truth about himself: that he is the holy Son of God. On the foundation of this inner honesty, he is able to demonstrate an outer honesty that vastly exceeds conventional notions. Not only are his words honest, but his actions are as well. He follows through with what he says. He keeps his word. He practices what he preaches. He embodies, in other words, a kind of ultra-integrity, to the point where all of his thoughts, words, and actions are completely in harmony with one another. There is a trueness that runs all the way through him, through his private thoughts and his public expression. At no level is he in conflict with himself,[27] and this gives him a peace of mind that we crafty magicians can only dream of.

3. Tolerance

In our efforts to tame the wilderness of life, we believe it is crucial to have high standards. They tell us what belongs inside our garden and what must be kept out. If we relax our standards and let anything in—rabbits, birds, substandard seed, cheap fertilizers, and those careless people—we'll not only lose control, but we'll also lose self-respect. At that point, we are no better than anyone else.

The advanced teacher, however, sees something we've missed: that this constant process of managing our world through judgment—judging what to let in and what to exclude—takes a heavy emotional toll. For one thing, it establishes a very narrow range of acceptability. It says things have to be just right or we lose our peace. For another, it makes us a rejecter, an excluder, one who cannot tolerate people unless *they* are just right. As a result, we sour on ourselves. We frown while we pound that "no trespassing" sign into the ground, because we are inwardly frowning on ourselves.

The teacher of God is unwilling to pay this price. Hence, he throws judgment away. He refuses to distinguish between pleasant and unpleasant situations, or between desirable and undesirable people. True, he makes decisions, based on his guidance. But in his heart, everything is just fine with him, and everyone is welcome. "Without judgment are all things equally acceptable....Without judgment are all men brothers."[28] This is how he looks on the world. He has found a tolerance as wide as the ocean, and thus, like the depths of the ocean, his peace knows no bounds.

4. Gentleness

Can we afford gentleness? We've all had the experience of trying politely to be heard while no one listened, only to finally get some action when we started shouting. The world is so set in its ways that railing against the injustices is, at times, the only force that can push the wheels out of their ruts. If we gently request that those wheels change direction, chances are that the only thing we'll accomplish is to get run over. In this view, maybe the meek shall inherit the earth, but first they'll need to be raised from the dead.

The advanced teacher, however, thinks this whole picture is completely backwards. He actually considers harsh tactics too *weak* to effect real change. In his eyes, gentleness is the strongest force there is, and he sees the evidence of this on a daily basis. He sees that one gentle touch can reach someone when nothing else will, that one gentle word can be more effective than all the shouting. Experience has taught him that the power of gentleness is the power of love, and is, indeed, the power of God. For love is gentle, and God is Love. Gentleness is thus more than just amiable behavior. It is a state of mind that mirrors the nature of God, and so taps into His infinite power. That is why the truly gentle have been known to perform miracles. And that is why the meek *shall* inherit the earth. According to the Course, "They will literally take it over because of their strength."[29]

5. Joy

Who of us does not want to feel joy? The problem, however, is that we believe it's not appropriate to feel joy unless something really wonderful happens. Consequently, in our eyes, anything more than occasional joy amounts to a state of being out of touch with reality. Given the condition of things down here, to be in joy all the time, you'd have to be mentally deficient.

The teacher of God, however, does not see joy as an isolated response to specific events. Instead, it is his response to the nature of reality, a radiant reality that lies just behind the drab appearances he sees. It is his "yes" to a God of boundless generosity, a God Who goes with him wherever he goes and Who covers him with kindness and with care.[30] His joy, therefore, has a limitless foundation. Hence, there is no need to scale it down to fit within the limits of caution and proportion. Further, being based on the nature of reality, it is no pipe dream; it is perfectly sane and rational. And since it is also based on that which never changes, it is not a fleeting emotion. Rather, his joy has become a fundamental character trait. He is able to look upon any circumstance, no matter how dark and threatening it may appear, and say to his God with perfect sincerity, "I am safe, untroubled and serene, in endless joy, because it is Your Will that it be so."[31]

6. Defenselessness

Life in this world appears to require a massive amount of defense. We need medicine to defend against disease. We buy coats to protect ourselves from the cold. We build roofs to defend against sun and rain. We make endless plans, which are nothing but defenses against future threats. We even drive defensively. All things considered, our personal defense budget takes up the greater part of our income. In addition to guarding against physical threats, we also defend against an equally long list of interpersonal threats. If people disagree with us, insult our dignity, dispute our intelligence, or challenge our character, what do we do? We get defensive. We do everything in our power to stop them from pinning that label onto us.

The truly advanced teacher is free of the need for defenses. Instead of seeing defenses as staving off dangers, he sees the defenses *themselves* as the danger. For each defense contains a crippling message: that he is "vulnerable, frail and easily destroyed, and at the mercy of countless attackers"[32]—a hapless fly caught in a raging torrent. Given this belief, no defense, however impregnable, could save him from chronic insecurity and fear.

His only defense, therefore, is his supreme confidence that Who he really is can never be harmed or injured in any way, that his reality was "created unassailable."[33] Given this confidence, what possible reason would there be to armor himself with layer upon layer of defense? And so he walks in simplicity, having no need for all the complicated structures we look to for safety. He laughs in the face of danger, because, quite simply, he sees no danger.

7. Generosity

Everyone feels the impulse to give, but there are costs involved. If we give too much, there will be nothing left for ourselves. Our giving is therefore constricted by a sense of caution, and overseen by a careful gauging of what we can afford. Granted, our idea of what we can afford often translates as what will not cut into our ability to accumulate at the rate we prefer. In this mindset, our gifts become investments, loans that we intend to call in at the appropriate time.

The teacher of God has left this mindset completely behind. His generosity has an extravagance to it, a lack of caution that we onlookers find both inspiring and unsettling. He might offer the shirt off his back to a complete stranger, or even an attacker. The reason is that he instinctively perceives giving as the way in which he himself gains, and sees keeping things for himself as a sure road to loss. As a result, his criterion for acquiring something is: "Can I give it away?" If not, he has no use for it. He can no longer even understand how something that is for him alone could have value. After all, every visible gift he gives—whether it be of his time or money or skills or possessions—is really just the wrapping for the gift of love. And the more he gives *this* gift, the more its radiance simply grows brighter within him. It is no wonder that he associates giving with gain.

8. Patience

So much of life amounts to standing in line. At any given moment, we are probably standing in about twenty lines, waiting for money to come through, for people to change, for our ship to come in, for our food to arrive. While standing in these lines, we try to wait patiently, yet doing so can feel like reining in wild horses. We silently wonder if our patience is too passive and wimpy, if we should just speak up in order to get the line moving.

Clearly, we are just putting a lid of patience over a cauldron of impatience. In contrast, the advanced teacher is *truly* patient, serenely patient, no matter how long the line is. What is his secret? "All he sees is certain outcome."[34] While his eyes gaze on uncertainty, his mind rests in the inevitability of a happy outcome. And so he can relax and "wait without anxiety."[35] His trust is so great that he knows that even the timing of this outcome will be perfect.

His patience, in other words, rests on his trust, the very first of his character traits. And this trust has a curious effect on the people he's waiting for. They actually move faster. For his patience sends them a message: "I am willing to wait for you without anxiety because I trust you completely." This loving message softens their hearts and kindles their motivation. Where before they would have dug in their heels, now they are drawn forward by the power of his love. Perhaps the Course is right when it says, "Now you must learn that only infinite patience produces immediate effects."[36]

9. Faithfulness

Most of us believe in some very high ideals, and we really intend to follow them, maybe even all the time. Yet we have a great many things to juggle, and while juggling those axes and chainsaws, we often drop the ball of our high ideals. Of course, that doesn't always happen. If we are spiritually inclined, for instance, we do turn some of our problems over to God. Yet we probably also believe there are certain problems that, if we gave Him the opportunity, He might solve in the *wrong way*. We decide we better keep those to ourselves. Who knows what bizarre and radical things He might do if we held nothing back and gave Him our whole life? In one of its exercises, the Course asks us to "think about all things we saved to settle by ourselves, and kept apart from healing."[37] It expects us to find quite a few, for it knows that we are not yet wholly faithful to our higher convictions.

That, says the Course, is the only difference between us and the advanced teacher of God. He *is* wholly faithful. If he did that exercise, there would be nothing on his list. He brings all of his resentments to the healing power of forgiveness, without exception. He gives every single problem into the hands of the Holy Spirit. That is why we look up to him. He actually follows through on his high ideals. For he has learned the priceless lesson that we are still learning: that he can "trust in the Word of God to set all things right; not some, but all."[38]

10. Open-mindedness

We probably consider open-mindedness to be a virtue. We value being open to new ideas and opinions. We respect those who will admit that they may not see the whole picture. But how far would we be willing to go with this? Would we open our minds wide enough to let go of every meaning we ever put on the world? That is what the advanced teachers of God have done. Not only have they forsaken trying to control their outer world, but they have also renounced an even deeper control: the control over the meanings they see in the world. As a result, they have left the world as they know it and stepped into the no man's land of total open-mindedness. They are not left hanging for long:

> They have in truth abandoned the world, and let it be restored to them in newness and in joy so glorious they could never have conceived of such a change. Nothing is now as it was formerly. Nothing but sparkles now which seemed so dull and lifeless before. And above all are all things welcoming, for threat is gone.[39]

The advanced teacher did not reach this profound openness overnight. It came, in fact, at the very end of his journey. The Course says that open-mindedness is "perhaps the last of the attributes the teacher of God acquires."[40] The reason is that through it, he was able to once and for all let go of the glue that held all his perceptions together: the perception that sin lurked within those bodies and forms out there. Open-mindedness, in other words, is the gateway to true forgiveness, and true forgiveness is the end of the road. The teacher has been forgiving up until now; by our standards, he has been phenomenally forgiving. Yet only here at the end does his forgiveness become real, because only here does it become perfect. Now it is the kind that can raise the dead. Now it gives him the power to "heal the world without a word, merely by being there."[41] And now he is ready to step off the wheel of time altogether, for having at last dropped his sword, he is ready to face God without fear and disappear forever into His embrace.

Conclusion

What strikes me about this portrait of the advanced teacher is just how qualitatively different his existence is from yours and mine. He has opted out of the game that we are all so busy playing, the game of managing our world for the sake of our separate self. We are constantly pushing and pulling, including and excluding, defending and attacking, tapping our foot when forced to wait, shouting when it will move things along, and lying as need be—all to make sure that we surround ourselves with the conditions that suit the self we think we are. As the Course points out, we spend our lives on the battleground.

In contrast, what we see in the advanced teacher is a shocking refusal to engineer his own security. He simply declines to manage his world for the sake of his separate self. He blithely opts out of this universal game; he walks off the battleground, for he doesn't need its rewards. His happiness is not dependent on the things of this world. He has found another reality, one which he rests on as trustingly as a boat rests on the water. And while we rush around trying to push our reality into the proper shape, he simply basks in his, happy, at peace, and without a care in the world. Of such people, the Course says:

> They want for nothing. Sorrow of any kind is inconceivable. Only the light they love is in awareness, and only love shines upon them forever.[42]

Resigning from the battle allows the teacher to be amazingly kind. Imagine what it would be like to be around such a person. He trusts you. He always tells you the truth, for he has no image to protect. He is supremely tolerant of you; no matter how you behave, he considers you his dear friend. He is always gentle, never harsh. He simply doesn't get defensive, regardless of what you say. He is uncommonly generous; he notices your needs and gives freely, even lavishly, to meet them. Even when you are impatient with yourself, his patience with you knows no bounds. And whatever mistakes you make, he forgives you, for he realizes that any perception of his that you are not perfectly holy must be his own mistake, which he gladly gives over to the Holy Spirit.

Who wouldn't want to be such a person? Who wouldn't give anything to have his sense of joy, his freedom from care, his trust in his Father? Who of us does not secretly ache to have that feeling of wholeness that comes from knowing that we are truly *good*? The Course assures us that all these can be ours. It is simply a matter of transferring our investment from the battleground to "the quiet sphere above the battleground."[43] As the Course points out, when we look honestly at the alternatives, the choice between them is no choice at all:

> Perhaps you think the battleground can offer something you can win. Can it be anything that offers you a perfect calmness, and a sense of love so deep and quiet that no touch of doubt can ever mar your certainty? And that will last forever?[44]

It is a long road from where we are now to the "perfect calmness" of the advanced teacher. Yet we will get there, if we can just keep from losing our way in the dark. What we need is "an easy path, so clearly marked it is impossible to lose the way."[45] What we need is a path of light. If we will just place ourselves on this path and keep putting one foot in front of the other, we will make it. This is the promise of *A Course in Miracles*.

Notes

A note on reading Course references

All references are given for the Second Edition of the Course, and are listed according to the numbering in the Course, rather than according to page numbers. Each reference begins with a letter, which denotes the particular volume or section of the Course and its extensions (T = Text, W = Workbook for Students, M = Manual for Teachers, C = Clarification of Terms, P = *Psychotherapy*, and S = *Song of Prayer*). After this letter comes a series of numbers, which differ from volume to volume:

T, P, or S-chapter.section.paragraph:sentence; e.g., T-24.VI.2:3–4
W-part (I or II).lesson.paragraph:sentence; e.g., W-pI.182.4:1–2
M or C-section.paragraph:sentence; e.g., C-2.5:2

Preface

1. R. Walsh, *Essential Spirituality: The Seven Central Practices to Awaken Heart and Mind* (New York: John Wiley & Sons, 1999).

2. W-pII.258.1:3.

3. G. Feuerstein, *Yoga: The Technology of Ecstasy* (New York: Tarcher/Putnam, 1989).

4. M-20.4:8.

5. St. Paul, Philipians 4:37, *Bible, Revised Standard Version.*

6. W-pI.185.Heading.

7. W-pI.158.11:3.

8. H. Smith, "Educating the Intellect: On Opening the Eye of the Heart," in L. Rouner, ed., *On Education* (Notre Dame, IN: University of Notre Dame Press, 1993).

9. Proverbs 4:5, *Bible, New Revised Standard Version.*

10. N. Angha, *Deliverance: Words from the Prophet Mohammad* (San Rafael, CA: International Association of Sufism

Publications, 1995).

11. K. Wilber, *The Spectrum of Consciousness. The Complete Works of Ken Wilber, Vol. I* (Boston: Shambhala, 2000).

12. Chogyam Trungpa, *Cutting through Spiritual Materialism* (Boston: Shambhala, 1975).

13. D. Anthony, B. Ecker & K. Wilber, eds., *Spiritual Choices: The Problem of Recognizing Authentic Paths for Ttransformation* (New York: Paragon, 1987).

Introduction

1. *A Course in Miracles* is published by the Foundation for Inner Peace, P.O. Box 598, Mill Valley, California, 94942-0598.

2. Richard Smoley, *Inner Christianity: A Guide to the Esoteric Tradition* (Boston: Shambhala Publications, 2002), p. 44.

3. "The Guru and the Pandit—Exploring the Future of Religion: Andrew Cohen and Ken Wilber in Dialogue," *What Is Enlightenment?* Spring/Summer 2003, p. 87.

4. W-pI.rV.In.1:5.

5. T-29.II.1:3.

6. T-12.II.10:1.

7. W-pI.rV.In.5:4.

8. T-12.V.9:4–5.

One

1. Kenneth Wapnick, Ph.D., *Absence from Felicity: The Story of Helen Schucman and Her Scribing of 'A Course in Miracles'* (Roscoe, NY: Foundation for "A Course in Miracles," 1991), p. 94.

2. Ibid., p. 106.

3. Ibid., p. 112.

4. Ibid., p. 125.

5. P-2.II.8:4–5. This reference is from *Psychotherapy: Purpose, Process, and Practice*, a supplement to the Course scribed after the Course was published.

6. T-4.VI.8:2.

7. *Absence from Felicity*, p. 201.

8. Ibid., p. 212.

9. Robert Skutch, *Journey Without Distance: The Story Behind 'A Course in Miracles'* (Berkeley: Celestial Arts, 1984), p. iv.

10. *Absence from Felicity*, p. 220.

11. This particularly comes out in her poetry, which is contained in *The Gifts of God* (Tiburon, CA: Foundation for Inner Peace, 1982). For example, speaking to Jesus, Helen writes, "My Lord, my Love, my Life, I live in you….I breathe your words, I rest upon your arms" (p. 53).

12. From Helen Schucman's unpublished autobiography, quoted in D. Patrick Miller, *The Complete Story of the Course: The History, the People, and the Controversies Behind 'A Course in Miracles'* (Berkeley: Fearless Books, 1997), p. 11.

13. *The Complete Story of the Course*, p. 16.

14. Ibid., p. 33. It should be noted that Bill Thetford took up an intense study of comparative religion and mysticism after the Course transcription began, and even though Helen read little in the field—and even then at Bill's insistence—the possibility of his study having some influence on Helen's later dictation cannot be entirely dismissed. There is, however, a remarkable consistency between the thought contained in the dictation she received before Bill took up this study and the dictation she received after.

15. T-6.I.15:2–3.

16. T-6.I.15:7–8.

17. T-6.I.9:2.

18. W-pI.rV.In.7:1.

19. *The Complete Story of the Course*, p. 14.

20. M-4.I.(A).6:11.

21. *Absence from Felicity*, p. 11.

22. *Journey Without Distance*, p. 107.

23. T-15.V.5:3.

24. Text, p. 350, First Edition.

25. T-18.V.3:1.

26. Exodus 3:11, 4:10, RSV.

27. From Helen Schucman's unpublished autobiography, quoted in *The Complete Story of the Course*, p. 12.

Two

1. Richard Smoley and Jay Kinney, *Hidden Wisdom: A Guide to the Western Inner Traditions* (New York: Penguin/Arkana, 1999), p. 66.

2. Ibid., p. 66.

3. *The Complete Story of the Course*, pp. 23–24.

4. W-In.1:1.

5. M-29.1:7.

6. T-1.VII.4:3.

7. As I will explain in Chapter 8, the role of teacher in the Manual is less like that of a classroom teacher, and more like that of a mentor, who works with pupils one–on–one to help them walk the path of the Course in their lives. This involves teaching the concepts to them, but also goes far beyond that.

8. T-31.V.1:7.

9. M-9.2:5.

10. Wouter J. Hanegraaff, *New Age Religion and Western Culture* (New York: State University of New York Press, 1998), p. 365.

11. *New Age Religion and Western Culture*, p. 115.

12. Matthew 16:17, RSV.

13. It should be noted that the Course never refers to Jesus as the Messiah. It does refer to him as the Christ, but portrays the Christ as a universal Self that is shared by everyone. Thus, in response to the question "Is [Jesus] the Christ?" the Course can answer, "O yes, along with you" (C-5.5:1–2).

14. Historical Jesus scholarship has arrived at many insights that strikingly parallel the Course's view of Jesus. See, for example, "Who Was the Jesus of History and Did He Write *A Course in Miracles*?" (available at http://www.circleofa.com/articles/Jesus_history_ACIM.html). In this article, I compare the Jesus of the Course with the historical Jesus as seen through the eyes of Marcus Borg, a leading Jesus scholar.

15. *New Age Religion and Western Culture*, pp. 37–38.

16. Galatians 6:7, KJV.

17. T-1.V.4:3–4.

18. See W-pI.rV.In.4:3.

19. There are certainly women in the East who reportedly have attained this state as well. The "classic pattern," however, generally depicts a man.

20. Greg Mackie, "Appreciating the Masterpiece, Part 1: Seeing the Course as a Great Work of Art," *A Better Way*, Issue #27 (August 1999), p. 9. I am indebted to Greg's article for much of this section's discussion.

21. W-pII.286.Heading. Interestingly, this sentence is also an alliteration; four of the five stressed syllables begin with "h."

22. T-26.IX.3:1–4.

23. T-14.X.10:1.

24. P-3.II.4:10.

25. For an extended discussion of this, see "The mechanics of perception" in Chapter 5 of this book.

26. W-pI.184.5:2.

27. W-pI.184.10:3–11:4.

Introduction to Part II

1. T-8.IX.1:7.

2. T-16.VI.7:5.

Three

1. T-31.V.2:7–3:4.

2. W-pI.21.2:5.

3. T-31.V.6:4.

4. T-31.V.5:3.

5. W-pI.51.5:4.

6. T-27.VII.12:1–2.

7. T-24.I.5:7.

8. The Course has a term for the mental images

we carry of the people from our past who didn't give us what we wanted. It calls these images *shadow figures*, and suggests that we are engaged in an ongoing campaign to prove to them that we really did deserve the special love they failed to give us. It even suggests that we unconsciously search for partners in the present who remind us of our shadow figures. Once we find such a person, we mentally superimpose the shadow figure onto the present partner. We then act out an elaborate dance of trying to extract from him or her the love the *past* person never gave us.

9. T-16.V.8:2.

10. T-17.III.3:2–3.

11. T-4.II.6:5.

12. W-pI.105:2:2.

13. T-15.VII.7:6.

14. T-13.III.6:4–5, 8:1.

15. W-pI.93.1.

16. T-30.V.2:4.

17. T-27.VII.7:4.

18. T-27.VII.12:2–3, italics mine.

19. T-20.III.7:2.

20. T-21.IV.2:7.

Four

1. T-14.IV.8:4–5.

2. T-14.IV.3:2.

3. T-1.V.3:2–3.

4. *The Gifts of God*, p. 126. I have laid each sentence out on a separate line for the sake of effect.

5. T-5.VI.10:4.

6. T-5.VI.10:8.

7. W-FL.In.6:1–3.

8. W-pI.169.5:4.

9. W-pI.132.12:4.

10. P-3.II.4:6.

11. S-1.In.1:3. This reference is from *The Song of Prayer: Prayer, Forgiveness, Healing*, a supplement to the Course scribed after the Course was published.

12. W-pI.97.2:2.

13. W-pII.14.1.

14. T-2.VII.6:1–3.

15. W-pII.11.4:1.

16. T-13.VIII.5:3.

17. T-15.V.10:10.

18. W-pII.12.3:1.

19. T-4.VII.5:8.

20. T-8.VI.5:7.

21. T-18.VI.1:5–6.

22. T-21.I.7:5.

23. T-15.IX.3:1.

24. T-11.I.3:4.

25. T-7.II.3:9, T-7.V.9:9.

26. W-pI.107.2.

27. W-pI.107.3:1.

28. T-27.VIII.6:2.

29. Though the Course does address *why* the separation occurred—the particular motivations that gave rise to it—it does not address *how* it could occur—how the separation could have happened at all in a perfect Heaven. This is a perennial question asked by Course students, yet the Course refuses to answer the question in the way it is asked. It does address the question, however, in a few places. What it says amounts to the following: 1) the question "How did the separation occur?" is inappropriate, for it implies that the separation *did* occur, something which the Course denies (see C-2.2:5). 2) "How did the separation occur?" is best answered not with an explanation about the past, but rather by looking at our choices to separate from God *in the present* (see T-4.II.1–3). 3) We should seek true correction of the error of separation rather than entangle ourselves in endless theological speculation about how it arose (see C-In.4).

30. T-28.III.7:4–5.

31. T-24.V.2:3.

32. W-pI.152.6.

33. W-pI.152.7:1.

34. T-26.V.9:1, 13:1; T-27.VII.12:4.

35. T-26.V.13:1.

36. T-20.VI.11:2.

37. T-19.III.7:3.

38. C-2.2:3.

39. T-27.VIII.9:1.

40. T-6.II.10:7.

41. T-18.II.5:8–12.

42. W-pI.132.6:2–3.

43. T-27.VIII.6:5.

44. T-9.VI.7:1.

45. W-pI.194.4:4.

46. T-26.V.3:5.

47. W-pI.158.4:5.

48. T-24.VII.7:3.

49. T-11.III.1:8; W-pI.64.3:4.

50. T-10.I.2:1.

51. T-4.III.9:1–2.

52. T-29.II.3:5–6.

53. T-27.VIII.10:5.

Five

1. T-14.IV.3:2.

2. W-pII.252.1:2.

3. W-pII.323.1:1–2.

4. T-5.I.6:4.

5. T-15.IX.1:1.

6. T-13.VIII.4:6.

7. W-pI.158.7.

8. T-17.II.1:1–6.

9. T-5.I.5:2.

10. T-6.V.1:5.

11. T-6.V.1:8–2:1.

12. T-6.V.2:1.

13. C-6.3:3.

14. M-8.3:3–5.

15. This discussion is drawn from passages all over the Course, but is particularly based on the discussion in Section 8 of the Manual, "How Can Perception of Order of Difficulties Be Avoided?"

16. M-8.4:1.

17. T-21.V.1:1.

18. M-8.4:6.

19. M-8.4:8.

20. T-13.V.3:5; T-21.In.1:1.

21. M-8.3:6–7.

22. W-pI.68.5:4.

23. W-pI.101.5:3.

24. T-29.IX.5:5.

25. T-19.IV(A).15:6.

26. T-19.IV(A).12:6–7.

27. Jane Lampman, "Forgive and Your Health Won't Forget," *Christian Science Monitor*, 19 Dec. 2002.

28. W-pI.134.3:2.

29. T-27.II.2:8.

30. Slightly paraphrased from S-2.II.4:5.

31. S-2.II.6:2.

32. S-2.I.2:1, et al.

33. W-pI.126.4:1–2.

34. Preface, p. xii.

35. W-pI.153.8:3.

36. T-31.VIII.6:3.

37. T-29.V.2:3–4.

38. T-5.IV.4:4.

39. T-27.VIII.10:1.

40. T-31.III.1:5.

41. Adapted from T-30.VI.2:7.

42. W-pI.161.9:3.

43. W-pI.151.8:4.

44. W-pI.78.6:3–4.

45. W-pI.161.11:7–8.

46. T-9.II.3:1.

47. P-2.IV.2:6.

48. T-13.VI.10:5–7.

49. T-14.II.4:4.

50. T-26.IV.2:4.

51. T-18.VII.6:4.

52. T-29.III.3:1–5, 5:5–6. I have changed a semicolon in the published version to a colon for the sake of clarity.

53. T-20.VII.2:1.

54. P-2.II.8:4–5.

55. T-17.II.2:6.

56. T-26.IV.2:2.

57. See W-pI.156.4:4.

58. W-pI.rI.60.3:4–5.

59. T-31.VIII.8:4.

60. W-pII.317.2:5.

Introduction to Part III

1. T-12.II.10:1.

2. T-5.III.3:5.

3. T-5.I.1:13.

4. W-pI.187.5:3.

5. T-9.V.9:1–4.

Six

1. W-pI.In.1:1.

2. T-11.VIII.5:3.

3. T-16.II.9:5.

4. T-22.I.6:1–4, 6.

5. W-pII.In.11:4.

6. T-4.In.3:11.

7. W-pI.rII.In.2:2.

8. W-pI.rI.In.2:3.

9. W-pII.In.11:3–4.

10. *Absence from Felicity,* p. 285.

11. W-pI.rIV.In.7:1–5.

12. See T-3.I.3:11: "I have made every effort to use words that are almost impossible to distort."

13. *Absence from Felicity*, p. 234.

14. T-23.In.3:1.

15. T-25.VIII.3.

16. What justice means in these sections is a fascinating study in itself. The Course bases its definition of justice on two core meanings in the word. The first is that justice treats everyone the same, regardless of social status. "Justice looks on all in the same way" (T-25.VIII.4:2). The Course carries this to its logical extreme, saying that true justice doesn't punish some while letting others go. It gives everyone exactly the same thing. The second core meaning is that justice gives people what they deserve. Since, in truth, everyone is the wholly innocent Son of God, justice "is bound to set them free, and give them all the honor they deserve" (T-25.VIII.8:2). In sum, justice gives everyone his due regardless of superficial differences. In the Course this means that true justice gives everyone *everything*, for that *is* his due, regardless of the superficial appearance that he has sinned.

17. T-25.VIII.8:1.

18. I arrived at this number by finding the average sentence length in a number of sections.

19. I did a count of themes in the two–page section "The Light of Communication" (T-14.VI). To count something as a theme, I required that the same term or similar terms had to occur more than once and mean basically the same thing each time. By my count there were forty–eight themes, represented by anywhere from two to twelve mentions. I list them here according to the terms by which I identified them: 1. darkness, dark; 2. ignorance; 3. light; 4. dispel (by the light), disappear (in the light), shine away; 5. understanding, understand; 6. fear, fearful, afraid, frightening, terrify; 7. concealed, hidden, obscure, kept apart, keep from; 8. perceive, perceives; 9. knows, know not, unknown; 10. meaning, meaningful, meaningless, means; 11. clear, perfectly clear, perfect clarity; 12. value; 13. shared, joint; 14. love, loved, love's; 15. Holy Spirit; 16. your Father, his Father; 17. bring to, brought to; 18. perfect; 19. openness, open, close; 20. power; 21. attack; 22. separated off, separate out,

remove; 23. breaking, disruption, broken; 24. interference, interferes; 25. door, doors, gates; 26. sentinels of darkness, guardians of illusions, strange ideas of safety, sentinels, guard; 27. safety, safe, unsafe; 28. protection, protect; 29. nothing, nothing at all; 30. life, live; 31. death, destruction; 32. truth, true, falsity; 33. guilt, guiltlessness; 34. one/the other, one/its opposite; 35. reinterprets, Interpreter, interpret; 36. restoration, re–establishing, restore; 37. made, you made, you who made, make, maker; 38. use, apply; 39. means; 40. purpose, holy purpose, holy cause; 41. teach you; 42. speak, say, said, expressing; 43. language, symbols, tongue; 44. communication; 45. carefully; 46. greet, welcome; 47. yield; 48. alien, strange.

20. T-31.VIII.9:1.

21. 3:1.

22. 4:2.

23. 3:2.

24. T-31.III.6:1.

25. 7:1.

26. 8:4.

27. 8:7.

28. 8:6.

29. T-2.V.5:1.

30. T-2.V.3:2–5.

31. T-2.V.4:4.

32. This does not mean that we do not need to use our bodies to convey the miracle to another. The section after this one, in fact, teaches that if we truly accept right–mindedness into us, Jesus will actually operate our bodies for us. This means that extending a miracle to another through our behavior will become an involuntary act.

33. T-2.V.5:1.

34. T-31.VIII.8:1.

35. W-pI.69.6:5.

36. T-15.VIII.4:1.

37. T-19.IV(A).16:4.

38. T-16.V.10:1.

39. T-25.VI.7:10.

40. *Absence from Felicity*, p. 229.

41. T-20.II.7:1–7.

42. T-13.X.13.

43. T-24.VII.2:2–7.

44. W-pI.44.3:4–5.

Seven

1. W-pI.In.1:1–2.

2. W-pI.95.11:3–5.

3. *Absence from Felicity*, p. 197.

4. *Absence from Felicity*, p. 285.

5. T-10.In.3:9–10; italics mine.

6. T-5.VII.5:1, 6:6–11; paragraph break not indicated.

7. W-pII.284.1:5–6.

8. T-7.III.4:1.

9. W-pI.94.5:9.

10. W-pI.97.3:2.

11. W-pI.98.5:1.

12. W-pI.rIII.In.4:4–5.

13. T-12.V.9:4.

14. W-pI.157.1:3.

15. W-pI.46.4:4.

16. W-pI.124.9:4–5.

17. W-pI.193.12:4–5.

18. W-pI.41.9.

19. W-pI.62.4:2.

20. W-pI.124.12:1.

21. W-pI.133.14:2.

22. W-pI.32.6:1–3.

23. W-pI.193.6:3.

24. W-pI.193.13:1.

25. W-pI.71.9:2–5.

26. M-16.5:7.

27. W-pI.122.2:4.

28. W-pI.rV.In.11:3.

29. W-pI.27.4:4–5.

30. W-pI.95.10:1–2.

31. W-pII.229.2.

32. W-pII.222.1:4.

33. W-pII.307.2:1.

34. W-pI.rV.In.12.

35. See M-16.

36. W-pI.95.6.

37. W-pI.153.20:1.

38. M-16.3:8.

39. The Epilogue to the Workbook suggests that the Holy Spirit will actually prompt you about when to practice and what to do during your practice periods (see W-Ep.3:3).

40. W-pI.In.1:3.

41 W-pI.20.2:3–6

Eight

1. W-pI.139.9:4.

2. T-15.VI.7:1.

3. T-31.VIII.4:5.

4. M-1.4:9.

5. M-1.2:13.

6. W-pI.65.2:1.

7. T-15.XI.10:9–10.

8. W-pI.191.10:6–8.

9. C-2.9:1.

10. T-5.III.4:6.

11. T-4.VI.6:3.

12. P-2.V.4:2–3.

13. T-13.VI.10:5.

14. T-6.III.4:9.

15. P-2.V.8:8.

16. M-25.1:5.

17. Preface, p. ix.

18. M-29.1:1–2.

19. M-In.5:4, 8–12.

20. M-1.4:1.

21. M-29.1:1–2.

22. M-27.7:1.

23. I realize this is a strong claim, but I make it for three reasons. First, the Manual's title clearly implies that it is for teachers who will guide others through *this* course. Second, the Manual opens with this role. Its first four sections are about the teacher of pupils. Third, several later sections (17, 18, 23, 24, 29) specifically counsel the teacher in how to lead students of the Course along this path.

24. The Manual discusses the new student of the Course in Sections 24 and 29. In 24, paragraph 3, it talks about how the teacher should handle new students of the Course regarding the issue of reincarnation. The answer is that he should not teach them that belief in reincarnation is part of the Course. For those new students who do not believe in reincarnation, mixing reincarnation with the Course would add an unnecessary burden onto the difficulties their egos are already having with the Course. For those new students who *do* believe in reincarnation, mixing it with the Course may cause them to rush into a premature acceptance of the Course, and instead they need to come to a *mature* acceptance of it. Clearly, the teacher here is shepherding new students of the Course as his pupils. They are not explicitly called *pupils* in paragraph 3, but they are in paragraph 5 (5:5). Then, in Section 29, paragraphs 1 and 2, the Manual discusses the issue of which volume a new student should begin with, or whether this person is even ready for the Course at all. Here, the new student is explicitly called a pupil three times. The answer is that his *teacher* should decide which volume he starts with, or whether he is even ready for the Course, and should do so by consulting the Holy Spirit. Thus, in both sections, the new student of the Course is called a pupil and is portrayed as being guided along by a Course teacher. And these are our only snapshots in the Course of new Course students. I think we have to assume that this is how the author of the Course envisioned new students. He saw them as pupils of a Course teacher.

25. This discussion is inspired by a study of the occurrences of the words "pupil" and "student" in the Course. These words cover a variety of situations—from learning the Course, to being

in school, to learning Christianity, to simply learning how to grow up—but they almost invariably depict a student being led along a "way"—a way of life, a path of awakening—by another person.

26. This is taught in *Psychotherapy*, in a section entitled "The Place of Religion in Psychotherapy" (P-2.II).

27. T-5.IV.5:1.

28. W-pII.14.2:5.

29. M-2.5:6.

30. There is no question that the Manual portrays the healer coming to physically sick people. It speaks of the healer treating a sickness which *appears* to have come to us unbidden (M-5.III.1:7), caused by our bodies (M-5.III.1:9), caused by various biological forces (or "non-mental motivators"; see M-5.II.1:8). In this sickness, it appears that the "body has become lord of the mind" (M-22.3:7), though in reality this sickness is brought about by the mind, "for a purpose for which it would use the body" (M-5.II.2:1). It is the kind of sickness which can be seen by our physical eyes, as we look on someone and see that he looks "'sicker' than others" (M-8.6:3). It is the kind of sickness for which we would seek out a "physician" (M-5.II.2:5), who would use "special agents" (M-5.II.2:8) to attempt to heal it. The healing of this sort of sickness would take "tangible form" (M-5.II.2:9), and failure to heal it would result in "continuing symptoms" (M-7.4:1). What else but physical illness would fit all of these descriptions?

31. M-7.2:1

32. M-22.4:5

33. M-In.5:4–7.

Nine

1. W-pI.161.6:1–2.

2. The Manual, in fact, states that it is inevitable that "the pupil comes at the right time to the right place" (M-2.4:4) to meet the particular teacher who has been appointed him.

3. M-24.5:9–10.

4. T-9.V.9:2.

5. W-pI.20.1:6.

6. T-30.I.9:3.

7. In this process of learning the Course's language, many students have found it helpful to use my book *A Course Glossary: 158 Definitions from 'A Course in Miracles.'*

8. T-22.I.6.

9. M-24.3:5.

10. T-31.IV.7:3.

11. T-22.III.2:1.

12. W-pI.181.4:2.

13. M-13.6:1.

14. M-24.3:6.

15. M-24.3:5.

16. W-pI.132.6:2–4, 7:2–4, 8:1; paragraph breaks not indicated.

17. M-2.3:6.

18. To read about these parallels, see the article referred to in Chapter 2, note 14, "Who Was the Jesus of History and Did He Write *A Course in Miracles*?"

19. M-23.6:1–4, 8.

20. M-24.3:6.

21. T-15.XI.1:6.

22. T-18.VII.6:4–5.

23. As I point out in Chapter 7, the Course does teach meditation. However, the meditation it teaches is different from what it describes here as "long periods of meditation aimed at detachment from the body," which "look to the future for release from a state of present unworthiness and inadequacy" (T-18.VII.4:9,11). Here, meditation is aimed at rising above the unholy bodily self so that one gradually *becomes* holy. In contrast, the Course's meditation techniques aim at uncovering a holiness that is already present and need only be recognized.

24. T-6.I.16:1–2.

25. M-24.4:1–5.

26. W-pI.42.7:2.

27. W-pI.155.4:2–4.

28. W-pI.155.5:1–6:1.

29. T-1.II.6:10.

30. T-4.II.5:5–8.

31. T-9.VIII.8:1.

32. T-15.II.4:6.

33. W-pI.94.5:9.

34. W-pI.rV.In.3:5.

35. W-pI.rV.In.2:1.

36. W-pI.rV.In.2:5.

37. T-12.IV.5:4.

38. P-3.II.4:10.

39. T-1.I.15:1.

40. W-pI.77.7:5.

41. T-8.III.4:1–5.

42. W-pI.153.17:2.

43. W-pI.154.1:5.

Ten

1. T-In.1:7

2. T-26.I.5:4.

3. T-27.IV.2:3–4.

4. W-pI.184.10:1.

5. T-15.I. 9:5–6, II.6:3.

6. John Hutkin, "A Holy Instant," *A Better Way*, Oct. 1991.

7. T-15.V.1:1.

8. T-25.VI.4:2.

9. *Absence from Felicity*, p. 98.

10. T-2.V(A).18:2–6.

11. *Absence from Felicity*, p. 122.

12. *Journey Without Distance*, p. 50.

13. W-pI.132.16:1.

14. W-pI.97.5:1–2.

15. *Absence from Felicity*, p. 118.

16. W-pII.310.1:2–3.

17. W-pII.273.1:1.

18. W-pII.286.2:1.

19. W-pII.232.1.

20. M-10.3:3.

21. M-10.3:5.

22. M-10.3:6–7.

23. M-10.4:7–10.

24. From the Course's standpoint, whenever guidance is wrong, it is because our own ego has gotten in the way. The author of the Course referred to this phenomenon in personal guidance to Helen Schucman, saying, "Do not assume that you are right because an answer seems to come from Him" (*Absence from Felicity*, p. 395).

25. M-4.1:4.

26. M-4.I(A).4:5.

27. M-4.II.1:8.

28. M-4.III.1:8–9.

29. T-2.II.7:5.

30. W-pI.41.Heading, W-pII.222.1:4.

31. W-pII.329.1:9.

32. T-22.VI.10:6.

33. W-pI.153.9:1.

34. M-4.VIII.1:3.

35. M-4.VIII.1:1.

36. T-5.VI.12:1.

37. W-pI.193.11:4.

38. M-4.IX.1:4.

39. M-4.X.2:3–6.

40. M-4.X.1:1.

41. P-2.III.3:7.

42. T-23.IV.8:2–4.

43. T-23.IV.9:5.

44. T-23.IV.8:7–9.

45. T-29.II.1:3.

Glossary of Course Terms

attack

The attempt to harm another for the sake of one's own gain. Harmful, unloving thoughts (called "attack thoughts"), words, or deeds. The essence of everything the ego does.

call for help/love

The real nature of attack. Attack is not a sin to be punished, but a mistake to be corrected, a sickness to be healed. When we are attacked, therefore, the attacker is the one who is truly in need. We give him the help he needs by offering him our love and forgiveness. That is what his attack really calls for.

Christ

The extension of God; God's one Son and one creation; the single Self that is shared by all minds, all of whom are equal members of the Sonship. Does not refer to Jesus, who is simply one of these members, one who has fully awakened to our shared identity as Christ.

Christ's vision
See **vision**

creation
The act of extending one's own being to bring into being "new" members of transcendental reality. What is created shares all the attributes of its creator, being an extension of its creator's being. Extending is how God created us and how we create our creations. Creation occurs in Heaven, not in this world.

creations, our
Our own creations in Heaven, which we create in unison with God and the entire Sonship. Like everything in Heaven, they are pure spirit, formless, timeless, and perfect. They are not our extensions or thoughts of love in this world, though such thoughts are *reflections* of creation.

defenselessness
The attitude and response that stems from realizing that Who we really are is invulnerable, and that we therefore need no defense.

dream
An imaginary experience the mind has when it loses consciousness of reality and projects its own fantasy world. The Course teaches that our entire experience within time and space is a dream, an imaginary experience that is occurring within minds that have fallen asleep to true reality, or Heaven.

ego
The belief in being a separate self ("I am me and you are not") whose needs are met through attack ("I am end and you are means"). This belief gives rise to our experience of being a separate entity bounded by a body. This experience is an illusion, since our true Identity is one with the All.

eternity
A synonym for reality or Heaven that emphasizes its timeless nature.

Eternity is not an endless stretch of time; rather, it is completely outside of time. It contains only "always"—the single instant of the limitless present, which never arises or passes away.

extension

The natural dynamic of the mind whereby the content within it is expressed outward. In Heaven, our function is to extend our very being in the act of creation. On earth, our function is to extend the love and forgiveness in our mind to other minds. Projection is the distorted use of extension.

fear

The feeling that stems from the belief in approaching danger, from the expectation of attack. The Course teaches that we only expect to be attacked because we secretly believe that we are sinful and thus deserving of attack. Fear is the essential mood of the ego.

forgiveness

The relinquishment of our false perception that another sinned against us, and that we are therefore justified in resenting that person. Releasing this perception that resentment is justified automatically releases the resentment. This definition contrasts with the conventional one, which assumes that we can let go of our resentment without letting go of the perception that causes it.

God

The eternal, unbounded Person Who is the Creator of all that is real, and Who is the goal of all desire. God is pure Mind, pure Spirit, and is only Love; there is no anger or attack in Him. According to the Course, God did not create the physical world. He created only Christ, His Son, to Whom He gave all of His Love and all of Himself.

guilt

The painful emotion that stems from believing that you have sinned and have thus corrupted your being, making yourself worthy of punishment and unworthy of love. The Course teaches that this belief is false, for your true nature as God's holy Son is incorruptible.

Heaven

The only true reality. The transcendental abode that God created for His Son, beyond time and space; a realm of pure spirit, perfect oneness, and absolute changelessness. Heaven is our true home; we are there now, merely dreaming we are in this world. We do not go to Heaven after we die; we awaken to Heaven when we have completely relinquished the ego.

holiness

A quality of divine innocence or purity, untainted by the slightest sin or impurity. Holiness is characterized not by separation from the impure (as in some traditional notions), but by the willingness to love and share and unite with all beings. Holiness is the fundamental and changeless nature of all that God creates.

holy encounter

An interpersonal encounter in which two people overlook all that divides them and momentarily lose sight of separate interests; an encounter in which salvation is given and received, and a sense of joining occurs. In the Course, these encounters are the primary catalyst of our awakening.

holy instant

A moment in which we temporarily set aside the past and enter into the timeless present, in which we momentarily leave behind our habitual, insane mindset and recognize what is real. A holy instant can occur privately—during meditation, for instance—or it can be shared by two people (which would make it a holy encounter). It can vary in strength; it can be anything from a relatively minor experience, to a life-transforming miracle, to a revelation—a direct experience of Heaven. Called an "out-of-pattern time interval" early in the Text.

holy relationship

A relationship in which two people have joined in a truly common goal. This allows holiness to enter the relationship at a deep level and gradually shepherd it to the goal of being holy on the surface level, where the relationship is acted out. Holy relationships are not restricted to romantic relationships; they can occur between two colleagues at work, a spiritual teacher and his pupil, or a psychotherapist and her patient (to use the examples in the Course).

Holy Spirit

The third Person of the Trinity, also called the Voice for God, Who was created by God in response to the separation as the remaining Communication Link between God and His separated Sons. His function is to guide us into the state of true perception or vision, from which we will awaken to Heaven. He also designs our special function and is available to guide all our decisions.

illusion

Something that seems real but is not. A belief about or perception of reality that is false. The Course expands this common definition to include anything outside of Heaven, anything that is separate, imperfect, finite, or painful.

Jesus

One of God's Sons, equal to all the rest, who became fully awake to his Identity as Christ. In his crucifixion, he taught that even the most extreme attacks can be met by forgiveness. In his resurrection, he brought us all closer to awakening and made God's Voice more accessible to everyone.

knowledge

The heavenly condition of knowing reality through direct and total union with it, unmediated by physical senses or mental interpretations. Knowledge is categorically different from perception and cannot be learned, only remembered.

love

The single emotion of Heaven. In love we view something as so attractive, so compatible with us, that we go out to it, give ourselves to it, and join with it. We can only truly love as God does, Who loves everyone equally and totally. Special love, which is selective and partial, is really hate masquerading as love.

mind
The aspect of the self that includes the faculties of awareness, volition, thought, and emotion. Mind is completely nonphysical; it should not be confused with the physical brain. Mind in Heaven is one with spirit. Mind on earth is separated from its true nature and split between the opposing voices of the ego and the Holy Spirit, requiring it to choose between them.

miracle
The activity of the Holy Spirit which shifts our perception from false to true and thereby grants us unconditional, instantaneous, and free deliverance from the imprisoning (yet illusory) problems of this world. We accept miracles into our own minds, extend them to others (which is the primary meaning of the word in the Course), and thereby recognize that we have received them.

miracle worker
One whose function is to extend miracles to those in need (called miracle receivers in the Course). The content of these miracles is the miracle worker's true perception (in his own mind) of the miracle receiver. These miracles aim at healing the receiver's mind but may also heal his body.

perception
The process of trying to know an object while separate from it, by interpreting or judging information received by our physical senses. Perception is generated less by the objects we are trying to know and more by our own mental processes, which means that we end up seeing what we believe and desire, rather than what is real. The goal of the spiritual journey is to move from false perception to true perception, from which we will awaken to knowledge.

practice
Repeated exercise in mind training, aimed at the gradual realization of true perception. Practice in the Course consists of a disciplined dwelling on meaning, usually in the form of words (repetition of impactful sentences), but occasionally in wordless form.

prayer

Asking God for that which brings us closer to Him, for the healing of the mind (our own and that of others) and for the revelation of His Presence. We ask in the confidence that our asking simply opens us up to receive what He has already given. For this reason, the prayers in the Course are generally affirmative statements designed to change our mind, not God's.

projection

The ego's distorted use of extension, whereby we take something within our mind and project it onto the world outside, making it appear external and unconnected to us, when in fact it is not. We project our guilt outside of us in order to convince ourselves that it is not within us, that we are innocent. We project our beliefs in separation and attack outside of us—thus producing the world we see—in order to provide external justification of our sense of separateness and our attack.

reality

What truly and permanently exists independent of deception, illusion, and subjective opinion. The Course claims that the only true reality is the transcendental realm known as Heaven or eternity, a realm of pure, unbounded, changeless spirit.

real world

The world we see with vision or true perception. When looking upon the real world, we look past bodies and their attacks, seeing only the loving thoughts in this world and the holiness in all minds.

response to temptation

Responding with right-minded thoughts to the temptation to engage in egoic thinking. According to the Course, whenever we notice any kind of upset, we should have a habit of instantly responding with a right-minded thought, especially our Workbook idea for the day.

salvation

Liberation from the entire separated condition in which we feel alone, afraid, guilty, and cut off from God. Salvation is of the mind, through the reversal of our thinking. It is not of the body, through purifying the body or forcing it to behave properly; nor is it of the spirit, which was never lost and so need not be saved.

separation, the

The event in which we apparently separated from God, which gave birth to the entire phenomenal universe. The separation seemed to be a real event in which we tore ourselves out of God's Mind and shattered Heaven into countless separate bodies and intervals of time. Yet it was merely a psychological event, in which we fell asleep to reality and dreamt of a separated existence in a separated universe.

sin

The violation of the laws of God or goodness. An attack that attempts to do harm for the sake of selfish gain and that succeeds, that results in real harm. Sin is an illusion, for no one can truly be harmed, since in truth we are all God's changeless Son. What appears to be a sin is merely a mistake, which calls for help rather than punishment.

Son of God

The true Identity of each person and every living thing. The one Son of God is composed of an infinite number of parts or Sons. Each one of these Sons is both part of the whole and all of the whole. It is these Sons who have fallen asleep and are dreaming they are human beings and other living things. This term does not refer exclusively to Jesus, who is merely one of the Sons, one who has awakened.

special function

Our special form of extending forgiveness to others; the special part that we have been assigned to play in the overall plan for salvation. Our special function is tailored to our particular strengths, adapted to our particular culture and time period, and involves certain people whom we are meant to save. Special functions mentioned in the Course include teacher, healer, therapist, and theologian.

specialness
The idea of being set apart from others and set above others. Having more or being more than others. Specialness is the great payoff promised by the ego and was, in fact, what set the separation in motion. We seek specialness through many means, but primarily through our special relationships. Because it is a form of attack, specialness brings not happiness, but guilt and fear.

special relationship, special love relationship
A relationship in which we have a special arrangement (an exclusive relationship) with and receive special treatment from a very special person, so that we can feel more special. This passes for love, but is actually an illusion of love; it excludes all but one person and is even a covert attack on that one, for it seeks only to get something from him or her. Once given to the Holy Spirit, our special relationships will be transformed into holy relationships.

spirit
The substance of which God created His Son, the substance of our true nature. Spirit is completely nonphysical, formless, changeless, holy, and perfect. It possesses only knowledge and is unaware of the ego. It uses the mind to express itself in this world, so that the mind can be restored to awareness of spirit.

teacher of God
One whose function is to teach others on behalf of God; a bringer of salvation, a savior, a miracle worker. The teacher goes through a lengthy developmental journey in which he first accepts his function, then joins in holy relationships with his pupils, then becomes an advanced teacher, and finally awakens beyond time and space, at which point he will be a Teacher of teachers.

time
The linear progression of separate moments that is the context for change, attack, birth, and death. The Course teaches that time is an illusion, a trick of the mind. In reality, there is no temporal progression; everything is happening all at once.

True perception

See **vision**

vision

An inward recognition of the holiness within all things, which overlooks bodies and their attacks. This perception comes not through our eyes but from a spiritual faculty in us called the eyes of Christ. Rather than seeing visual forms or color, it "sees" pure meaning, the meaning of holiness.

world

The realm of time, space, and form which is the context for separated existence and is the opposite of Heaven. An illusion, which was not created by God but rather is being dreamt by sleeping minds in Heaven as a projection of their psychosis, their break with reality. When those minds awaken, the world will disappear. The term also has a second meaning in the Course: the collection of separated minds in this world. This is the world that God loves and that we are meant to save.

Index

Headings in **bold print** indicate a chapter or section devoted to the subject. After the initial listing, *A Course in Miracles* is referred to as "ACIM."

Index

About the Author

Robert Perry has been a student of *A Course in Miracles* (ACIM) since 1981. He taught at Miracle Distribution Center in California from 1986 to 1989, and in 1993 founded the Circle of Atonement in Sedona, Arizona. The Circle is an organization composed of several teachers dedicated to helping establish the Course as an authentic spiritual tradition.

One of the most respected voices on ACIM, Robert has traveled extensively, speaking throughout the U.S. and internationally. In addition to contributing scores of articles to various Course publications, he is the author or co-author of nineteen books and booklets, including the hugely popular *An Introduction to* A Course in Miracles. Robert's goal has always been to provide a complete picture of what the Course is—as a thought system and as a path meant to be lived in the world on a daily basis—and to support students in walking along that path.

Circle Publishing is a division of the
Circle of Atonement Teaching and Healing Center.

For more information about the Circle of Atonement,
please visit our website at www.circleofa.com.
If you would like to receive a free copy of the Circle's newsletter,
as well as a catalog of books and tapes, and information on
upcoming speaking events, please write, phone, fax or e-mail to:

The Circle of Atonement Teaching and Healing Center
P.O. Box 4238 • West Sedona, AZ 86340
Tel: (928) 282 0790 • Fax: (928) 282 0523
E-mail: info@circleofa.com
Website: www.circleofa.com